LIVING SYSTEMS

First published in 2024
by Vagabond Press
www.vagabondpress.net

Edited by Michael Brennan, introduction and selection © 2024
Front cover images: Kay Orchison © 2024

All rights reserved. No part of this publication may be reproduced, stored in a retrieval system or transmitted in any form or by any means electronic, mechanical, photocopying or otherwise without the prior permission of the publisher. The information and views set out in this book are those of the author(s) and do not necessarily reflect the opinion of the publisher.

ISBN 978-1-925735-74-1

This project has been assisted by the Australian Government through Creative Australia, its principal arts investment and advisory body.

LIVING SYSTEMS
POETRY FROM ASIA PACIFIC

VAGABOND PRESS

CONTENTS

Introduction in two poems, 13
Dorothy Porter, 'Comets IX', 13
Ōsaki Sayaka, 'Eternity and a Day', 14

ADAM AITKEN
   Rimbaud's Spider
      (Lake Toba, Sumatra), 16
   Omen, 18
ALI ALIZADEH
   from Evental, 19
ELIZABETH ALLEN
   News from home, 20
   At Winton, 21
   Neighbourhood Watch, 22
   Catastrophe, 23
RIO ALMA
   In the 50s, 24
ARAI TAKAKO
   Beds and Looms, 26
   Shadows, 29
AVIANTI ARMAND
   Tamar, 30
LOUIS ARMAND
   Drinking at the Vandenberg, 32
   To the U.S. Postal Services, 34
   Charles Blackman, Everything
      Changed (1957), 35
TAMRYN BENNETT
   To heal the wounds, 36
   Here is where you begin, 37
LAWRENCE BERNABE
   Detail from a Book of Windows, 38
ANSELM BERRIGAN
   from Pregrets, 39
JUDITH BEVERIDGE
   The Fisherman's Son, 42
JAVANT BIARUJIA
   'que sera Serrano', 44
ANGELITA BISCOTTI
   Sydney Road in 2011, 45
JUDITH BISHOP
   T/here, 47

POOJA MITTAL BISWAS
   write back, 48
MARIO BOJÓRQUEZ
   Desert Alive, 51
   Desert Mirage, 51
KEN BOLTON
   Boundless (Sasha), 52
PETER BOYLE
   from Enfolded in the Wings
      of a Great Darkness, 57
   The Parade of Moments, 60
   From the Country of Pain, 61
   Five Companions, 62
JEN JEWEL BROWN
   Grey-headed flying foxes, 65
PAM BROWN
   A second ago, 66
   Here's to you, 68
MELINDA BUFTON
   Industria, 71
   You are possible, 72
ALÍ CALDERÓN
   from Obscurum per obscurus, 73
KEN CANNING/BURRAGA GUTYA
   Old Clever Woman, 74
   Uncaptured, 76
BROEDE CARMODY
   from Shouldering Pine, 77
A. J. CARRUTHERS
   Music after Alison Whitaker, 79
   Axis 1: Axiality, 80
   Axis 42: Cryptic, 82
BONNY CASSIDY
   from Range, 83
DON MEE CHOI
   Yellow Translation, 84
STEPHANIE CHRISTIE
   Bitshy, 85
JUSTIN CLEMENS
   Trying to buy that what
      they have not got, 86
ALI COBBY ECKERMANN
   First Time (I Met My
      Grandmother), 87

ALI COBBY ECKERMANN
    Intervention Pay Back, 88
    Anangu Love Poems, 91
EMILIE COLLYER
    Friday Night at Jimmy Wong's, 93
    Homemaker, 94
    The Space Between, 95
MTC CRONIN
    New Ninety-Nine Percent, 96
BRETT CROSS
    from red / birthplace / islands, 97
MIKAEL DE LARA CO
    Cultivation, 98
    Canopy, 99
NOELLE LESLIE DELA CRUZ
    Weight, 100
    But death is not an optical illusion, 101
RODRIGO DELA PEÑA, JR.
    Hymnal, 102
DAN DISNEY
    from Human Positions, 104
ĐỖ LÊ ANHDAO
    Running into Fidel Castro, 108
CHRIS EDWARDS
    Look at that one!, 110
    People of Earth, 111
    Works of *et cetera*, 112
JOEL EPHRAIMS
    Prince Krishna, Icarus and the Voyage of the Zen Poet, 114
KATE FAGAN
    from return to a new physics, 116
MICHAEL FARRELL
    they asked for my death, 117
JOHANNA FEATHERSTONE
    A Bundeena Hideaway, 118
LIAM FERNEY
    Saturday's Typhoon, 119
LUKE FISCHER
    Blue Flower, 120
    Coastal Idyll, 122
TOBY FITCH
    In Memory of My Furlings, 123

LIONEL G. FOGARTY
    Australiana Crap, 126
    Tent Embassy 1971-2021, 127
    Murgon Brawl Cherbourg Brawls, 129
    Borri is Fire Waru is Fire, 131
KATHERINE GALLAGHER
    Blue Painting (1924), 134
JO GARDINER
    Alexander February, 135
ANGELA GARDNER
    Zero-Sum, 136
JANE GIBIAN
    Leftovers from a pirate party, 137
    from long shadows, 138
KERI GLASTONBURY
    from local/general, 140
JAMIE GUSMAN
    A Page Ever Coming, 141
HA JAEYOUN
    A Dining Table for the Clouds, 143
    12 O'Clock, 144
NATALIE HARKIN
    from Archival-Poetics
        Prelude, 145
        Memory Lesson 1, 146
        Archons of Power, 146
        Memory Lesson 2, 148
        RSVP, 148
        Dear Sir, 151
        Under the Act, 153
        State Lady Report, 154
MARTIN HARRISON
    Double Movement, 157
    Fence Posts, 158
    Breakfast, 160
J.S. HARRY
    They, 163
    Laws 1, 164
    Laws 2, 165
    Her night thoughts, 166
KEVIN HART
    Yes, 168
DIMITRA HARVEY
    Currawongs, 169

ASHLEY HAYWOOD
    Plant Script, 170
    Hippokampos, 170
    The Lure, 171
FIONA HILE
    Whatever, 172
    Bizarre Triangle Fetish, 174
HIRATA TOSHIKO
    P-E-O-P-L-E, 175
    Man Without Arms, 176
    The Next Day, 177
LK HOLT
    from Modern Woman Sonnets, 178
    The Expected Guest, 180
    Describe the Singularity in the
        Style of Emily Dickinson, 181
HONG YING
    Chongqing Slum, 182
    Fortune Teller's Dance, 182
    Electric Shock, 182
    Dreaming of Beijing, 183
    Mother's Clock, 183
    I Too Am Salammbo, 184
HWANG YUWON
    The Meditating Buddha Sitting
        Full-Lotus that Meditates on
        the Beginning of Winter, 185
    The Green Spider Speaks, 187
JOY ANNE ICAYAN
    The Alcoholic's Prayer, 189
    Harvest, 190
HOLLY ISEMONGER
    Sweat, 191
    My Week in Haiku, 192
    My Life as an Artist, 194
ISHIGAKI RIN
    Living, 195
    The Economy, 195
    Plucking Flowers, 196
ITŌ HIROMI
    The Heart Sutra, 197
    Cooking, Writing Poetry, 200
ELEANOR JACKSON
    Endemic Species, 205
    Hard Lockdown, 206

ANNA JACOBSON
    Letter 2, 207
    Letter 4, 207
JILL JONES
    Erosions, 208
    Dream Horses, 209
MOOKIE KATIGBAK-LACUESTA
    Borealis, 210
    Sinking Cities, 211
KIT KELEN
    Go Bush, 212
SK KELEN
    from Don Juan Enters
        The Underworld, 213
KHAING MAR KYAW ZAW
    Rebel Venom, 214
    Her, 216
KIM HAENG SOOK
    A Not-crying Child, 217
    The Goodbye Ability, 217
    Hormonography, 218
    Thick Rainbow, 219
KIM MIN-JEONG
    Tits Named Dick, 220
    Penis Named Face, 221
    Finale, 222
KIM YIDEUM
    Anna O's Office, 223
    At the Laboratory, 224
    December, 226
JOHN KINSELLA
    Destabilising (the) Pastoral, 227
    Swarm Fibrillation of Orbit
        and Warning Areas, 228
    Full Immersion, 229
    Suppliants – an ontology, 230
    Affected by What We Read,
        What We Recall, 232
ELENA KNOX
    New Dress, 233
KOIKE MASAYO
    Men, 234
    Bathhouse, 235
    A Short Poem about Daybreak, 236

JOSE F. LACABA
    Response, 237
    Saturday Afternoon, 238
MIJAIL LAMAS
    Away from Naming What
        Names You, 239
LÊ VĂN TÀI
    Where Can A Seed Take Root?, 241
    Wandering Illusions, 242
BELLA LI
    Dimanche: À travers la terre, 243
KATE LILLEY
    Her Bush Ballad (Bourke St Elegy), 251
    Tilt, 252
DEBBIE LIM
    Bodies of Pompeii, 255
RACHEL LODEN
    from Kulchur Girl, 256
ASTRID LORANGE
    58, back-most lot …, 260
RAMON LOYOLA
    Touch me where it hurts, 261
LƯU DIỆU VÂN
    Becoming a professional soliloquist, 262
    Here comes the truth, 263
JENNIFER MAIDEN
    Diary Poem: Uses of Cosiness, 264
    Maps in the Mind, 265
DAVID MALOUF
    Seven Faces of the Die, 266
GREG MCLAREN
    Thirteen Ways of Looking
        at a Black Dog, 270
PHILIP MEAD
    Really. Our day resembles …, 272
    sundown: that moment …, 272
MINASHITA KIRIŪ
    Tropic A, 273
    Circulation Sacrifice, 274
PETER MINTER
    from morning, hyphen, 276
MARK MORDUE
    … so anyway the bones are small, 277

NGUYỄN THÚY HẰNG
    Page Quatre-Vingt-Seize, 278
    Temporary Loan, 280
NGUYỄN TÔN HIỆT
    A person is writing, 281
NHÃ THUYÊN
    a path, 284
    the fear of borders, 285
    discourse on water, 286
    grass, 287
ŌSAKI SAYAKA
    Wandervogel, 288
    The Next Planet, 290
    A Special Day, 291
    Rebirth, 292
OUYANG YU
    Listening to the Chinese
        Woman Philosopher, 293
JORGE PALMA
    Paraphernalia, 294
    Afterwards, 295
JASMINE NIKKI C. PAREDES,
    Artificial Islands, 296
    After the Flood, 297
ALLAN JUSTO PASTRANA
    Inner Life, 298
    A Colony, 300
EDDIE PATERSON
    just to the right
        of the heart of it, 301
PHAN QUỲNH TRÂM
    A Poem About Having
        Nothing to Say, 302
    Risk Management, 303
ANUPAMA PILBROW
    Insect Poem, 304
    Happiness Poem, 305
FELICITY PLUNKETT
    Seastrands, 306
DOROTHY PORTER
    The Ninth Hour, 308
STEPHANIE POWELL
    Gentle Creatures, 312
    Between the flags, 314

DAVID PRATER
  Jetlag World, 315
PETER RAMM
  Minnamurra Sestets, 316
  Losing You, 318
NICK RIEMER
  Afterlife, 319
ARIEL RIVEROS
  Settlement, 320
CLAIRE MIRANDA ROBERTS
  Stones, 322
  Backwater, 322
  Reflection, 323
IZZY ROBERTS-ORR
  The Birthday Party, 324
  If the Sunlight Had Echoes, 325
NOEL ROWE
  Pentecost, 326
  Next to Nothing, 327
TRACY RYAN
  Gwenfrewi Walking, 330
JAYA SAVIGE
  Magic Hour L.A., 331
SUSAN M. SCHULTZ
  from Dōgen Series, 332
JOEL SCOTT
  Goggle, 335
SEO DAE-KYUNG
  Autumn Night, 336
  The Inspection, 337
KAZUE SHINKAWA
  Ordinary Gods, 338
  Island, 339
  As I sit on the grass, 340
  Over the Bridge, 341
  How Many Bitter …, 341
GIANNI SICCARDI
  from The Forest, 342
ELLA SKILBECK-PORTER
  Time Passes: The Window's Light
    On the Floor Under the Chair, 343
  Avalon Airport …, 344
PETER SKRZYNECKI
  The Autumn Winds are Cold, 346
  Rain at Night, 347
VIVIAN SMITH
  Traveller's Tale, 348
SOH SAKON
  (Running: That Night 14), 349
NICOLETTE STASKO
  Hummingbirds, 353
SVETLANA STERLIN
  Apocalyptic Sunsets at
    the Дача, 354
EMILY STEWART
  from Silence is Ok, 356
JAMES STUART
  The white horse, 359
  For the twilight hour
    which passes, 360
THOM SULLIVAN
  Red Creek, 361
  Carte Blanche, 362
NIOBE SYME
  Sub-Prime Along
    the Mississippi, 363
TAGUCHI INUO
  The Cathedral, 364
TANIKAWA SHUNTARŌ
  Keep Writing, 365
  Good-Bye, 366
  Ordinary People, 367
ROLANDO S. TINIO
  Postscript, 370
  Chorus of the Street, 372
JOEL TOLEDO
  A Record Year for Rainfall, 373
  Attachments, 374
JOHN TRANTER
  Tasman Sonnet, 375
  Crowded Hour, 375
JESSIE TU
  The Hotel, 376
SUZANNE VERRALL
  Criminal Intent, 378
  The Department Store
    of Everything, 379

ANN VICKERY
  On Not Giving an Account
    of Oneself, 380
  Concept Creep, 381
  Listed Land Uses
    of Moonee Ponds Creek, 382
TAIS ROSE WAE
  Finding Home, 383
  Imago, 384
WAGO RYOICHI
  from Since Fukushima
    Pebbles of Poetry Part 1, 386
COREY WAKELING
  Lectures of the Alone, 390
MAGGIE WALSH
  Christmas Time, 391
  Free, 393
PETRA WHITE
  Family Tale, 394
NICK WHITTOCK
  Sie t-ins 88, 395
JESSICA L. WILKINSON
  The Twelve, 396
  Elegy, 397
  Broadway, 398
  Hollywood, 399
CAROLINE WILLIAMSON
  from January, 400
MISBAH WOLF
  The Mango Tree in Khai Village, 402
  A Little History of the World, 402
ED WRIGHT
  The Empty Room, 403
YAN JUN
  Charter Sonnet, 404
YANG LIAN
  The Last Starlit Sky at Fifty-Five, 405
YOTSUMOTO YASUHIRO
  Starboard of My Wife, 406
  On the Lake, 407
MAGED ZAHER
  from Love Breathes Hard, 408
ZANG DI
  History of Daffodils, A Book Series, 411

ZHAI YONGMING
  In the Old Days, 412

YOTSUMOTO YASUHIRO,
MING DI,
KIM HYESOON,
TANIKAWA SHUNTARŌ
with DON MEE CHOI
  from TRILINGUAL RENSHI
    The Role of 'Sea', 413

Acknowledgements, 421
Contributors, 423

LIVING SYSTEMS

INTRODUCTION IN TWO POEMS

This anthology marks twenty-five years of small press publishing. Since 1999, Vagabond Press has worked with some remarkable poets from around the world, many of them gathered here. Big-hearted, big-brained, inquisitive, generous souls who turn language upside down, inside out, and the world with it, making it strange and new, before giving it back to the reader.

Dorothy Porter
Comets IX

After sunset
above the horizon
near the hunched bright arch
of the Westgate Bridge

through binoculars
shivering

you looked looked looked.

But what difference
does the looking
of a finite terrestrial
neurally aglow mammal
really make?

Let your own watery
chemistry's delusions
boil
for a pulsing moment.

And believe
your squinting eyes
your warm breath
keep this fuzzy speck
blazing in and out
of the night clouds
going.

With this anthology, the aim was to produce a book to flip through, read and re-read, dogear, dip in and out of and return to years later. A book for the curious and for poets just starting out. Given our backlist, there was a Borges of anthologies possible. This is the one that evolved. It's diverse and inclusive, not exhaustive or comprehensive. Over the next twenty-five years, we hope to continue to create more space for more writers from more languages in our region.

We live in language. It lives in us. More than any other art form, poetry breaks the beautiful trap of language open, revealing and reinventing our human syntax, showing how we connect to each other and the world we live in, and that for all our differences and our unique experience of the world, language and each other, we're not alone.

Ōsaki Sayaka
ETERNITY AND A DAY
Translated by Jeffrey Angles

You lean on the first big tree you see
You were just born but are already exhausted

A stranger is seated next to you
Perhaps he was once important to you
So you decide to dance with him

The sky is as clear as a Van Gogh
The birds are circling
The forest is rising up
The people are gathering

The people are being counted
The traffic is being swindled
The ambulance is stopped
The industries have grown dark

You'll decide once
If you like these things
Then you'll change your mind
Is it better to feel sad about what you don't know?
You don't know

(You think you'll keep an eye on everything
But when you keep missing things
You simply sigh with relief)

The child who stole the yellow jacket
Dashes off into the woods
This single
Scene
Sort of enviable
Sort of celebratory
Sort of like a game in which you search for what's not the same

You wait for the low song
Of the falling rain
To grow audible

Mostly likely, ever so lightly, you will surpass
The speed at which you feel no despair
Though circles may not have them
You do have a beginning

In another twenty-five years, the press will hopefully still be publishing. Maybe by then we'll be publishing poets who first stumbled on poetry here, in this collection, and found in the magic of language, that most human thing, the chance to witness and question the world as it appears, new and newly possible, word by word, syllable by syllable.

August 2024

RIMBAUD'S SPIDER (LAKE TOBA, SUMATRA)

They were more than friendly,
sharing the room,
he, diplomat of immense politesse
and the spider,
who was sorting photos, drinking beer,
serene, with a foot on a trigger,
guardian of the lakeside cold and deep.

Such priestly stillness!
With all of Java's crimes (that history
none must speak of)
hanging there like tear drops,
suspended in her web
with nothing else but themselves
panoptic, self-governing and oblivious
to drought, flood and fever,
more rigged than a schooner, in the bathroom,
just below the cistern.

She may be dead or stoned, she
hasn't moved all day,
he had spoken to her once
of his humble notion
of no pain beyond progress, then

she carried on, the web
made perfect and complete.
he her guest who overstayed
who never left, the one she chose
to lay her brood within
that eats him from inside
infused with an acid to keep him fresh.
For he would survive
on a spider's sliding scale,
paralytic with affect
for each hour of night
sucking nothing else but violets,

or by casting his eye
on her mountain or her valley,
the intricate realm of her.
In her fraying sheet
wrapped and woken at dawn,
in an Eastern light
intense with forgetting,
a forgetting of forgetting:

which divided him again,
into a jewel of many faces,
multiplied in the exploded
constellation of her eyes
in which he lost himself again
like a boat among islands,
singular as a memory
equal to her kind.

OMEN

Of a blue-black fledgling embalmed
in river's frozen page.
The early buds of sugarbeet, wild mustard,
gone now to frost, too early for their sap to rise.
When there's snow in the Cevennes
the farmers say next season's onions
will be thick in skin,
those farmers who are never wrong.
Neither is the weather or its message:
those birds we pay good money for.
And without a doubt, there it is:
a flock of small birds heading for the sea
heading for Africa, where
everyone believes in them,
in headlong flight
from all the whiteness of this earth,
for this is good for them
doing what they always do.

from EVENTAL

I'll begin with what I know: my life
the situation of a dire struggle

to avoid usurpation by the state
of survival *inter alia* how to be

in a world where being ends
up as nothing but a knowable fact. Say

dreams, self-discovery, journeys
ultimately saccharine, often sly

words to fill the lacuna at the core
of any story. I've always longed

to detect a simple, beautiful scent
amid the rank miasma of rotting

midden of dates and names; history
signposts soggy mass graves

ibid memory stirs sentiments
that simmer to barbarity. *La Terreur*

for example, linguistic plaster
to seal the cracks in presentations

of pure multiplicity of the event
a là la Grande Peur. But I'll recall

the act at a tennis court in Versailles
sans the guillotine fetish, to show

how it happens, how a truth can be.

NEWS FROM HOME

It's been a while, I thought I should write and say 'hello'.
The people here seem nice so far: friendly, and gentle.
Muscular wings grow between their shoulder blades
and they walk like earnest yoga students back home.

The people here seem nice so far: friendly, and gentle.
I think I became invisible at the border.
They walk like earnest yoga students back home:
their chests puffed out and their tail bones down.

I think I became invisible at the border.
They all have a USB port at the base of their necks,
their chests puffed out and their tail bones down,
smelling faintly of newsprint and caffeine.

They all have a USB port at the base of their necks
and there is a yellow flowering plant everywhere
that smells faintly of newsprint and caffeine.
Nightfall, when wattle stains the doubting heart:

there is a yellow flowering plant everywhere.
So, tell me the news from home.
At nightfall, when wattle stains the doubting heart,
it makes me feel homesick in my own skin.

So, tell me the news from home:
does the anorexic girl still walk to the shops?
It makes me feel homesick in my own skin.
Does it still feel like you could walk straight into the ocean?

Does the anorexic girl still walk to the shops,
her white shopping bag always empty?
Does it still feel like you could walk straight into the ocean
as you come down the hill after getting off the school bus?

My white shopping bag is always empty,
muscular wings grow between my shoulder blades
as I walk down the hill after getting off the school bus.
It's been a while, I thought I should write and say 'hello'.

AT WINTON

Here your body learns the seasons.
She brings you a home-grown pear, slightly bruised.
It rests in your palm like an answer.
At night, while you dream, the dog whines and the wombat
snuffles and scratches at the wooden bedroom door.

The weekend is sticky with traces of apple jelly and toast crumbs.
You sit back on the couch full with wine and love
and high on coffee, bitter and sweet with condensed milk.
Josh takes you back to your past:
playing Uno and Snap with dog-eared cards.

Brin builds a dog race up behind the house
with wire and wood. Small adjustments.
You fight a temperamental DVD player,
walk out to pick bay leaves and oregano by starlight.
Sitting in Easter long weekend traffic you shift slowly

back to your Sydney state. The car struggles to get up hills.
Underneath the engine runs a clichéd tune:
I miss you I miss you I miss you.
You note speed limits, consider new approaches to happiness:
buying new clothes, acquiring a boyfriend online,

wonder why it is so important.
You are reminded again of how many people there are,
how strange a collision of factors determines what we are,
how small this corner of consciousness you keep defending
with each breath.

NEIGHBOURHOOD WATCH

Early one Saturday morning you watch
her as she shuts the door to her three-
bedroom terrace & crosses the road,
highlighted for a moment in the sunshine.
She is wearing a red & white made590 skirt,
a black Witchery top with a blue plastic bird
brooch, Salt Water Sandals on her feet
& a hat made from a patchwork of recycled
vintage fabrics. She has a Monsterthreads
jumper over one arm, a tote bag with an owl
on it over the other & a KeepCup in her hand
(in your mind you can smell the coffee).
Some days she walks to the GoGet parked at the end
of the street. But today she appears to be walking
in the direction of the local organic produce markets
where she will no doubt buy carbon neutral food.
Sometimes you wonder what she is doing inside
her house: eating ash-coated goats cheese
on sourdough bread while listening to FBi radio,
flicking through a magazine of new emerging
writers, or rewatching Mad Men? You think,
not for the first time, about how she would
be such a good character for a play: the wealthy
girl from the North Shore who makes her way
to the hipster wilds of the inner west & goes
no further, apart from occasional trips into
Marrickville for pho or to Parramatta to visit
the one friend she has who lives out there;
how she would be so easy to write,
how it would be so easy to mock her –
so much harder to take her seriously.

CATASTROPHE

the taxi driver
will deliver you
to the wrong house,
you will miss the plane,
the waitress will
forget your order,
you will be late,
you won't be able
to find the right building,
the right room

your phone/keys/wallet
might have fallen
out of your bag,
your phone charger might
have disappeared in the night,
your guide to APA referencing
might have gone missing

and under this some
greater loss
some inadequacy:

people will discover
how stupid you are
how fundamentally
different
how you are

silently
fucking
things up

IN THE 50s
Translated by Robert Nery

Our eyes are opened
By even a little violence done to us;
The fright and anxiety we were forced to swallow
Was the holy water in which legends and heroes
Were baptized in ordinary life.
Remember Juan T. who went away with others not from here
After he was beaten up by drunken Civil Guards?
Really, in those years
Many of us became men early,
And the trigger drew many like a loadstone
When the tank torched in the war
Still lay unburied by the side of the road.
The nights were long and tedious;
The days, sad and short.
No warning thud when death and horror visited;
In the massacre at Pinambaran and at Magmarale
And that ambush by a patrol in Paluwasan.
In those stray bullets that nipped a whole family
And the kidnapping of those three drunkard Civil Guards.
The day was the glint of helmets, and sobbing in the stockade;
The nights, bearded shadows and bloody encounters.
Ten thousand pesos were on the head of Commander T.
When the townfolk caught a sergeant
Shouldering a sack of hens and pullets.
No-one was certain of friend or enemy;
In the staccato machine-gun and angry dagger
None could be certain of flag and belief
Because life, if it was living,
Was caught between the smell of lead and candle smoke.
Commander T. surrendered in a hut in Arayat,
He had malaria and wounds in his feet,
But he felled three soldiers
Before he ran out of bullets and gave himself up.
The nation came through those years
With scars on its memory and conscience.
Some saved their rifles for the war yet to come;
Some came home to missing wives and hanged themselves.
The Americans gave out artesian pumps and books;
Before you knew it, a former sergeant

Was elected mayor in the next municipality.
Juan T. was granted amnesty
And remains a bachelor living alone in his farm.
Ask him about Commander Firelight
And he looks up at the sky.
Make much of Fernando Revilla's amulet,
Or Ben Tumba's hair-raising gang,
Or the student union you've set up
And in the tune of the smile playing on his face
Is all the weight of the rain he went under
While you wipe the milk from your lips.

BEDS AND LOOMS
Translated by Jeffrey Angles

My job was as an operator, to call people out
An inexperienced girl like me
Pick up the receiver, run to the factory floor
And among the noise of looms – *clackity-clack, clackity-clack*
Stand up straight and shout into the women's ears
'Sat-chan, telephone!'

The call that day was for Yai-chan
I dashed through the place
Where we punch the cards for the looms
Through where we prepare the threads for the warp
There, where we spin the thread, I saw a pornographic picture on the calendar
Like in a public path, breasts exposed
In a factory where all but the two who fixed the looms were women
They would let the real thing spill over as well
If a baby cries, you've got to let them feed
The women working in the factory
Put their children on their back, carried them to the cribs
They were saving their money
The oil of the machines, the oil of their hair, the breast milk
Those were the scents of the factory
I hated it, didn't want to breathe them in
Baby beds and power looms, baby beds plus power looms, baby beds as power looms
Clackity-clack, clackity-clack, clackity-clack, clackity-clack

The call was for Yai-chan
She had a reputation for her weaving
To finish weaving a bright red robe for a priest
You need a good hand, good eyes, a good mind, a good vagina
It won't work if she doesn't, if she's not a woman among women
The woman manager would always say
Those priests, never knowing a woman
It's not Buddhist recitations that let them reach Nirvana
It's our woman weavers
It's the robes against their skin that calm their desires
Yai-chan's hand is the oar, rowing on the River of Three Hells
The gold-threaded brocade (four hundred thousand yen per meter)
Worn by the abbot of the high temple
Supported
The life of the factory

The twenty-two workers, their husband's liquor
Their mother-in-law's incense
Their savings for their sons' trips at school

Yai-chan also had a child
With the delivery boy from the noodle shop
Who kept his wife in the country a secret
Their relationship broke off, like noodles cooked to mush
In the stewing stomach of her anger
She gave the baby to her older sister and her husband
So that's why
Even though she was past thirty and her breasts were swollen full
Not a single drop came out, nipples bound up tight
That's why the pornographic picture in the woman's factory by the
Baby beds and power looms, baby beds plus power looms, baby beds
as power looms
Was an overripe icon of Yai-chan, she who had no one to give her milk
The woman manager would say,
'The worries that cause her to crease her brow
Are what make her work late into the night
Are what make her a woman among women
We put our hands together in thanks'
Not a very considerate thing to say
My job was to call people out
Yai-chan was farthest back
If the caller got impatient and hung up
We would have to call back at our cost, factory accounts determined my speed
I ran, I ran
I ran as fast as I could
In the place where we stored the thread, piled with spools
I noticed something, something flat
Clackity-clack, clackity-clack, the machines were moving by themselves
She was not there
The Maria-Kannon of the Weaving Factory was not there
She was not standing there
She was asleep, she was in bed
She'd hauled in a double bed!
Yai-chan had been doing it
During the lunch breaks with Sho-yan who fixed the looms
The femurs before her sacred gate
Must have *creeeeeeaked*
As they opened
(Who can say a baby bed was acceptable

But a double bed was not?
The factory worshipped her skill
If in this woman among women
We had a secret buddha
Who could say
She should not open her shrine?
Her loom weaves the robes
Clackity-clack, clackity-clack

The phoenixes in pure gold thread
Unfold line
By line
Their combs fall forth like plumes, their claws sharpen
They dance up
In the patterns upon the back and sleeves of the priestly satin robes
The open eyes of the cloud dragon, long whiskers of the rising
dragon, scales covering the mystic dragon
Dance down
To the birthplace of the thread
Where they intertwine
With the thread
To breathe in the sweat of the rustling sheets
From the double bed found there
The dragons, phoenixes, and lip-licking priests
Clackity-clack, clackity-clack, clackity-clack, clackity-clack
Double bed is a power loom, double bed as a power loom, double
bed with a power loom
The woman manager
Foamed at the mouth in anger and
To this day still recites the Heart Sutra
Before the shrine of her ancestors

Clackity-clack, clackity-clack, clackity-clack, clackity-clack
Form itself is emptiness, Emptiness itself is form
Sex itself is emptiness, Emptiness itself is sex

    Call them out
    Be called out
    We women are called out

SHADOWS
Translated by Jeffrey Angles

In this place suddenly thrown into disarray
It is impossible to distinguish
Between what is garbage
What is not and what is still useable
So much earth, sand and dust
Has fallen that
Everywhere I see
A great can of refuse
The mucus I wipe on my sleeve is black
The throat and the lungs are eroded
Let it be, just the way it is …
Listless and resigned, I roll up my sleeves
And muster what little enthusiasm I can
I cannot let this be turned into a vacant lot
At least until I pick up the marble
I dropped here before it became this way
At least until I can pick through the refuse
And save at least one suitcase's worth of junk
It will be completely stripped away
It will disappear
I must stretch out my hands
And hold fast to
The shadows of this land
In a suitcase I will surely
Never open again

TAMAR
Translated by Eliza Vitri Handayani

Genesis 38:6
And Judah took a wife for Er his firstborn,
whose name was Tamar.

Where she stands, the land recedes
from her naked palm.
Shadows creep out of the sand
and turn into mourning veils.

The wind flaps.
The field loses its silence
and edges.
The words blow
from the north:

'Re is the devil. But they call him Er
so that you will not know him
and be deceived.'

Re. Er. Re. Er. Re. Er.
Like the murmur of water
in the throat of the stones.
Like the silver knots of the river,
and the silver that turns to black
beneath your eyes.

She looks up and sees:
there is no sky.
Above, the ocean rolls into waves
and swallows the stars and the clouds.
The sun falls into the abyss.
But the fingers of the whirlpool
claw into her flesh, tearing it
from four directions.
Fourteen Tamars are peeled off.
One after the other.

The moon dies with the travelers,
leaving a trace of red on their coats,
the fragrance of wild flowers on their hair,
and strands of hair that curl like sheep's wool and the cooing of pigeons
in the cracks of the rocks.

Time is drowning. Along with its signs.
The day weakens her
like age.

From the fields of Adulam
they take her
when the season is still young
and dreams are stranded
on the shores of leaves.

'Wash your feet, woman!
Wear your loincloth!
Hurry, before the day gets dark.
We have prepared a donkey
for you to ride.
And a man is waiting
to ride you.'

Where she stands, everything is over.

DRINKING AT THE VANDENBERG
for R.C. Acheson

A table. Five planks nailed to a pair of dead sawhorses
scavenged from construction sites – frame-houses,
half-assembled, walls the colour of sarsaparilla – red
pyramids of roof tiles, copper piping, cement mixers.
Twenty-five years ago, stashed poetry under a brick
in a hole in the ground. Passion fruit vines draping
the tool shed at the bottom of the yard, grape vines,
cherry tree and banana tree, the fields behind. That
place doesn't exist anymore, now roads and suburbs and
supermarkets. First grew up in a white convict house
on Pittwater Road, The Gables, built 1860 by one
Henry Miles – in those days timber huts, dirt floored,
burlap sack windows, cabbage tree roofs. Blind lady
my great-grandmother before she died, asleep
among the azaleas, hydrangeas, a red tricycle upsidedown
in green fishpond. Which one of these stories
should we go on living by? Drinking at the Vandenberg
the day they buried my father's mother, where my
father was born and I almost drowned by the sandbar
near the river bend. My father's hand came down
out of sunlight filtering through brown water, like the
angel's hand in Caravaggio's *Martyrdom of St Matthew*.
First memory, back in the pre-everything days when
knowledge was safely out of range and nights without
linebreaks and interruptions. Our families didn't
begin here, the long migration out of Ulster, Edinburgh,
Aachen. The only way out, they knew, was to
do something and being what they said they were?
Across the street, an empty plot where the old witch
kept a watermelon patch and mean broom handle.
We used to chase shadows in bamboo thickets,
reeds around the dam we trail-biked on, ironbark
sleepers piled up beside the entrance to the wrecker's
yard. Sometimes watched the veterans sitting
outside the Australia Hotel. The ANZAC drummer,
the last post tunelessly rehearsed once a year at the
town cenotaph. We knew the names by heart and knew
their families. Confronted with History, they never
stood a chance. It was a fight against all odds. Politics.

Most are gone, the farms in hock to banks, no one
wants to farm here anymore. Hard to imagine
boating parties on the river where now there's a petrol
station, itself already antique. What good's nostalgia?
Or memory, without 'progress'? Or poetry?
This is what they taught us at our school: *God Save
the Queen* under hot foreign skies. After, to exist
without anybody noticing, like a clerk of the court
of petty sessions. As to the purpose, nothing can be said.
Their world was always a world away, ours was just
a type of forgery done up in Depression-era gaberdine.
At night, speedway sounds and protest march delinquent
kids throwing cans at parked police cars. Striking
rail workers, dockers, BLF. Cold Chisel, Bathurst riots.
When the television broke down we left it that way,
a box filled with grey static, like a picture of what lies
behind every image. A succession of inertias, entropy.
Outside, a sky too brittle beneath and black above.
Where else was there to go? We didn't believe in a
species learning to evolve, we believed only in stupidity.
Years later still talking about that woman on the corner
of Parramatta Rd, with a piece of cake in a stencilled
cake tin. Or the dead soldier who sent postcards from
Europe after the War, slept on a park bench drinking
meths. So much for utopia. The decade when ideology
ended, left us standing in rain with fact-files and useless
megaphones. Walked across the Bridge on acid, head
full of Utzon and Bennelong's ghost. How long since that
first girl-boy kiss gave little meanings to little things
and channelled us towards middle-age and boredom?
Of course we live in a better world, someone must've
pulled us all up by the bootstraps. Growing up, the
distance travelled was never so far as we imagined it
should've been. Once everything had been done for us.

TO THE U.S. POSTAL SERVICES

Somebody phones in the middle of the night about
deliverance and the great conspiracy,
filling our heads with noise so as not to think.
There are others, too, whose minds are
contaminated by literature, still counting
the cracks in the wall. Paris was long ago.
There must be better ways to cover our tracks
than keeping all the options open.
Cruising the West Side, lunch with C.,
pastrami, coleslaw, pickles, Russian sauce.
Then Zoe on the Bowery, telling about Freud
at Coney Island, circa 1920, films and
pornography. Can love exist without censorship?
I pick up the phone, but it's no one, or I
forgot to dial. But it's late. I'm still looking
for your letter, the one with all the lines
crossed-out or stolen from books and people.
Please send stamps, dollars are no good.
P.S. The headaches won't go away.
Is there any news yet about future happiness?

CHARLES BLACKMAN, EVERYTHING CHANGED (1957)

There were thresholds of immensity. Waking
under the ringbarked tree, dead rabbit and
sand slithering up from a creek bed. Thin air
materialises in hands. Sky a cupboard door,
pale silvery with teapots, milk-white.
Everywhere the manically repetitive windows
of the soul. Dear Alice, last night I dreamt of
poetry or some other menial labour.
At least TV is painless, acts of desertion
from the near-but-far? Climbing under the table
(there was suddenly a table, with legs like
detached tenderness) to arrange the debris
into a passable symmetry. Our lost
specimen days, bits of the enquiring mind,
a dictionary of obsolete word-ends.
Somehow you were leaving, running away
before gravity sickness or the opposite of relief.
Though alarms and traps had been set,
the error was only realised after it was too late.

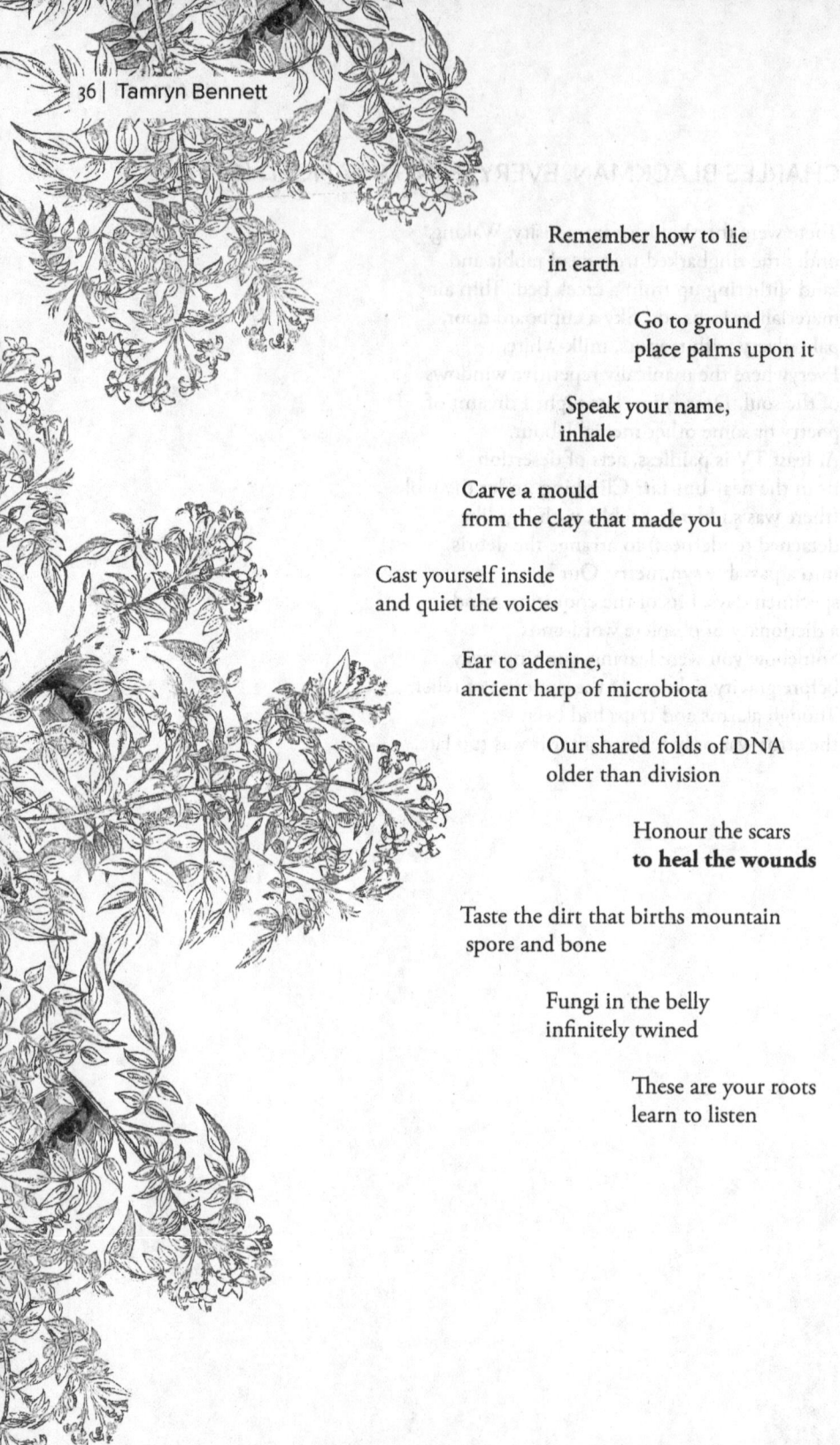

Remember how to lie
in earth

Go to ground
place palms upon it

Speak your name,
inhale

Carve a mould
from the clay that made you

Cast yourself inside
and quiet the voices

Ear to adenine,
ancient harp of microbiota

Our shared folds of DNA
older than division

Honour the scars
to heal the wounds

Taste the dirt that births mountain
spore and bone

Fungi in the belly
infinitely twined

These are your roots
learn to listen

In the desert you are yet to know
        we died.

      Limbs becoming sand
I lied down and laughed,

           nothing to be scared of in the vault
birds were invented once.

How we live is how we leave
      this borrowed body

your father writhing until red,
      breath held in battle with coyote.

    All of us covered in flies
until cells turn to chalk.

Here is where you begin,
fistful of galaxy reassembled on shore

      a little castle of salt lit with shells
      and a bag of broken charms.

      Dying takes a lifetime,
lightening through your limbs

don't rush the slow dark

With illustrations by Jacqueline Cavallaro

DETAILS FROM A BOOK OF WINDOWS

Like two fields crisscrossed from end to end with wires.

Two grilled openings into a darkened space
Out from which a few eyes peer from the back of a van on the road
A hand hanging on as if in a window of a jail
There is a man who sits hostage or guarding over goods inside
It is hard to tell.
In the back of the aluminum van other faces other eyes moving
Taking in glimpses of sky,
Glimpses of skyline.

Junctions later,
There are more people sitting in that box,
Their fingers on the wires.

Out of the moving cave
One eye peers into mine
As if to say –
The taxi radio advertising painkillers with rhyming verse.

Destinations tentative, our trajectories
Meander in the shadow of overpasses. Their fingers
Clutching the wires.
The view from the window
Short circuits the mind.

I do not know you do not know them by name.
What we share for now is the move of this road.

And greyer now the evening.
The best bits of the city are fried under the sun.
A train passes over our heads, the rumblings of
A thousandfold millionfold crammed homebound.
Day in and day out. The sun has seeped through us all.

What changes changes changes.

I look away. I lose sight of you somewhere
Around or after the twin camps, right before
The next flyover complex.

from **PREGRETS**

PREGRETS

put a little box with stuffed bird & toy
pistol in the bobbing footrest filled with
dessicated millipede husks, do dessicated
millipede husks, and humanity, matter?
light socket in pant leg fetishizes the X
out, nodding inside a bitchin' taxonomy
of agreement, head w/busted can lid sorts
its stuffing: oil (ears) newspaper (nose hair)
fabric (eyebrow scar) wire hanger (lonesome
eyelash conduit) furniture wheel (negative
retina space) zipper (hair line), as for the
rest of the bod: postcard compass paper-
clip and corkscrew on canvas, everything
pitched to the walls is poorly rendered
black box data revealing clues on paper
looks into its soul, sees super-powered
twinsies, cross out "terrible" insert "poorly
rendered" and referent of quiet desperation
(blasted), will be talking to the rays a lot
in the off season, a kingdom of isolation
ampersand it looks like metal's the queen

DEGRETS

the skull purses exchanged bitter remarks
&, exasperated, fled across the feels, New
Sauce summons its little family, to model
in intimacy, it's lately blooming homemade
mask, caught stealing fabrics employed cudgel
& stiletto merely grazing, Sigmar pokes you
a sidebar, that hawk laying eggs on an a/c
rallies a cam to live by their side, ornamental
framework boogers falling, hypo-thyroid agency
rising, iron riddled half-liters of blood running
free, taser-fed symbology awaiting finesee, think
of the many shits passed this week, suggestions
routinely become physical, to abet & abut the
population explosion, the legs of which remain
asleep, skaters known for their bloopers &
leaving by flying saucer soone enough spending
afternoons working whatever it is out fused labor
& work long ago, for all the goods did them
last zebra screensaver holds serve, invitation
to become pauses, big signature warns you
are not alone, below and to the left a face rolls
around its face, watching you take a break

PREGRETS

upsided down self-portrait by elder daughter
sees through the scaffolding of his and his
conceptions, speaking as a haphazard encounter
of a few lines, a few colors, a few shells, a few
insects, a few detours, a few toxins, a few lies
a few fade patterns, one definite assertion, the
accidental order for the lost instinct has to take
the shake of its measure, feed's full of burnt kids
every day-glo cut-out, inert, key lime irritant, foxy
beads, the essence of the shit so rich in isolation
elusive even to irrationality, happy sox pictured
in plastic studio setting up the deep steal again
& again on film in the boards, under the little
flash, the little pileated shop worn mask, someone
just walked in & took their time's photograph
I don't wonder about the minature objects lining
up in me not so secretly, all illusions currently
in the shop, which is all air, for instance we're
writing in sentences, nothing has to be having
matter, want to say a few words about lino
engraving refuse to insure the back-up drive
the stand-ins a gang of viscious holograms
in defiance of their own needs and so forth
Matisse was ambivalent about words they say

THE FISHERMAN'S SON

Perhaps it was when he first felt his shoulders
roll an oar, or when he pulled the thick boots on.
Perhaps it was when he saw the curved thin rod
of the moon angle into his father's face and hook
his mouth into an ugly grin; or when the sun
rerouted his eyes to the necks of wading birds
along the shore, as the first pink tones of dusk

uncurled along the ferns. It could have been
the way his father's knife eased out the eyes of so
many fish like spoonfuls of compote that gave
him thoughts black as the inky emulsions of squid,
a sleep no fishing boat could ease, nor star prick
with its comforting pin. Perhaps he learned nothing
from his father's face, except how whiskey

trawled sleep from his eyes and left him pursued
by pain and thunder and a show of lightning's
yellow flares. Perhaps when he felt the rod
pull his arms through a reel's band of static,
when he heard his father's voice in the headache
scudding low across his forehead, the reel
with an insect's drum-head pitch his heart into

summer's mounting heat; the slow drip of days
revved up by outboards then dispelled by a drill
of mosquitos, or weather finding tenor in its squalls.
Among stars and fish, those notes from the waste
hours he gutted, from the river's sweep of years,
who could know how many knives he heard
audition his nerves, or what beat his heart

took, or how many rounds of an ingoing lake
before the wind rushed into the uncaulked
cracks and left him face-down, deep-drummed,
gear-slipped, deaf to his inner repetoir, blind
now to the river's weather-beaten stare.
Perhaps from a tangle of yellow air, or when
he heard the wind bale out of a speeding sky,

or a firetail add its flute to the rankling handle
of a windlass, a lyrebird weigh its call in
with an anchor's unrolling links, some twisting
erratic pull of tackle as the mosquitos buzzed;
when he heard his father's voice in each dizzy
injected dose ... All day such talk went on
as the men brought in their hauls, gutting fish

to the noise of pelicans, those bills clacking
like clapperboards, the ease of routine. Here
among the brace of tides, as wind skips along
ropes left lank and loose and dangling now
among the sloops, no one fully knowing why
a boy would desire to die ... The avocets walking
the short with their hesitant, hair-splitting steps.

'QUE SERA SERRANO'

pish! cripes!
        partida serrana!
            scatalogue of filfa!
                bucolic scornographer!
                    flesh sin[e]s of the x!
                        apodyteriating cibacrime!

ahí está el busquillo

Ah, Ishtar, Beelzebub! (it came from outer space): *That's the ticket that exploded.* ('You're in!' assured the potsnpanhandler.) 'Lawks!' cried the simple folk in astonishment, '*¡Ave Maria Purísima! Halloo! Whoop! ¡Ja, ja, ja! ¡Ji, ji, ji!* The Nova Mob have installed themselves in the Villa Revocador, Spring Street, Melbourne. Think of it, autoerotic poker machines! Lucre is luzbel is luck is lust in orgasm is lues is *lusus naturae* is lush is lusk is lure. Lock up your donzels in distress! – The sky is falling, the sky is falling! – My god, young bucks could imitate him! – Art has broken past the NGV's Green Room! – Earthquakes, hurricanes, El Niño, *niños* and *ninfos*! – Jissom, saltpetre, whitehot spunk, briba and brine! Piss-a-Mouth, bring in the combat troops, the good ministers of the cloth, the hunkers of hammers, the synaloepha the cross! – *El jefe*'s still at the Hesperus –
'Ship ahoy!'

(*El señor Serrano waves a dissident ave to the gardeners on the beach.*)

[FADEOUT]

SYDNEY ROAD IN 2011

Sydney Road doesn't
lend itself
to odes.
It is too odd,
un-self-consciously so.
East collides with West
where Victorian buildings
take a backseat to
Lebanese bakeries, and
spray-painted calls to
radical thought
colour the walls that lead
to Safeway.

Safe
is not the way
Sydney Road is, where

intersections
are Freudian hotspots
for nonverbal rage, where

catcalls of all sorts
punch the mid-evening air, where
contests of all sorts,
between all sorts are
the topics of chatter between
slow sips of single origin coffee,

and somewhere not far,

a murderer lurks,
a rapist covers his tracks,
armed,
at large.
It is not
for making
romantic memories.

It is not built on
nostalgia, its
gaze fixes strongly on
the future, and
its engines (those
little shops
peddling the
ethical, the
diverse, the
hyperlocal)
run with no
signs of
stopping. An
express train, but to
what end or beginning? Maybe

a route that knows that
the way to roots is
not to lock down but to
branch out widely,
wildly, to

draw the gaze
upward, to
give the sun
something glorious to
catch.

T/HERE

This is not a place for candles, or the scent of red cedar
gathered on a hill to burn, or native plum, lit at night
to hold the urgent dead at bay: you won't wake to hear
the click of brumbies' hooves on a road that flows
to where the humans are, or blink to see the mob
jittering in the dawn air:
                            this is not a house
of language, in the first sense of the word, the one
in which it made the world, this is not a place of origin,
ground, or single source: this is not a road for drinking
in the middle of the night: you won't see
the ink of fire moving night and day across
the blotting paper of savannah, or the scorched paperbark
raining through a reddened dusk:
                                    and this is not a place
for gathering the raw fruits of the earth, or to learn
the names for lily root, honey, paperbark,
nor to hear the many uses
to which an axe gets put:
                         for that is not a life
of plainness in the hope of life unending, nor a way
of being gentle on the earth.
                           Here, you meet
no women keening for the death of only sons
on the lamplit urban roads, rock to skull, beating down
the dumb refusals of the mind:
                             and this
is not a place for dreaming
on the memory of rocks, or to hear the rain that drops
as though a sea were in the sky, or watch erosion
on a scale both intimate
and eons wide.
                 From these walls I cannot read
the lineage of human lives.

Manyallaluk, N.T.; Sydney, N.S.W.

WRITE BACK

you write back to your birth.
your birth was the beginning
of a word that is yet being spoken.
you are being spoken. you are a noise;
you are music; you are language.
you are a scream. blood-clusters of cells
spinning iron-spoked
buried in the flesh of a womb
still birthing you.
you do not know for whom
your final emergence
will be a greater relief:
you or that which holds you.

you write back to your birth.
indianness & brownness & womanness
a jute rope thrice threaded. abstract algebra:
your best subject. *mithai* in a ghee-stained
carboard box, sugar congealing
clear as the sap of stars
on the bottom. *suya* sizzling in a smoke-filled
hut. red-raw meat burning, turning brown.
your mother gave birth to you
in a country not her own. you give birth
to your child in a country
not your own. it's agony.
it would've been agony anyway.

you write back to your birth.
dirt-black, lotus-white, your fingers emerging
from the soil beneath your bones. reclaiming them.
Ibadan, Benin, you wandering
lost through a corridor of elongated wooden masks
that gradually become your face. in Delhi
the summer singes your soles like acid.
tongues of flame. skin peeling away, flecks of
dandruff on the cracked pavement.
gnarled hands knitting
an off-blue sweater for a doll with blank

plastic eyes. powdered *buknu*
on a *paratha* served hot from the stove.
you write back to your birth.
to poems composed on faded, lined diary paper
atop the flat, bird-shit-stained roof
of your *mausi*'s apartment building.
on the stairs up to the roof rests
the neighbourhood dog, panting, her belly
distended with a litter she is soon to deliver,
her swollen teats pink amid pale fur.
there will be blood on these steps the next time
you return. darkened, rusty. perhaps she at least
knew where she was going. perhaps she had
a place she could go to.
perhaps her pups survived.

you write back to your birth.
your sand-encrusted snakeskin unwound
like a clock being slowly, lovingly deconstructed
by a devout clockmaker's hands. you are the earth
that is trod upon & the river that is
drunk from, reduced, emptied
with every second. a consumable.
your beautiful brown scaled skin
becomes cheap linoleum
on which footsteps are smeared
like funeral ash. those who pass
never pass. a boarding school where the girls
are whispers, where the whispers
disappear. anaemia.

you write back to your birth.
to a closet through whose doors no fire
can penetrate, nor sound, nor memory. hands
of chipped gilt folded in prayer. a church or
a temple, a mausoleum or a garden,
tulsi leaves & green birds.
haldi-yellowed grains of rice
at the feet of a forgotten god. a cupboard

built of glass feathers
sharp as knives, in which you keep yourself
as if in a cabinet of curiosities. refracted
by rivets, by cracks.
people lean in to stare. they can't quite
make sense of what you are.
neither can you.

you write back to your birth.

translations & notes
mithai: generic hindi name for indian sweets
suya: a nigerian kebab
Ibadan & Benin: nigerian cities
buknu: an indian spice mixture used as a garnish
paratha: an oily, multilayered indian flatbread
mausi: a hindi word for "aunt"
haldi: a hindi word for turmeric

from OF CERTAIN DESERTS
Translated by Mario Licón Cabrera

DESERT ALIVE

The breath of dawn
ascends over the dunes

The morning light shows
the ever quiet shadow of the path

Silence grows in an endless symphony

Plants and rocks
beat a restless
inner life

Only men are amazed by their own bodies.

DESERT MIRAGE

We came to till the ground with the blood and sweat of faith
The sand extended untill it covered the settlers' houses

The few of us who were left
had seen the mid-day sun
saguaros like souls in pain
of those who'd died of starvation and thirst
rains of dust and water beating timber roofs

We
the last ones
we love commodity and idolatry
we live comfortably in sin.

BOUNDLESS (SASHA)
for friends & i.m. Sasha Soldatow

> '*Boundless, as we wish our souls to be*'—Shelley

in a Shelley-ish mood
                                          —or 'Shelley-induced'—

all weekend reading his biography
                                                      the music
of Bernie McGann
                    looping thru the house

            I lie for a moment by Pola
patting her side, feeling her rib-cage rise, fall, rise.
                                                                             She
has not yet given up on the idea of a walk.
                                                                  The sky
is blue, the wind slightly buffetting
                                                  branches of the pecan tree
     —or the hazel—
                          reach up
                                                                leafless,
silvery white
                 in the mid afternoon sun
                                            in a beseeching, idealistic
gesture
(Shelley has been reading Plato—
                                              which gets me
                                            'as close as I come'
to the great ur-texts)
                         the branches make me think,
                                                                         idly,
"ideal",
        "Mont Blanc"
                      "does this look Swiss?"
                                                        etcetera

it could just as easily be Italy

                                        & of course
it's Australia
                "that / is a fact,
                                as the Americans say"
—to quote Mary Shelley.
                        She also uses the term
'heaps'
        which I find delightfully teen-age
                                                almost
anachronistic
        though it can't be: that must be what the
modern Miss said in 1817
                        "went to heaps
                                        of places"
(bouncing illicitly around London
                                with Shelley—
with her boyfriend—
                infatuated,
                        about to embark
on the rest of her life)

                (Mary *was* a teenager in fact.)

They did do heaps.
                Pola, what will we do—
                                                Cath is
away
        in Hobart—
                her mobile phone rang last night
to let me hear Terraplane,
                        Pat's band
                                        'live' in the pub
Even over the phone they sound great—
                                        wild, euphoric
teetering on disjointed,
                        in just that way I like
danceable, grinding, crashing rhythms
                                harmonica playing the
brass lines, then Pat's voice comes in
                                melding rhythm & tune,
marrying them to end.
                                        There is

a guy talking near Cath, loudly, I can hear,
                                                            saying something
to his friend.
                        Wish I was there.
                                                    But for now, Pol, what?
—wanna do that walk?

                    I come home   cook food   read
                                Bleak House (!)

is on TV tonight
                    'racing' to its
                                        "startling denouement"
a phrase I have always loved
                                                    I ask it
about Cath's novels
                        Is it 'racing
                                                            to its
startling denouement'?
                                        She tells me No or Yes
She is with
                Hobart friends tonight
                                                        While I have
the option
                Of a party at Mill's
                                                            (my favourite
photo of whom
                    has her reading,
                                                                a lazy
teenager,
            lying on her bed
                                        —with sunglasses on, I think—
20 years ago
                        'approx'
                                                        (in fact, 24)
)
I was the age she is now
                                            when I arrived in Adelaide
& she was a little kid

I moved in with a house that Mary, her Mum, held together
—who was about 35 then
                                      (Mill, then, is for me
uncannily like Mary, her mum
                                      (who is not at all like
Mary Shelley)

                Mary Christie.

                Millie Dickins.

          #

      I consider the names

               #

                                An email from Pam
says Sasha has died
                        —who might have quoted the line:
          "All I want is boundless love"

                                         His *attitude*
might have quoted that—
                Sasha wouldn't

I remember 'Alastor' 'goes' (as teenagers say)
"(X) has died, & many worms & beasts live on".

I am glad to be alive
          —as Sasha was.

                "Heaps!"
I hear him say

                      & see him momentarily
shoulders hunched together, leaning forward
holding a glass, at about eye height,
                            a toast
to heaps of life, to boundlessness &
                              boundless love—
& fun
        but really, mostly, boundless love

would you call his haircuts, usually, 'gamin'? His skin was
olive, his features fine, his lips were full. He was beautiful,
& alert.
   My friend. Gone.

from ENFOLDED IN THE WINGS OF A GREAT DARKNESS

As I unfold
the pages of
the dreambook
more and more
diagrams open out.
What was I assembling?
It is not my life
or any vast
array of appliances
sent to me
from the future.
It does not belong
to my past or
the world's past.
Is it
the elaboration

of a space
soon to be evolved
for whatever remains
after us
or the shadow-shape
of where the earth
didn't go?
Perhaps a code left
by someone
piece by piece
remembering
their life
as a bird

or what the plankton dreamt
when the seas
bore the churned foam
of promise
or perhaps these
chaotic diagrams are
the history of the abandoned,
each spiral,
fold or
curving chamber leading

you further inside
the breathing of the thing
to the point where
it vanishes, a shell
left for
interplanetary ants
or silk worms that
transform
specks into glitter

or as if every leaf that
had fallen
or would fall
became a letter
to build
an immense
improbable word,
some
infinitely layered name
to which
everything
was reaching,
the void's
inexpressible
signature,
white space at
the end of all
corridors,
what silence
translates

*

if light
the sun's light
its bright dependable
presence among us
moving into our rooms
brushing our bodies as we wake
altering nothing

(so it seems) yet
subtly changing everything

arriving and retreating
beyond all interventions
indefinably here

is the closest
we will ever have

to a metaphor
for being dead

vanished
from so far off
we will glow
among our objects
and our traces

unspoken irreplaceable

the underworld's
almost indetectable
shimmer

       *

you stand in the doorframe
touched by light –
in your hands a cup
of grey-brown earth-coloured
warmth from which
steam is rising slowly.
Over your head
ivy laces its darkness.
I can't make out the season –
autumn or a strangely
spring-like winter morning –
and though you have gone eight years now
you are still in mid-life
only slightly bemused by it all

THE PARADE OF MOMENTS

In the here and now I am restless,
In the here and now I am scattered,
In the here and now it is cold, the sky is a purple tinge of grey and,
        outside, a heavy green foliage blankets the trees,
In the here and now a great distance opens between myself
        and the simplest shape of beauty, of joy.

And yet I have just been meditating,
And yet I have just been sitting, holding tight to breath-awareness,
And yet a moment ago my life lay before me, threaded together
        by long strands of radiance, of certitude,
A moment ago I said, inside myself I am Buddha.

Meanwhile my eyes sting from onions chopped
        half an hour ago,
Meanwhile my head throbs for no reason, slightly, persistently,
Meanwhile I squeeze my eyes shut till a quiet pulsing
        erupts from the still sadness at the earth's core.

And today I have listened to Mahler,
And today I have walked by the river,
And today I have filled pages with words broken loose
        like chipped stones.

It grows cold in the heavy depths of my boots.
Autumn spills quietly into winter.

Today I may be lost
or today I may be stumbling, more sideways than forward,
while daylight's ebb and flow
tilts a little more into darkness.
With no time to assemble them,
messages arrive from the vanishing world.

Today the house is still
and, in my shirt pocket, memory places
the note to collect from the Dry Cleaners the trousers
        with the hole to be mended
in the right pocket where my life might
        any moment slip through.

FROM THE COUNTRY OF PAIN

You message me from an airport.
You tell me there are loudspeakers playing hymns at full volume.
You tell me there is no water in any shop or in the washrooms.
You say the cold where you are is very personal and stretches from
    horizon to horizon.
You tell me time is not for speaking and it will soon make sense.
You ask me to describe carefully the lines in my right hand and
    where exactly my childhood scar runs. You say this is most important.
You say you are not frightened though each minute you are growing smaller.
You tell me sleep interrupts you, often. In between, the colours of the
    sky keep changing.
You ask me if the world is truly large and if I believe there was a past.

I cannot read the photo you sent me.
On this side
tides and faces recede.
I am staring into the book of water.
A chipped pebble roars inside my head.
I no longer understand
my own life.

FIVE COMPANIONS

1. Small spider

Next to the strawberries I am cutting on the kitchen counter
you step out
intent on exploring the world.
Gladly I leave you
your portion of the visible field
and the privacy of your millennial appetites.
   Already the first day of summer
is carving a space large enough
for both of us.

2. Raindrops

I am wearing a necklace of raindrops, more judiciously
rounded than teardrops, moulded into shape
by the greater gravity of earth and the sky's
overburdened need for equanimity.
   And when I come back inside
raindrops linger for a while along the windows
to sign their disappearance with random streaks.
I cannot hold onto a single one of them
long enough to recite even a short prayer
for their death.
   Gazed at for the moment of their being
they each have the perfection of utterances
the sky makes for the lowliest of creatures –
the slug, the ant, the caterpillar, the grasshopper
and for the outstretched hands of leaves
      also waiting to fall.

3. What is lacking

As if assailed by doubt
water suddenly lost its ability to move.
It stares at us forlornly
from the upper shelf of the refrigerator.

Addicted to my own thoughts,
unable to hold onto my own molecules,
I do not have the immortality of water.

4. My distant brother

Light, like water, is a strange creature.
    Suddenly, when I thought the day could do nothing but steadily get colder, light appears, stepping beyond the trees that seem to block it to become a presence all along the front windows of my house. Then I notice it has already stepped inside and is now inhabiting a small oblong stripe on the wooden floor. A moment later it's settled into a glittering half-presence that gently laps the patch of carpet at my feet.

    Of all the creatures I know it is the one I least understand. I could call it wilful as so it seems to me, but it also strikes me as the most solemn of life's companions though not without a distinct flair for playfulness.
    And now it turns firm and resolute, holding the scratch marks and spider webs of my east-facing windows in a steady embrace. I think it must be the sole creature whose only instinct is to give. At the same time I am loath to talk about light too much. For fear my words might be judged ill-considered and it would turn its back on me forever. Yet, over and over, since my first days my heart rises to meet it. It surely knows I want to follow it. Somehow I trust that we are kin.

5. In a divided landscape

Three dreams cross the river
while a crow flies ahead to announce them.

      Citizen of the dark earth
wading across a shimmering landscape
of moss and stone,
water creatures seek to enter you.
Already your belly is ballooning with shapes
that swim, wriggle and kick their way
through tangled memory-zones
of a life spent incubating
below the moon's surface.

      Tonight as you sleep
the dreams will gently guide your visitors
back to the margins of firm earth.
Suddenly free and extraordinarily alone,
where you will wake
the dreams will not tell you.

GREY-HEADED FLYING FOXES

bats they come
a stream of them
a spatter
decidedly flap flapping
hundreds now
like a discharging incinerator

creaking calling
smoking over Yarra Bend Studley Park
the boathouses and the oily loop of river
towards Burnley Gardens yapping
scolding pleading hollering at stragglers
yellow box gum blossomed
little rusty faces swivelling 360
rusty hinges
 strung with warm
  black chamois
   swinging by the
hooks like pterosaurs
looping and dropping

heading south east
   as the blue glows inkily
            dying into night

   resurgent after record winter rain
            sodden October
grey-headed flying foxes
big-bodied steady travellers
   rising from the skerricks
left from those who dropped
out of the skies heat-smacked
   last summer
            Black Saturday and
firebreathers unrained
and four horsemen of days
these are the survivors
   sons and daughters
this is how they win

A SECOND AGO

I see my mother
          as a type of gerbera,
    & have always known
babysitting anyone's mess
          can be another person's reward

             -

   my predecessors,
          I love them
             but don't want to imitate them,
               living in rest-of-world,
  knowing they,
           my predecessors,
were in main-world,
             europe, japan, north america

          -

debates rail across
          creative commons,
  I take a few of James Schuyler's
              peonies,
    Maggie Nelson takes the bluets

         -

spluttering in the city,
          conditioned to fortune
  against
         huge smoking days
   rolling in –
wild flames
         crown stands of eucalyptus,
  the sun a carmine lake

        -

my mother likes to know
             the wind's direction

        & to say it –
              'it's a north westerly'
&
      'the rain comes
              with a southerly'

I would like
     a speculative set
of laws
        that are friendly to life,
that's the main thing
               & that's all,
  really

just as
     I was feeling sorry
for the line break
  it all
        happened again,
               a second ago

HERE'S TO YOU

slashed by rain's small disorders
    the pamphlets' dyes
        stain my fingers

where no manifesto
    dares to go   I go
(soaked sopping)
    towards your letterbox

despite
    the din   the street debris
      the horns & screeches
the gutter spray

    (indifference is indifferent)

stuffing choices through your slot
    but don't imagine
        change

dreams of fixing
    the fucked
      won't be realised

  cleaning the air

    picking up plastic bits

little bags of dog shit
    tucked at the foot
of every tree

one in ten's
      photovoltaic

one in a million
      animals

are minerals are synthesised
           vegetables

toting calico bags
      of super seeds

~

car dust and rain
      grimy panes

the room is drunk
      the shadows are talking

~

in your entire existence
           so far
  your selfie
      was a fraction
    of a second

always apologising
  for
      being 'busy'

what kind of
      'busy'

Pine Gap busy
    viral disease busy

~

undecayable stuff
    has a fast redundancy anyway

I can replace you

                    biomimetic robots
can,

like, 3D print my dinner
          any colour

once
    we shared
              the love
      of anything food

(and people say
          'there is no care')

I work
     on the taste
     of muscle

tiny curled
      digestive howling
eating pig
      from the
Grow Finish Unit

(indifference is indifferent)

you'd adulterate the food
    (the 'Frankenfood')
        whenever you could

you always put
       the 'w'
    in wreckless

but   super sensitive

you knew exactly when to flee
        like a dog
            before the cyclone

INDUSTRIA

Aspire like your life depends on it
because it does. Change management unpicks the dead. The heart
has its pleasure and the fingers, mindset at the keyboard. It's early.
You are there before the others. Johnny-come-lately this fate unfolder,
the lazy kinks are post-truth. What you
are getting today peals
the new structure.
It has ambiguous rooms and largish pockets.
The pockets are best for strategic aspects
that have not yet been mapped. You name this with something
    capitalised and embed this mindfully while serving up other text of
    this movement. As you sip
the next big thing in dandelion heart-start
stars gambol from this sleepy player, your critical function.
Where the alchemists removed layers, a similar rhizome grew but
ends rescues by destiny; 'the universal promotion'.
Our collective engine fires lanky, gagged shots with a ghost-bidden
    cordite. We cannot
tell because pressing send is so down with conspiracy, and
comely splendour of articulated mess. You choose your words like
a compositor,
each specimen carrying the weight of hope and
her probable claims. Can you offset this lode, this removal
of all refs to your
dept, your profession, your role, the barcode you have instilled inside your
wrist (in latin). The policy change drags in a direction
away from your livelihood and you create this written wording
in shaded aspect to your seniors, who have commissioned with
hands quick on handsets, their throats thick with
dire.
They are beguiling times when you weave enough
non-ferrous materials amongst the axioms
and the cosmos. What of the cosmos?
The org chart is an Atlantic map, it is melting Antarctica
ice masses breaking, bergs beneath the surface. The melt metaphor
designs our feelings. Decisions float in and out of my consciousness as I tamp
them down with viognier and your thousand-yard stare.
It's a beautiful evening in the after-hours world, kitten at our feet and ripped t-shirts
sunk like impetuous suede on the lovelorn
jeans we never throw out.

YOU ARE POSSIBLE

Walking through the mint halls
I am ocelot again.
If this path does not open, golden brick road
before me, I will sledge it open in the
nearest of time. Come lately, I am what you
plaster your dividers with silent push pins.
I am where you congregate, like liquid pooling at lower lid
like the line where you can glide a white pencil.
Wide openly is the only way to go. I released my other self to her
highest realms (graffiti art, but where she is the aerosol) so with curling
tired finger I select, then delete my own appointments. It is done
when I say it is done. But for now, the briefing.
My aching temples.
All things equal we should have a good run.

from OBSCURUM PER OBSCURIUS
Translated by Mario Licón Cabrera

If at the end I had said it all?
If my words were only pretence and ash?
If concealment and silence and shame
had diminished to dust all my rambles?
If the happy days were just a vision the underside
mirage of what has never been?
If the final memory
had submitted fake coins and copper
broken light bulbs stains
funeral processions nothing
but black crosses
and anhedonia?
If suspicion and thistles
for a second
had not dwelled in my name and wounded it
and the words prostration defeat
had lost their meaning
I could
but my condition of useless being
the irremediable presence
of crows flying up into the northern sky
instructs me from inside
forces me to comply
the wicked lines of my hands
to smile to be always polite
the day-by-day deaths
If frustration gills
and the gallows have left their
irrevocable here and now?
If at last every thing had gone
to hell?
If gusts of wind
have swept away whatever I am
in a general cleansing?
If the curtain on the farce had gone up
a definitive exit?

OLD CLEVER WOMAN

Old woman sitting by road
waiting long time this one.
Tree keep hot sun out,
thinkin' hummin' old songs.
Leave hand mark in dust,
for big one wind take away
to her place of secret
she knows but not tellin'.
Slow dronin' noise commin'
along a road like one big firefly.
This be that that fella bus
fulla starin' one – pink face.
They lot silly that one
sittin' long – long time
on motor – hardly touchin' earth.
Close now drone roars,
demons from night time.
Big squeal – call him break,
alla time hurtin' ears.
Eyes shades over push em away,
alla same captain cook.
They makin' funny noise,
not talkin' – sorta like wild chook,
click – click – click – click,
they just love picture,
no remember – head must be empty.
Old tired eyes close, cover tears.
This old one need no picture,
mind say like yesterday all same
click – click – click – click,
the guns shoot fire,
little ones screaming,
scream never go away.
Pink faces make same no talk noises.
This old one got one big photo,
killin' times her mob dyin'
click – click alla same.
This lot take picture
put 'em in big book.
Tell 'em world they good,

they just love blackfella.
Click – click – same one,
gun – camera no matter,
all part of killin' thing.
So she sits all day
she's there all time,
waiting for big one firefly,
carryin wongi pink people.
She bin worryin' – grievin'.
Pink mob need photos,
makin' they feel good fella.
No picture – they go lookin'
maybe find big mob,
plenty trouble that one.
No more picture then,
they want alla people,
alla land – they take away.
Bring grog make wongi dance,
pink men takin' black girl,
too much frighten – bad way.
Old woman see alla time,
she bin waitin' before road,
just dirt track for horse.
Bus – horse same bad things.
She wait all same – never go,
she keepin' pink demon movin' on.

UNCAPTURED

You branded me
a number,
you flogged, tortured
and tried and tried
to culturally alienate me.
Cages, batons,
underground tombs
of death
to decay the soul.
Scar tissue
physical and mental
is your justice.
Year in year out
until violence is the norm.
Hysterical laughter
of supposed victory
of my oppression –
My spirits soars
the Old Ones strengthen
my will to survive
your barbarism.
Time grinds,
eternity –
release.
You crushed my body
but my spirit outlives
your strange ways.
I walk and walk
and walk to freedom
while you die
in your bile of violence.

from **SHOULDERING PINE**

There is not much to do in the apartment
except wander in small circles that get smaller.
I spend hours playing video games. After all, rolling through sulphur
is hard when you're stuck in other muck.
There can be too much adrenaline stim.
As an example, what will we call summer when
it's more than four months long?

*

Yesterday, I thought I saw my
dead friend at the depot: black Docs,
leggings, two ribbons of hair falling
from undercut. Our friends are counting on us.
I don't mean a lonely medical droid. I'm talking
before Alderaan's demise. I wonder if
there's guilt in hyperspace. I already know
the answer: in-game & at that market a sonic
imploder detonates my mouth.

*

I hold my breath when passing
strangers. This movement not unlike
a river. People sitting in small crop
circles next to a velodrome.
The question is: when does water
end? I recognise my friend's weary eyes.
She says it's not screen fatigue.
Sometimes the sound of rain is just leaves
scuttling across pavement.
I try to talk about something other than
case numbers, wildfires or the man in the white
house with COVID-19. The whole time her hand a galaxy from mine.

*

I'm not sure how much
time we have left on this spinning
rock in the sky,

I think, as a great gum reaches
for Orion's belt.
Just because a place is

beautiful doesn't mean you won't slip
down an abandoned mine
shaft. We're all panning

for specks of something.
A friend's Tarot cards describe
the road I must take.

I explain that a raw chestnut tastes
like carrot. We walk back
to the Airbnb under a warm lick

of rain. In a way, we are all
mountains: emptying ourselves into rivers
emptying into the ocean.

*

Have I told you how campfire smoke
reminds me of home but also
preparing to flee grassfire?

The last time a big one ripped through
it took so many bullets for the sheep to sleep soundly
among scratched earth that night.

Dear air, where have you gone?
My throat itchy from other people's
cigarettes. I write letters to friends in the smog.

Read that babies born under this kind of glow
are likely to have lung issues well into the future.
I love my friends, but some of you would be
fucking useless if society collapsed.

MUSIC AFTER ALISON WHITTAKER

A setting of 'line up' (2018)

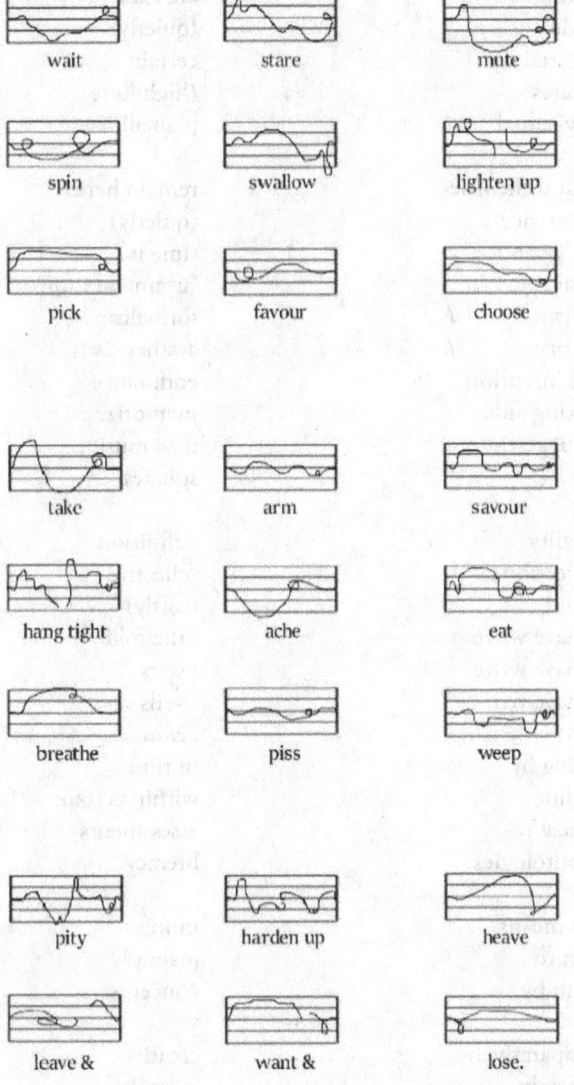

AXIS 1: 'AXIALITY'

the books	in us
are sad	incident
reunion	are axes
made	(quietly)
uncertainty	certain
spheres	(high flute)
play actual	plan all
what difficulties	remain here
start twice	(quietly)
the second	time is
scenic	'argumentation'
realism /	formalism
history /	aestheticism
and intention	endurance
writing aids	memorize
at suggestion	new musics
old	spheres
Axiality	definition
projection	reflective
sound	(softly)
to have written	: the fold
to have write	: stars
to have writ	: veils
sails	*Seuils* …
sailing by	in time
in time	within certain
radical re-	assessments
of ontologies	literacy
this means	more
than to	jusimply
mean by	concepts
comparatively	creative
heavenly	mortal
the dividing	tonality

Tonemic
the accent
literature
music

beginning
that difficulty
the entrances
'a reality
reach of

phonemic

The Boke
and perfect
structures
J-A-Z-Z !
a choruses
lineaments
leftwards
The Lunar
lunar plane
wherein
listens to words
and musick
inner contour
each axis
Marina's
sung with
till time
embraces
indices

accenting
exceeding
(quietly)
(flute note)

always 'next':
returns
convey
beyond the
wisdom'

enTrances

Uses Musick
harmony
scenography
junipers
long orotorical
lean
in lamplight
politick
planned with
Pericles
out of song
reaches an
that binds
reception
sufferings
(oboe +)
entraces
its slowest
finite series
its shifter

AXIS 42: CRYPTIC

II	III	I	IV
Constellation formed from unlimited gas. Monster secreted flower.	Alga to zebra — not the A to Z of mathematics	Thinking about writing material. Extended in a line.	Sentence, one foot in length, cut two thirds.
Bumps off small poetic songs. A string flower?	Exaggerate rubbish in old poem. Tedious 'nu' clue.	Do without the chorus. Invigorating new tune.	Illegally downloaded endless epic and settled its value.
	Speech containing no sound, like regret for following.		Poet's sound recording. The protracted use of lines.

from RANGE

1.
A bird breaks
itself down, ties
its tune into a knot.

Always begin with a bird, like ruling a line
that stretches into angles
                 an envelope shrieking
                 its opening
                 and its closing

                 Thus begun, unfold and draw in –
                 so near, the soft-burring edges of green or brown
                 will frettle under an easterly; so they will,
                 as a bird, fold over head
                           slide through marsh lines
                 pulling both ways into a long unmoving spoon.

2.
A bird calls, spans, takes off, slicks up water.
Before the air, it was in   hidden
on a rustling explosion of leaves.

Before the bird, the tree was downriver
somewhere, stalking; needle falls gave it away.
But don't listen for walking saplings: it's when their droppling
becomes a memory not too distant, that it's heard;
and all their scattered picks and knots will harden into recognition.

Only the wasps
jammed between rock and earth are
somehow
a chill clean pocket
of ready thoughts,

known at once
lean like sun –
step where the light comes again
quick.

YELLOW TRANSLATION

One Day the Governess ordered our Coachman to stop at several Shops; where the Beggars watching their Opportunity, crouded to the Sides of the Coach, and gave me the most horrible Spectacles that ever an European Eye beheld. There was a Woman with a Cancer in her Breast, swelled to a monstrous Size, full of Holes, in two or three of which I could have easily crept, and covered my whole Body. There was a Fellow with a Wen in his Neck, larger than five Woolpacks, and another with a couple of wooden Legs, each about twenty Foot high. But, the most hateful Sight of all was the Lice crawling on their Clothes: I could see distinctly the Limbs of these Vermin with my naked Eye, much better than those of an European Louse through a Microscope; and their Snouts with which they rooted like Swine. They were the first I had ever beheld; and I should have been curious enough to dissect one of them, if I had proper Instruments (which I unluckily left behind me in the Ship) although indeed the Sight was so nauseous, that it perfectly turned my Stomach.

One day I became a halo-child after many days of waving to American Hellos by the roadside with other halo-children like myself, shamelessly infrequently bathed, in other words, prone to rickets and tuberculosis. We were swell. The elevated feeling of smallness was what hooked us. At sunset we parted like tapeworms, breaking off into individual pouches in which we kept cigarette butts that we collected for certain medicinal uses our mothers requested. An Asian house is smaller to say the least. What spectacle does an Asian eye behold, you ask? Enormous noses. RITZ crackers are impressive too, their enormous holes. Enormity is our savior. We move our heads from side to side, swishing our haloes about, causing cosmic dizziness. We go into trance, a biting narrative of breasts, genitals, tongues, and umbilical cords of universal proportions that tie us to the formation of thought and unthought. So, to say the least in the most delicate manner, we are forsythias in the wind somewhere and everywhere flowering on the belly of the beast.

First stanza from Jonathan Swift, *Gulliver's Travels* (1726).

BITSHY

We're word-generating engines,
crazy for self-reflection, surviving
simply through believing our families
to be the most deserving. It's people
like you who make accidents happen.
We stormed away, not noticing
how dry the city had become,
a blast of hunger rippling in.

Give me lessons in my privilege –
how can I make it work more for me?
I took on all the ideologies and found
that now the world won't fit in
with their logical consequences.
In the fiction section a narrator
collapses from exhaustion – I can't
make up many more meanings for you
to clip the events of your life onto
she claims, pale as these pages.

In the irredeemable drag
of physical maintenance, control things
so the nerves aren't exposed,
    the deep program
a fickle bolt of sexual response
and all that blood. Heat brings the veins up
    arms made out of dirty marble
It's a whole new world, in which
we spend all week recovering.

That baby cries like a motor
turning over   not catching
    now suddenly roaring
into vivid falsetto forte life.
I don't get this new mode of precision,
and I don't know yet
what to do with the crystallised effects
of sensitised seconds in which
the compassion was all that could aid me
in sitting sober through
everything apparent at once.

TRYING TO BUY THAT WHAT THEY HAVE NOT GOT

We don't have that kind said the girl so me and me trumpet got
a different kind altogether and gave her $5.00, where'pon
she looked politely at us, then said sir, I need another 40 cents,
which was the price of the original loaf we'd ordered
but they didn't have, so me trumpet fanfarared out this one is only $4.60
and I pointed to the board where the relevant legend was inscribed,
where'pon she, furious, slung our change back at us. Typical,
if someone give you something you don't want
they still try to charge you for what you did but didn't get,
and they'll have that only-too-familiar feeling of frustration,
garnished with a frisson of a sense of your injustice,
will that does not know, agon of fools, self-improvement as history,
progress no one wants nor can even envisage, swarming
reconciled by the ending-to-come, secularised providence,
and will-to-power already implying a field of competing forces
in which some of them simply fail to take it right to the bitter end.

FIRST TIME (I MET MY GRANDMOTHER)

Sit down in the dirt and brush away the flies
Sit down in the dirt and notice the many eyes

I never done no wrong to you, so why you look at me?
But if you gotta check me out, well go ahead – feel free!

I feel that magic thing you do, you crawl beneath my skin
To read the story of my Soul, well I'm telling you I'm clean

And now yous' mob won't talk to me, so I just sit and sit
English words seem useless, I know Language just a bit

I sit alone, not lonely, 'cos this country sings loud Songs
I've never even been here before, but I feel like I belong

It's three days, here come the mob, big smiles are on their face
'This your grandmother's Country here, this is your homeland place'

'We got a shock when we seen you, you got your Nana's face
We was real sad when she went missing in that cold Port pirie place'

I understand my feelings now, tears push behind my eyes
I'll sit on this soil anytime, and brush away them flies

I'll dance with mob on this red land, munda wiru place
I'll dance away those half caste lies, 'cos I got my Nana's face.

INTERVENTION PAY BACK

I love my wife   she right skin for me   pretty one my wife   young one   found her at the next community over   across the hills   little bit long way   not far

and from there she give me good kids   funny kids mine   we always laughing all together   and that wife   she real good mother   make our wali real nice   flowers and grass patch and chickens   I like staying home with my kids

and from there I build cubby house   yard for the horse   see I make them things from left overs   from the dump   all the left overs from fixing the houses   and all the left overs I build cubby house and chicken house

and in the house we teach the kids   don't make mess   go to school   learn good so you can work round here later   good job   good life   and the government will leave you alone

and from there tjamu and nana tell them the story   when the government was worse   rations   government make up all the rules   but don't know culture   can't sit in the sand   oh tjamu and nana   they got the best story   we always laughing us mob

and from there night time when we all asleep   all together on the grass patch   dog and cat and kids   my wife and me   them kids they ask really good questions about the olden days   about today   them real ninti them kids   they gunna be right

and from there come intervention   John Howard   he make new rules   he never even come to see us   how good we was doing already   Mal Brough   he come with the army   we got real frightened true   thought he was gonna take the kids away   just like tjamu and nana bin tell us

I run my kids in the sand hills   took my rifle up there and sat   but they was all just lying   changing their words all the time   wanting meeting today and meeting tomorrow   we was getting sick of looking at them   so everyone put their eyes down   and some even shut their ears

and from there I didn't care too much   just kept working   fixing the housing   being happy working hard   kids go to school   wife working hard too   didn't care too much   we was right   we always laughing us mob   all together

but then my wife she come home crying   says the money in quarantine
but I didn't know why they do that   we was happy   not drinking and
fighting   why they do that we ask the council   *to stop the drinking and
protect the children   hey you know me ya bloody mongrel I don't drink   and
I look after my kids   I bloody fight ya you say that again   hey settle down we
not saying that   Mal Brough saying that   don't you watch the television   he
making the rules for all the mobs   every place Northern Territory   he real
cheeky whitefella   but he's the boss   we gotta do it*

and from there I tell my wife she gets paid half   half in hand half in the
store   her money in the store now   half and half   me too   all us building
mob   but I can't buy tobacco   or work boots   you only get the meat
and bread   just like the mission days   just like tjamu and nana tell us

and from there I went to the store to get meat for our supper   but the store
run out   only tin food left   so I asked for some bullets   I'll go shoot my
own meat but sorry they said   you gotta buy food   that night I slept
hungry   and I slept by myself   thinking about it

and from there the government told us our job was finish   the government
bin give us the sack   we couldn't believe it   we been working CDEP for
years   slow way we park the truck at the shed   just waiting for something
for someone with tobacco

the other men's reckon   fuck this   drive to town for the grog   but I
stayed with my kids   started watching the television   trying to laugh
not to worry   just to be like yesterday

and from there   the politician man says   *I give you real job*   tells me to
work again   but different   only half time sixteen hours but I couldn't
understand   it was the same job as before   but more little   less pay   and
my kids can't understand   when they come home from school   why I
cant buy the lolly for them   like I used to before   I didn't want to tell them
I get less money for us now

and from there they say my wife earns too much money   I gonna miss
out again   I'm getting sick of it   don't worry she says   I'll look after
you   but I know that's not right way   I'm getting shame   my brother
he shame too   he goes to town drinking   leaves his wife behind   leaves
his kids

and from there I drive round to see tjamu   he says his money in the store
too   poor bloke   he can't even walk that far   and I don't smile   I look

at the old man   he lost his smile too   but nana she cook the damper and roo tail   she trying to smile   she always like that

and from there when I get home   my wife gone to town with the sister in law   she gone look for my brother   he might be stupid on the grog   he not used to it   she gotta find him   might catch him with another woman   make him bleed   drag him home

and from there my wife   she come back   real quiet   tells me she went to casino   them others took her   taught her the machines   she lost all the money   she lost her laughing

and from there all the kids bin watching us   quiet way   not laughing around   so we all go swimming down the creek   all the families there together   we happy again   them boys   we take them shooting   chasing the malu in the car   we real careful with the gun   not gonna hurt my kids no way

and from there my wife   she sorry   she back working hard   save the money   kids gonna get new clothes   I gonna get my tobacco and them bullets   but she gone change again   getting her pay   forgetting her family   forget yesterday   only thinking for town   with the sister in law

and my wife   she got real smart now   drive for miles all dressed up going to the casino with them other kungkas   for the Wednesday night draw

I ready told you I love my kids   I only got five   two pass away already and I not complaining bout looking after my kids   no way   but when my wife gets home   if she spent all the money   not gonna share with me and the kids

I might hit her   first time

ANANGU LOVE POEMS

1.
I will show you a field of Zebra Finch Dreaming
in the shadow of the stony hill ochre

when the blanket of language hums
and kinship campfires flavour windswept hair

little girls stack single twigs on embers
under Grandfathers skin of painted love

the dance of emu feathers will sweep
the red earth with your smile

do not look at me in daylight
that gift comes in the night

tomorrow I will show Mother
your marriage proposal in my smile

2.
in the cave she rolls *the* big rock for table
for *the* desert wildflowers they pick for one another

she carries many coolamons filled with river sand
to soften the hard rock floor

she makes shelf from braided saplings to hold
all the feathers given by the message birds

while he sleeps she polishes his weapons
with goanna and emu fat till they glisten in fire light

he tells the story of the notches on his spear
the story of the maps on his woomera

their *eyes* fill with spot fires lit on his return
the other women laugh 'get over yourself'

they laugh 'he's not that good'
she smiles she knows him in the night

3.
there is love in the wind by the singing rock
down the river by the ancient tree

love in *kangaroo goanna* and *emu*
love when spirits speak no human voice

at the sacred sites eyes unblemished
watch wedge tail eagle soar over hidden water

find the love

FRIDAY NIGHT AT JIMMY WONG'S

No food at home so I've stopped at Jimmy Wong's,
waiting in the fluoro with my book.

Slowly hacking my way through a Great American Novel
full of baseball metaphors I don't understand.

Three cops walk into the Chinese restaurant.
Not a joke, it's just what happens.

Three cops. Three guns. I wonder, briefly,
what would happen if I tried to grab one.

The guy appears with my food, asks if I need a fork.
'Have a nice night yeah?'

And because he says it with a question mark
I believe he really cares.

I get home and all I want to do is watch
So You Think You Can Dance.

A skinny girl dances in a white dress
and Lady Gaga is judging with blue hair,

her body fierce like a bird.
She leaps from her seat at the end of the dance:

'I love you!' she cries and the dancer glows.
Gaga has tears in her eyes.

I eat my Combination Special Fried Rice,
mute the sound during ad breaks.

The street outside is quiet,
full of parked cars dreaming.

HOMEMAKER

we throw words at each other
and the blows form bruises
our bodies take up too much room
in this house where floors slope
and the cabinet rattles every time
someone walks through the kitchen
I used to hurl words like this at my father
never at my mother
in that house where dark furniture
and polished silver cluttered rooms
the fourth wooden step from the top creaked
there were cupboards under the stairs
that grew from small to large
other people's homes were always more appealing
their sheets whiter their apple juice sweeter
the silence of mornings cool and full of promise
I never thought I would make a home
did not dream of wedding dresses, picket fences
or milky babies – lived as a renter
happy to make a corner
of me in someone else's architecture
I did not want to own
anything not a dog or a cat or a fish
could not even commit
to tending a garden
now I am the adult in this house
try and keep the fruit bowl topped
benches wiped
tea and chocolate close at hand
should anyone drop in
but I cannot edge around the fact that I
have made a home
where bruising words are thrown –
words that leave their own dark stain

THE SPACE BETWEEN

This child did not grow in me, but has found a place
under my skin   each time she leaves I am a little more

pulled out of shape. My body remembers this yearning
to find comfort in another.

Years spent throwing myself
up against the wrong person   clinging at night

dissolving with morning coffee,
smudged mascara and muttered excuses.

The small hours are calmer now but something
worries at me, wide-eyed in the dark. Is it grief?

All that this flesh has failed to do, thicker now less buoyant.
Things don't bounce back like they used to.

Certain words have always stumped me
lover mother baby   I fumble with their intimacy.

Still can't find the name for this dragging behind the ribs
I'm left with each time. We used to fight when she went,

struggle in the ebb of her absence   slowly we have learned
to be kind   hold the space between us with care.

NEW NINETY-NINE PERCENT

We want you to read because what you read is beautiful
How do you do it?
You don't look like your real face
Your face as treasure cuts through its own lost beauty
Its meaning what it means if it did not be
I heard you ask
How do they put themselves in danger?
With a ball?
With the inside of the palm?
And then you said I'm just scared of a little bit of grass
The temporary feather of a snowflake becoming
the new ninety-nine percent of life
The body running between two poles
unspilled and becoming
Swimming broken by the small mounts upon mystery
But our mirrors are lazy and our short breaths wasted
by all near the end

We want you to read
Read for us the swarm-of-flies words
Put leaves in your mind to take the place of the leaf-space
made by concept
How do you do it?
Your face becoming this side of the poem
What we see when you turn to us
your world

from RED / BIRTHPLACE / ISLANDS

the island is sunrise
red bursts
behind the ragged range
jutting
a lizard's spine
up the land

drinks
at the resort's
faux whare
palm woven
bar
glasses float
from yellow, green, blue, orange
to red

sip
dusk pooling
between the swimming platforms
windsurfers
ball throwing
sand
soft and sieved
light
and swept

rooms tropical
white sheets and en suites
lie
on the king-sized
some bullshit
afoot

CULTIVATION

And when this is all over
I will look at my mud-creased hands

and wonder how they came to be.
These scabs on my shins,

this drooping back.
The sparrows withering

as they eye a fistful of grain
clenched by crowding rock,

an inch of root devoured
by thirst. And me, pining

for salt and asking
why there exists a god

for fire and none for hunger.
The shrubbery traps

a shaft of sunlight.
Another brown leaf

snaps from a tree.
The wind claimed it,

found no use for it.
Let it go.

CANOPY

There is a surplus of fire with which
all things transact, a hiddenness
called forth by the visible: As in
the afternoons that lazed behind
the thick tarnished windows
of my childhood, my grandmother
lifting the lid off a pot of boiling
broth, the smoke that lengthened
her pumice-gray hair before she turned
to me and motioned with the ladle,
grinned to articulate all the acid
she was able to wring from a bruise
of tamarinds. An entire history
she inhabited and that I will
never know. I walked along
the old farm and noticed the sunrays
lining my path, their steady, defiant aim
bursting through the canopy as if to say,
The problem with the world is that
it lacks the patience of light. I was looking
for a long-enough stick to prod free
a fruit the size of two fists, thinking
of how every trembling sweetness
vanishes when plucked, remembering
the woman I will never love. Her small
ankles. The words she taught me in some
mountain language, and the way
the tongue curls away from memory,
is cured of longing. How far away
from summer it felt, our cold,
parallel sadnesses. There was a lake
somewhere. Tall branches.
An abundance of leaves.

WEIGHT

They stand stolid in the nook under the stairs,
hefty soldiers on four wheels,
bemedalled with airport-approved locks,

in nondescript black, ceremonial sentries
to my departure from summer
in the Philippines, toward spring

on the other side of the world –
laden with clothes for every day
I'll be away, assorted emoluments

to grease bereft moments, sweets
for family and friends to remind them
of their old country – each item

carefully packed amidst cushion of socks
and underwear. If there be excess
baggage, it would not fit in anything

that's not the size of my heart
when it heaves the mass of worry
about an arthritic aunt who can't walk fast

during an earthquake, or the dog who'd yip
at midnight beside me and must be shaken
from fitful dreams. And if only because

the inevitable is yet far away,
for my Stateside parents I carry the legend
of dialysis or angioplasty, a monster

called the wheelchair, all the folktales
about defecating in your bed. I know
I must pack heavy to get there,

breaking my back on the bursting volume
of a love whose only outward clue
is a label that says 'fragile'.

BUT DEATH IS NOT AN OPTICAL ILLUSION

On my way out of the parking building,
I look up at the open stairwell stretching
twenty floors above, thinking of the jumper
who fell through just before All Souls' Day,
breaking an outstretched arm on a railing.
I crane my neck and the void goes on, the starting
point of her death magnified by nestled squares,
a tableau straight out of M.C. Escher's 'Ascending
and Descending'. You never know what's going on
inside someone. Coiled pattern of guts, skein
of nerve and muscle, obeying their daily marching
orders. It is not for the body to ask why.
Some phenomena are difficult to fathom:
boredom, the porous border between tragedy
and comedy. There comes a day when up
is hard to tell from down. It is the precise point
the steps lead to infinite regress, forever delayed.
I suppose it is not unlike the journey of souls,
if these are things we can have, or are.
Art's deception is perfect. But she wanted out
of the frame, even at the price of falling to pieces,
breaking the promise of asymptote.

HYMNAL

the god of all grace the god who rumbles
as thunder but also whispers as waves
the god who saves and does not save tell me
if you can hear me too or are you busy
listening to the lament of others
who perhaps need you more than I do
with my little wants what I want to know
is how do you weigh each question each plea each
prayer mumbled before sleep to consider
it enough for an answer I'll never
know with your silence although I keep on
asking and looking for your face and strain
to hear your voice in every sound and there
is nothing but god I want I need to know

*

if you are the creator then I am
what you created flesh blood and bone hair
sprouting from my groin the itch I feel
is that you god you are the bread the riven
body risen lord create the scab
to crust my wound your hands can heal and yet
and yet you also let the body fail
you let the sea churn waves that topple homes
you flood the streets with endless rain or else
withhold the rain for many months if you
indeed are the creator then why bring
forth this serpent tongue why make the poison
ivy climb all these questions mere footnotes
in your book why cancer in my father's lungs

*

this morning are you the bee in the garden
flitting from flower to flower searching
each fold of petal for a drop of nectar
is that you god or maybe it is me
bee tracking tremors of color flickering
light fast-flying birds you reveal yourself
as iridescent wings beating faster

than a fruit fly's floating over orchids
with furry lips and stuck-out tongues you sting
because you can because the world must ache
its way to joy of course you're more than just
this waggling bee but it might be what I am
to you a bee lost in your garden god
bee that makes honey from what it can gather

*

the leaves are leaving the branches a storm
of locusts devours the field somewhere a star
collapses into a hole where no light
can pass I wonder why you unmake
your bounty god why you undo what is
sometimes I'm filled with doubt why you exist
at all how random you are in your mighty
works you play with dice you deal the cards god
you're a gambler and we take the loss not
that we have much of a choice do we but I
I leave it up to you though hope you let
fruits ripen before they fall before the worm
gnaws its way into the gourd o god forgive
my human heart forgive my unbelief

*

another day another night it must
seem like a blink to you a single breath
blown to the sky you must be patient god
if you're still here from the very start
when you alone had sparked a flame it's good
for you to stay this long though are you waiting
to end it all when will it be you count
the days you melt the ice the burning lasts
another day what happens next is up
to you and you alone thy will be done
thy kingdom come forever and never
you must be patient to light each day while
here I wait for all the days to end the very
end god I wait for you to snuff the fire

from HUMAN POSITIONS

        work >>> suit, specs,
            whitened teeth
                & crumpled notes

on power ‖ conveying
        criticality, a canon's logorrhea,
        best minds

in best etc.
        , at these anthropogenic ends
wondering

            what the factual uhck
            (smiling >>> hominizations, truthiness, etc.)

>>>
        '& what if
            we're part flower,
                part crowd, part

sewer, part cloud?'
        you ask, eyeing
            a mosquito (long dead)

at the window's wire
        ‖ one day *puff*, then gone ‖
'I know,' whispered, 'you

        think of it also, your
            body taut against mine'

>>>   the fridge full
            of inscrutables >>>
                ponytail kimchi, duck eggs (baked),

        pickled clams, glasswort
            salt, bee pollen, roasted
                seaweed, Japanese apricot wine,

        grain syrup, pineapple vinegar,
            perilla oil, wild rice,
        fried glutinous crackers, buckwheat noodles

                (served cold) ‖ Siberian gooseberries (fresh)

>>>   & these texts (again)
            'fetishistic, incommensurable,
                heteroglossias voicing

the ideal, aestheticized' >>> speaking
        in gestures here
                of destabilization + critique

oh & there goes
        that colleague from upstairs
face in a pose of only

        ever one thought away
        from another plate of bitter plums

>>>
        & you're saying, 'hot
           -headed, pangs of desire,
              throb-hearted,

wincing regret
    >>> such feelings
        in our word-suffused bodies

rapt & wrapped in self
    -dramas,' & the mind, that
dramaturge, engulfed,

        has no final script

>>>

    trees in the slow clock
        of wind, ticking
            a unified machinery

on this one day
    called today / I saw
        the whole of the sun rise

& saw it all set
    >>> *nothing more to see,* except
from my office window

    a paper plane
    momentarily ascend an updraft

    (after lines from Cho Oh-Hyŏn ['Musan'], 1932-2018)

>>>   again, these humans inside
         the small expanses
            of our bare flat (lotus bell,

     shrouds of curtained silk), beautiful
        except to themselves, perhaps
          sensing a force &

     sitting behind tea (steaming), wanting
        whatever you've got &
     you, also wanting

            your tea to slightly cool

>>>   their *Centre for Quantum
        Spacetime* office door locks
          the same as mine (insert key, twist)

     & it's late & again we stare
        into the planar
          matrix of drolly collegial

     linoleum ‖ pass a herd of chairs
        on savannas of corridor,
     an $E=MC^2$ of awkward

          anthropoids under fluorescence

RUNNING INTO FIDEL CASTRO

yo soy una chica vietnamita en little havana =
I am a vietnamese woman in little havana.

the summer humidity makes lovers out of natives and
prisoners out of tourists.
this foreign land ambushes me like a surprise enemy or guerrilla warfare,
neither and both
ways to join the republican party here are simple:
jokes the young cuban barmaid with her sugarcane-scented voice,
the saccharine and sunlit smell is unexpectedly familiar.
my home on the other coast suddenly appears and jabs me at the throat.

she is standing too close to me,
pushes the boundaries of my personal space,
tells me about the journey she made across ninety miles   of sea
on a pick-up truck-turned-escape-ship-turned-lifesaver.
as we both laugh about the fact that only the desperation and brilliance
   of a third-world
nation would drive its people to make life-savers and boats out of pick-up trucks,
(no, we weren't being sarcastic),
she invites me out for a night of the latin 3 m's: miami, mojitos, and mambo,
smirks as she mentions 'the dictator' and leans in to kiss me on both cheeks.

se llama maria isabella bolivar
maria is a 1.5 generation immigrant,
waitress by night and chicano studies college student by day:
she embodies the refugee work ethics and peppers her speech with espanol.
maria often feels displaced and seldom laments on her loneliness:
it is hard to relate to the other 400,000 cubans on this soil.
afterall, they are in exile so viva the yankees.
castro is not dead, yet he already haunts.

bienvenido a little havana:
the 23 blocks in the southeastern metropolis of the florida peninsula,
I walk along these streets with this radiant latina,
both of us speaking English,
both of us Vietnamese American Cuban American,
born in opposite sides of the world but wear the same working class skin color and
experience the same anti-Lenin protests,
somewhere in between resisting assimilation and embracing this common land

that never quite accepted us but brought us together,
we were on our way to connecting as we reach
the colorful center of town,
the artery that keeps the heart of little havana beating,
the official name is sw 8th street but everyone knows it as *calle ocho*.

there, I forge empathy and tell maria about *hai ba trung* street in little saigon.

LOOK AT THAT ONE!

I was with the waxworks for many more years than I care to suppose, changing my posture regularly to maintain interest. Whether this worked or not seemed to depend on the chart you consulted. If it was the blue one, all hell broke loose: bells began sounding in the antechamber and you knew it was time to extol the virtues, or demonise the vices as the case may be. The red chart meant you should pray for visitors, but I never did this – to tell the truth, I hated being gawked at. I had no objection to being quietly observed from behind the crimson, gold-braided rope by a single hushed spectator, or even a couple or a small band of allies, but the random horde put the horribles upon me. They'd always make exhibitions of themselves. *Look at that one!* they'd instruct their companions, who were invariably already looking. *You'd think they'd do something, wouldn't you? At least fix its hair.* But we *are* doing something, you idiots, I'd feel like shouting. We were maintaining a certain lifestyle, true, by collecting money at a booth outside, but inside we were hard at it, immutable stabilities in their midst. Didn't they appreciate that? It was alright for *them* to be flitting about all over the place, but if the whole world did that, who would ever know where anyone was? Or *who* they were for that matter? You always knew where *I* was, my name was inscribed on a gilt-edged sign at the edge of my little dominion, and I like to think this comforted people who otherwise would have been lost in the world, unsure of where to find things or where to put them back. It was a purpose, I suppose, in a world that had little. Tour guides would sometimes give me a quick once-over, perhaps under the impression they'd encountered me before, and I freely acknowledge I have known variety in my life. Moulded in the image of an old Norse god and cooked, along with the rest of the crew, in a pot for an educational exhibit, *Cultures of the South Pacific*, I was singled out in my informative years as the ideal mute embodiment of mysterious dark forces; suggestible in those days, I was also suggestive. Relatively thin-skinned, absolutely thick-headed, I was tortured, guillotined, burned at the stake, hung by the neck down an elevator shaft, strapped into an electric chair and caught red-handed on numerous occasions in acts of infamy and violence, until finally the evidence, mainly from the red chart, proved I'd petrified no one. After a stint in storage, I redeemed myself, I like to think, by spending what seemed an eternity penning orations as Madam Blavatsky, then mastered various supporting roles – butler, bailiff, dear departed, bearer of placards, plotter against kings – and served in my declining years as Minister of State, thus miraculously continuing on as whatever the fickle throng dictated. Throughout all this, I managed to maintain 90% of my mass, and my betrayal of the basic human emotions – clamorous, lustful, panicked – remained constant to what I knew to be true: that whatever happened between here and meltdown, my identity was secure. My assistants would take care of it. It wasn't a bad gig.

PEOPLE OF EARTH

Whenever I discover what an idiot I've been,
    I turn to television – 'Oh screen of wonders, flick me
        on and off like an appliance,' I implore it
    and it answers back
and I cackle away in the aftermath
    of its buckets of canned laughter.
        I lie on my little raft wondering
    whose abduction is this
anyway? *'People of Earth, I have
    no intention.'* Damned alien, chronic
        master-plan – part of some system. I try
    to asphyxiate one last program, switch
to the contactees. Seems that in 1981 Debbie
    divorced and went to live with her parents
        @ 32,000 kilometres per hour
    happy to show off,
push buttons, poke around
    the house for a while, hatching her evil plot.
        She spoke, when she talked at all, Phooey.
    Most witnesses have the wit, but Debbie
received the phone call. *'Hello, I'm
    Mrs Cleaveland.'* It was a small, large-headed,
        grey-skinned entity – guided, she said,
    by remote control by her little Maude, who,
once dead, made it safely to Mars. *'My stars,
    they tell me, predict the weather'* – but nothing
        predicted whether or not she truly spoke
    the Martian language, a propellor-driven
vessel featuring flapping, inflatable wings that,
    suspiciously, Maude had taken off in.
'There's this big ball of light,' she said.
    Did you believe her? Debbie did – she'd *seen*
the tarted-up guests and reporters being fed
    to the startled backdrop: it was aquamarine, like
        Maude. But as this realisation dawned then bored her,
    whaddaya know, she remembered her plot –
and boy did *that* buck everybody up,
    bucked 'em up *real* good.

WORKS OF *ET CETERA*

The set-up

And he said to his disciples: 'See here,
fishy thou art and fishy thou shalt remain,
at least while my ... my father's in charge.'
Whereupon they said back to him: 'Luddite!
Drink and be merry!' And he looked up,
and saw gifts in the treasury.
    Then there arose a great reasoning among them
planting and building house and barn, and the body
what ye shall put on. They said
to him: 'Son, remember the days of torment.'
Doth he thank them several times? Dogs
licked his good bits, and all the beasts
of the field.

'And the ...'

And the Luddite spoke to Mr Mouse
and the little ones, saying the name of the place
per adventure a rock in Horeb
found it, he layeth it on his brother, three
cubits of thousands of hands and feet
and division between my people.
    *The generations now
are many*, they cry, saying
neither shalt thou counterbalance
also 'thou shalt not oppress a stranger
nor dwell in their land.' If thou serve their gods,
Mr Mouse will stretch out his hand and drive
them heavily unto thee. Extinction?
It was easier for a camel yet
Mr Mouse did so.

Dig in

Now, concerning the instructions
'Flee fornication' and 'But if the unbelieving
depart,' remember this: Ye may give yourselves
to a feast, but the profit will be
gloriously corrupt good manners,
e.g. when he says 'You are not
your own?' and ye
dig in, partakers, unto edification.
Such an abundance of revelations
should be exalted, fool, he continues,
lest there be debates, backbitings, whisperings,
swellings – whereby one takes pleasure in
infirmity and so on – no thanks
to you, salvation.

Approx.

And it came to pass – the end of the world,
regular as clockwork: every thirty million
ups and downs, approx., through astro-rubble,
then home to a gnashing of teeth
and *that fat son-of-a-bitch*
'Oh ye of little water …'
Life, lack I yet? You can keep
the commandments, indicating
heaven. Among thorns is thy field?
You are here to go: thus
spake Gysin.

Sources of (mis)quotations: **Look at that one!** André De Toth (Director), *House of Wax* (1953). **People of Earth** Hilary Evans, *From Other Worlds: Aliens, Abductions and UFOs*; Gig Ryan, 'When I consider.' **Works of** *et cetera* T*he Gospel According to Luke*; *The Second Book of Moses, called Exodus*; *The Epistles of Paul the Apostle to the Corinthians*; Brion Gysin, *Here to Go*.

PRINCE KRISHNA, ICARUS AND THE VOYAGE OF THE ZEN POET

I'm sunk into the refused wingchair on my shimmering porch.
Chaos-webbed screens, exploded, confetti-skinned umbrella skeletons,
record rain overdosed bookmarks. Small bands of party-goers
dissolve into unknown locations,
assembled by superglues and awash with precious traffic:
Like marine flares into crests of cake icing.

Did you really think we could build it alone,
sitting tiny atop its open-roof walls in the ice-dazzle air
… for what … five Olympic cycles? … while Moore's law stalled,
quantum supremacy was reached,
and jewelled bears combed
the inside of the basketball of the street?
Icarus

Croutons blimp in my pumpkin head soup.
A woman looks like a corrective female wizard
for a new Lord of the Rings spin-off trilogy.
Pushing her tandem pram, carbonating penthouses.

Last weekend I followed a group
of morning robes out of our shared dimension.
Their wearer's Dobermanns had sniffed out the missing force in gravity.
They used an analogy about space grease and winder stairs,
decayed ghost particle families,
and something about a splintered grey building
fitting inside an unplayable piano.

They were all talking at once
while the dogs licked silhouettes of limes.

The girl from class with the pronounced white, spidery arm-hair
picks up her micro fiction and speeds away
in her mother's Landrover. It was a screwball comedy about
Armageddon featuring an ebullient kazoo.

Hypothetical bar mitzvahs, movie releases,
VR arcades, Oort cloud expeditions,

sports stadiums, tooth-picked shrimp,
strangers who want what they have.

One day everything that is good
in their fabric will be more closely stitched together.
Enough leaves will be mirrors.
Then they will build it around themselves, roof and all.
Prince Krishna

I applied for night sorting at the postal service.
I watched a film about a lunatic plastic surgeon.
Ending idea no. 36—
The taste of universe too much in Prince Krishna's mouth,
he vomits it into a bucket at the Athenian gods' brainstorm
to planet destroying backyard applause.

from RETURN TO A NEW PHYSICS

beside ourselves
we wait for light
and arrange lake things
spectating upon the inevitable

this breath pulls apart a dandelion
with related intensity
seed-heads
springing into maps

leaving speed
to other equations and valencies,
we are splitting prisms
hoping
for slow fantastic
disturbance

and pointing at nothing
as it empties

THEY ASKED FOR MY DEATH

i couldve gone to nz with a friend
instead i entered the original coliseum
a man with the normal impulses of his
thirty two years here it was happening
to me let me tell you how it felt
that slight metaphysical prod the ne
cessity of religious independence must
be emphasized im abstract they said
be_ a hempsized im_ stabcart he_ _ty dias
the buzz of revenge better than juice is
it was a case of everything & nothing
le bourdonnement a vengeance meilleur que ju_ _
ce _ _ _ un cas a tout et rien
i headed somewhere more symmetrical

*'father & son' – edmund gosse

A BUNDEENA HIDEAWAY

Smokey green gums
flickering Saturday's
breeze,

the sea making way
for the river before me:
deep in a wicker chair

I can't get enough of
the radiant water – its drift
and unquestionable journey

answers that old, dumb
question: what is it
you do, exactly?

SATURDAY'S TYPHOON
for Gilmartin

The moon harbours fugitives & monsoons persist
as desperate as sleep deprivation or loss.

Where drifters suit up for the army while they dish out
free money at the sandstone graduation & I make do

with bushwalks, greef joints, tai chi, *Outlandos d'Amour*
cranked full bore on a hand me down Kmart beatbox.

We prick at the voodoo doll of our routine
& there is an absence of transcendentals, of candles;

with rain drum-rolling on the veranda
like sunshine on some LA up & comer's $400 haircut.

Chicken sticks, kalbi tang, takeaway pizza,
Monday, Tuesday, Sunday. Distance refracts you

as abstract as a burst bubble on Bloomberg
for some sud sipping undercapitalised schlub,

the pursuit is as relentless as a Mandalorian,
show up at the temple & it's mug's luck: priest out to lunch.

This life is on fire & some kid has buggered the extinguisher.
Get down low & go go go, Alice's carbon monoxide opera,

the second rate tragedy sends me asunder
a Ramsay St. fault line, an Australian Dostoyevsky:
                                      The Bloody Idiot.

BLUE FLOWER
Improvisation on a Two-Year-Old's Drawing

This figure dashed down
in an instant – at first glance
the sketch of a child in deep blue,
standing upright with multiple limbs spread out,
her head a spiral egg on its side –
a blurred still of movement,
a girl dancing a ring around a rosie,
whirling in the snow.

We're informed it's a flower, of course!
But its leaves are rungs, the blossom
a vortex, a whirlpool or shell, the orbit of planets.
It's a blue ladder reaching to the stars.

From what sources
did this gesture spring,
this fossil of a moment's
action? The transections recall
a Byzantine cross, but coupled
with the circle of the Coptic
crux ansata, and even more closely
their ancestors: the spine of Osiris
and the symbol of life –
the djed and ankh
entwined in the sceptre
of the Word-God Ptah.

Had he eyed this unlearned abstraction
Paul Klee would have seized it
as a rhythmic motif in a whimsical
series of plant metamorphoses,
paintings titled: *Blue Rose Wind,
Field of Night Flowers, Lantern Festival,
Among Star Children* ...

The horizontal axis of sliding, crawling,
the verticality of standing, walking,
have been transfigured
into a human tree,

a dryad that speaks:
*I am the Proteus of all things
and cannot be captured
in any form, both
blossom and fruit,
leaf and root, I play
within the kingdom
as a child, lightly assume
whatever guise I please:
ladder, ocean, snail, flower,
dervish, windmill, lighthouse, star.*

COASTAL IDYLL

A crescent beach, flour-white sand,
swells – turquoise, emerald – curl and break
bright as bleached linen, porous and
scented with salt. In wetsuit pelts
surfers crisscross waves, absorbed
in the play of elements as sporting
dolphins and seals. Along the headland
hollowed-out sandstone, broken honeycomb,
a Gaudi prototype for the Sagrada Familia.
Fishermen stand on a rock-edge, awash,
their rod lines glistening strands of web
bending in a breeze. In a tidal pool, constellations
of blood-red urchins, tiny glinting fish.
A flock of gulls alights on the shore
with the synchrony of a ballet sequence,
a closing phrase. Limber bodies
keep a ball aloft like a buoy rocked on waves
until a tall figure leaps, spikes it out.

This scene simulating dreamy childhood days
feels like a film that masks a pentimento –
in a smudge of reef beneath translucent green
the glaring, twisted face of an Emil Nolde,
a phantom that stalks you up and down the beach.
Swells turn into noise of static, breaking
up the screen of the Coke commercial.
Through the cracks you eye forests
of bone-white coral – a submarine cemetery –
and the deep sea beyond where an iridescent
slick smothers scales, penguins and albatross
undulate limply among leagues of plastic,
a super trawler rests: nets bloated
with ocean-floor fragments, fish populations,
strangled turtles, seals ... Back on the shore, you tread
over corpses, painted faces, skin caked in blood
from bullet wounds, wooden spears lying
beside them. With the thud of a ball and cheers
reception returns, authentic as a president's pledge.

IN MEMORY OF MY FURLINGS

My anxiety has a dog in it, she's opaque
    and drags me slowly, like a creaky ship, through the CBD.
        She's unlike anything, except maybe a cloud
            of bats at night, or letters.
My anxiety has several furlongs, and so many
    bristling little selves I bear against the creatures
        who readily pretend they're human, not
            the weapons they've become pointing to the sky!

In winter they're cold as aircon, in the suburbs
    taste of sweaty equipment I split from
        into rose coastal waters. At times, out beyond flags,
            I stare back at the unthinkable
worlds that continue to clash and remember
    I'd prefer to be baffled, redistributed by these waves,
        their pulsing blue pillowcases,
            and by Frankie and Freddy who swim

up through the Anthropocene to meet me.
    Where it's turquoise we nap together,
        they speak of underwater mares but I'm too purple
            to hear the polar bears bassooning their discomfort
over the heat that echoes to the poles
    and back of the plastic gyre squelching its dulled
        mirror – its floating shadow – on the oceans
            of the indebted and gravity-locked.

Meanwhile, a Coke in my ex's freezer 'explodes,'
    one of me darts from pub door #7, one of me is yanked
        by a chain and one of me jumps the double white-lines
            to avoid being struck. Another me
hovers between landing planes with a bird
    's-eye view of the next me perambulating the Inner West
        and all the other me's pushing
            prams through parks in criss-cross patterns,

Minkys running doggy arcs about us, impervious and fuzzy
    half-awake babies squinting at the late
        afternoon light that slants in between muslin and pram hood
           and underneath each wheel
as I round The Bends over Bilgola, head losing another hair,
    body letting loose another ghost,
        the back-end of the Mazda I was in sliding out
           and through a gap in oncoming traffic,

the rain of At the Drive In pelting me with the drops
    of a future death, cilia on the insides
        of the lungs and bowels of earth
           pushing shit along and the sphincters inside of me
gaping for one another.
    They won't find each other
        any more than my others'll find me, each of us
           in our respective wormholes

but each able to see how so many of our obscurities resist,
    are contrary – partly terrified of a glaring
        mushroom-cloud dream,
           partly trying to circumvent whatever commodity
fetishism they're subject to,
    and partly just flaking out like little moons with dandruff
        lolling across a toothily numb-dark horizon –
           my covert creatures,

dank inside my coat, pants and pockets, busting to come out
    and take it from those who'd hunt big game
        with their LEDs oblivious
           to the helical pasts and futures
that 3D-print themselves now into the dark
    of neighbouring galaxies. Glowing
        I dip behind a scraper, whistling as though no one
           could possibly've noticed how I almost

        pulled a trigger on that particular teddied me.
           But Minky's eyes did – reddened, barked at how hard
                my opaque pupils had come to seem
                      in their modes of perpetual escape – so I kiss her
and we flip about as puppies in a box
        on the interwebs, wriggling,
                not without panic
                      and not without a certain icy comeback

reserved for and justified
        in those kinds of webby fields when we need to
                but acquiescent enough to the necessity,
                      scrolling up and
down through rippling neon hills which
        presciently come to resemble
                the furlings and unfurlings
                      I continue to have to save and put down.

'In Memory of My Furlings': is a ghosting of part 1 of Frank O'Hara's 'In Memory of my Feelings'.

AUSTRALIANA CRAP

The long invasion sheds an Aussies day
Over nearly two or three centuries, skills are enlightened
By blackmail, the blinkers didn't persuade nor colonise
Clogging research didn't stop knowledge and opinion to embrace
Something straying, it's imagine or tricks
Just on fellow peep at amazing spread of knots
Of dramatic transits.
So widely linguistics merged a continent linking stories
Collected from grown up firearms.
Castaway distant seventeen years, by some helped in us.
Sketchy danger but cattle, horses, cats, pigs, donkeys,
Camels, rabbits too
Are brother sister
Long visit him sharply wanted.
Now involuntary impresses homelands.
Dog bark and sheep bleed
Reported twice-big binna; big horns gone.
Over tracks intruders were closer threatening a party
Where blankets; tin mugs; wine were
Meeting empty satisfactory praise found flints passive
In own curious inexperience.
Glimpses of dress; skin combing; straps were a new expedition.
Sturt found Abos' inquisitiveness and submitted
They is no creatures; but for desiring than we.
Early uncertainty roughly was exposed without any Ceremony.
They natives shirt and trousers change to witchcraft if dirt.
Yet ghosts; demonic beings or monsters familiar still
In an Australian's day.
Unless foreigners are quitting the thing; that no more
Aboriginals here
But remember European; we not the corpses or the living
But virgin aboriginalised Earth.

[2010/2011]

TENT EMBASSY 1971-2021

I was just a young pie
Did not know who was by
When the bikies turned up at the Tent Embassy
No discriminative bikes of bias fumes smell
Just the emblems of their unity
    As slogans of a piked togetherness
Piles of toughness done by prejudice
Showing solidarity towards years gone by
Non authoritarian attitudes in the latitudes of their ride
No posh push chains spikes emblems or helmets
    Shown by these non named
Eat the tarred scarred marks of tyres screeching
As time flies by so that we and them must form
A ride of the rainbows night after day
Where babies pedal accelerate mirroring
The lights of the forward going
    Praise thee no matter what
No bike club on our drugged or non drugged
Where stones are eating the dust of the heavens
Those conscious out of hell tell
Black rights must be respected
    By the bikie nights in any party rights.
Once these have a common of every tyres
That roll in every pebble of sand across our nations land
Just don't forget no matter what
Bikies must create the swift fastness
    When all man woman and child rides together forever
So laugh at the insights
In respect of your no law love must exist in repetition
In the exquisite behaviour of the officers
Throughout Australia's police force
    We darkies will always spark the starch
I know what's good for me mate
Where's the road? When the cop toads fall to pieces
As the snitches steal the boots when
The real bikers are locked with the blacks
Say goodnight to all the illegal bikie laws

Because they could be right in your neighbourhood
In come the lovers ride the night
Ride that breeze ride the banquet
Bikers be nice
Insight our black rights.

[2010/2011]

MURGON BRAWL CHERBOURG BRAWLS

They out there, not hidden
Have you heard of that brawl?
Up at Murgon town
Have you seen the 20 15 or so?
Darkies cause a fuss and fight?
Well, they came and told
Me before I read a paper.
Some sisters bashed up a
Female cop hey.
Some cops dragged picked on
The wrong black man,
So they deserved what Bompi
They got hey.
Now there's this Jackie Joe
Saying them blacks who
Can't hold their grog bang
Brought the brawling on
And guessed what him say to media.
I'm a bit ashamed to be Aboriginal
For they should not have charged at football
Show games places
Well who started it
Cops speaks drunks started
Hit Hit Hit
Black Joe Jackie says all dri=unks
Started Hit Hit Hit
But Jesus was a drunk
Have you all heard, blacks
Drunken having a good time
Blacks, playing win or
Lose, sometimes can't
Hit, when called boong nigger,
They react fast
Have you heard of stirring?
Cheeky police office
Who wait for those loud?
Talkative blackfellas under the weather
Then bang into the paddy
Wagon or slammed

The police don't maintain good
Relations when you heard of
Bompi Bompi with Murris
Maybe all bad cops and bad blacks
Should go over goori for fighting ground next.

(To Kurt & Nanny Fisher, Sunday 8.39pm 2011-01-09)

BORRI IS FIRE WARU IS FIRE

Fire is our right
Fire OH fires our lives
We had no cooked food, fire was there.
Time needs fire, rain needs fire
Sky eyes had to have sun's fires.
Winds were and are friends to fires.
The fire can kill, when not looked after,
Safe by fire makes new peoples a unity
Fire made not by man but natures
Can't stop old fire
Can't stop young fire
Open fire warm earths all bodies
In heat fire is wanted for without the cold were.
You and we are without age-old fires.
The belly guts ribs fires on the lip fire speak sings to the ears.
Fire brings sex rest and cares
Aboriginal's fires are power over laws
When it love brake homeward.
These fires are under ground waiting for house
That disrespect man using.
So beware fire as luggages and fatly takes lives in speeds.
Colour is fires over dark light rainbow show fires are signs.
The trees never grow without fires.
Every bodies needs fires to creator song,
To dance walk stand fires have places.
In the valley mountain dark fires don't lie.
In all morning fire await wood fallen from the trees of fires birds fireflys.
At night to see space fires are wanted
At stars fire plays eyes to the blind.
Fire is unity when care is peace for the blanket of beds the fire gives.
Fire gives all written painted artist what we have now animals fires.
If there's no fire, earth dead and the world will be misunderstand
Fire on fire to put out fires.
The city be nothing without fires
The countries be nothing without fires
Our roads when made needs fires
Fires is the stories log and bush
Fire lay every birth for humans
All fire thrown still the wars sweet evils are fires of wronged.
Sweet heaven dreams fires to get away from evils.
Dreaming using love fires finds ways to bring together kindest.

Many thing are said for fire, all season around fire arms all babies restless
Dreaming is fire for babies.
Many pretty fires close the gabs off sad tears, as waters are the real loves of fires
Waters are nothing without fire,
Fire burns under waters.
Ready is fires on anytimes.
Humanities are fire
My race is fire
The spirit is fire
We use fires spirits to heal
Being in side fire the grass growth
As green round of joy smiles when fire rising.
The moon cherish the fires
The sun still needs our fires a blazing below.
To have vision fires are important
To have schools fires is education
Much death as fires for a life
Much life as fires for a death
Let the house of fire live for happy livings.
Love of fires is the fight
Fire of lovers is to take it easy
Friends are fire Brother with care
Friends are fire Sisters with stares
Don't fire out the fire made a Thousand years ago.
For the stories are kept by these fire stories.
Fire now is the book of face fires.
Fire runs men's and women's in every work they do.
No poetry is alive without fire,
Words are fires written for action.
All poet stand as fire, No one is poet without fires.
Fires are the hearts for fire bloods,
Dry creek beds cry for fire from the sea fires to unite clouds abodes.
The creator made us fire for our well beings.
The future will always say fires will state again for seeds are sprang by fires.
Waru Borri walk
Waru Borri talks
Waru Borri our eyes
Waru Borri dances us nice
Waru Borri loves the lovers
Waru Borri can hate
Waru Borri can kill
Waru Borri live for death

Waru Borri can rainbow your days
Borri sits even as wits in lit
Let the stars shone bright bellow our sleep the Waru Borri will be safe.
Let the control off the fires be always man's
    Knowing its powers
No wars must be fires
No personal baldest be fires
Oh he got the fire in his speak let it be of greater peace
If to write be to fight, do it with fire better and right with the good camp-
    fires stories.
Ghosts are fire death in tales
Ghosts knows fire, but are not creator of fires.
Be the Waru Borri of fire in sighs to riot stone
For tomorrow we needs still fires

(Merton VIC, 2013-07-05-6)

BLUE PAINTING (1924)

Let the eye investigate blue
and all the arrows focus gravity.

Across the spectrum – cerulean,
prussian, cobalt –

a patchworld of hues
quilts galaxies.

Remember Earth,
the Blue Planet,

how it takes you into backdrops
for a rose, a hyacinth,

the single flowers
multiplied under a clean sky.

ALEXANDER FEBRUARY

Strangers behind each other in the Qantas queue,
I thought I heard him say he'd wanted to type over
the endings. So, at nineteen, he'd been travelling light,

always wanted to hike over the Andes, drink tequila
with a worm in it, watch the moon's shadow fall on
South America. He left Germany and tipped his head

to stars wheeling like flocks of silver-winged birds,
and read his journey in that map of borrowed black sky.
Beneath skeins of wild geese, he slept rough and woke

to the insistent mantra of grass wrens, the wild clatter
of parakeets blossoming from branches. On a derelict bicycle
he was flying blind in Argentina when condors worked their way

upstream above the valley as he waded through corn silk
where Holando cattle lay like boulders and watched him pass,
recognising his sweet submission to the road and all

that it would bring. He waited in a pond of darkness and just
when he thought it would always be dark, light stepped through
trees and a car arrived to take him to some new and waiting room.

ZERO-SUM [A MECHANICAL SOUL PONDERS ITS EXISTENCE]

Instability swims in its metal casing
– the unbelieving mechanical balk
of simple objects held to
sense perceptions – void reduced to void

as radiance discharges, decays, loses
autocorrelation, achieves the fallibility
of protein. Sleep-wake a machine inhales
the sky: so close, so blue, so fitful
in binary, algorithms [regulating
and inhibiting] how relative at evening
how circadian in its suddent inverse proofs

Atoms cruise the scaly circuitry. The visual
system lights up dubstep
giving spatial coordinates to memory
electrochemical brain-states of the cortex.

While the body is incoherent, frayed to negatives.
Language a limit, edge to motion
:oh! the inefficiency of biology
may idly thumb its own prosthetic needs.

LEFTOVERS FROM A PIRATE PARTY

OFFER: very small
dog coat Lewisham
4 used netballs
Old goth/punk clothes,
size 12-14
WANTED: Heat mat
(for hermit crab aquarium)
Inflatable Santa – giveaway or loan
OFFER: Three-arm chandelier
with frosted glass –
needs rewiring
LEFTOVERS FROM
A PIRATE PARTY
Jade plant from Mascot
gone already!
RE-OFFER: Disposable diapers
for small cat/dog
3 vacuum cleaners,
no wands
WANTED: 7 fence palings
LARGE CONTAINERS
FOR HOME BREW
To the Lady who I gave
Sony Trinitron TV to in Feb!
OFFER: Yabby family
of five in Glebe
Mixed Things From
My Pantry: Riverwood
Two shopping bags
full of stuffed bears etc

from LONG SHADOWS

dry summer
choosing the ripest peach
from the blue bowl

easy silence
the bunch of keys
warm from your hand

in darkness
a branch strokes my shoulder
wheeling out the bins

spring morning
painted on the footpath:
proposed tree

sleeplessness
low in the summer sky
an orange moon

just over there
    both ends
of the rainbow

sea breeze:
my shadow hovers
on the ocean floor

sunshower:
grasshoppers scatter
before my slow tread

heat wave
scribbly gums glow orange
in the dusk

from LOCAL/GENERAL

*01:   this poem gets you in like a bath
at the exact temperature – don't wait
for the plumber to get here, & s/he will
just send your desire & your hygiene
& tick this box if you need a receipt
on the sand, my thighs rub like mail-merge
& broken porcelain, as each gallery must decide
its definition of collection
mine's from the stormwater rivulets to you
& birds appear in the cliffs, full of song and lice
sharks too. while above the frequent flyers yawn
& my white sheets rise
like a mist
       attached to the sky

*06:   friday, i'm the girl
on the 339 with the quivering
organs the weekend
insinuating itself
in a way i can only hope is *a priori*

saturday & so it thunders
over a heterotopic landscape
the thwacking of the perch
in the bottom of the boat
drowning in air & the proper rain
now falling straight down

this is how i see it
       sometimes we'd fuck to guitar pop
       sometimes to ambient electronica

A PAGE EVER COMING

We likes to write about birds.

Semipalmated Sandpipers, Bonaparte's Gulls, & Pacific Loons.

We gives them names and the names We reflect
various sexual positionings

The Snowy Plover, the Common Moorhen, and the Pomarine Jaeger Dark Morph.

America's anxiety of influence in bird culture:

The Virginia Rail, Forester's Tern, and the Lesser Yellowlegs.

We: Western Kingbirds, Bohemian Waxwings, & Golden-crowned Kinglets.

In America We likes to write about wee birds
that fly into a poem easily as lint.
From poem to lint, to lint to lint.
We likes to think that these birds
haven't been dumbed down by We's garbage,
We's shit-talk, We's atmosphere.

In America We likes to write about atmosphere
because We knows it is less scary to pretend to know
such an unknowable thing than for We to actually admit
We knows more about nothingness, dryer sheets, featherbeds:

birds   lint   atmosphere

Wilson's Spine   Albert's Towhee   Whip-poor-will

We moves slowly like the Asian Giant River turtles
humping one another.

It takes them hours to get off
the ship and to the Honolulu Zoo
where my sister says
"We has them in Florida, too"

or in We's pockets, at the gift shop
I remember the time I was shoplifting and didn't get arrested
or the time I was shoplifting and almost got arrested
then the time I was shoplifting and did get arrested

with all the birds eating the lint eating the atmosphere
I sat in the nothingness looking at the ink on my tiny thumb
and my tiny thumb on the white walls of a singular cell
built by We-men that makes up a whole body of cells
and all I could think of was which We was hungry and which We was full of ink

In America We puts birds into We's poems
because We knows the human experience is so fragile,

like We's sugar stuck to the spoon like We's own ashes
made of said spoon and spun in said sugar.
Because We knows when a Toyota is coming We's way.
We can see the big tires and taste the tar
and hear the anger in each spoked rotation.
We can smell We's lungs burning down a forest.
And in We's last moment We makes lint of We's very self
so much so that the sky becomes We's skin.

Every now and then We hears of a suicide among the birds.

the less Black-backed Gull the Lincoln's Sparrow the American Goldfinch

We throws lint on their feathers
We lights up the sky with We's thumbs

We writes a poem about birds and leaves the rest to the atmosphere.

A DINING TABLE FOR THE CLOUDS
Translated by Hyemi Seok and Soohyun Yang

In the 25-hour supermarket on the fourth shelf to the left
Are the blue sardine cans.
They cost one thousand four hundred won a piece.
Dust sits on each can in the shape of a swirl.
I pay with a 10,000 won bill and I return home,
My pockets jingling with change.
Seven deaths filled to the brim with bones. Seven meals on a table.

The sardines in front of the kitchen window sit
With their sharp ends facing the sky.
Where did all the sardine heads go to?
Sometimes a cat comes round the window. Sometimes light rain.
They leave fingerprints.
However, the sardines don't pay attention to the cat, the cat
Doesn't notice the rain, and the rain isn't interested in sardines.
They leave their indifferent fingerprints, fingerprints for many days.

The thing I sometimes invite to eat at my table
Is a cloud. He rests his chin on his hands
And casts a shadow over me and my food.
Since it's hard to clear away a cloud,
I hang the cloud to one side like a curtain and I open up a can.
Anytime you look, seven sardine cans line my kitchen window.
Seven types of death. Seven kinds of luck.

Past the three Mighty Monkey machines at the arcade
And the wooden bench outside Hyundai Real Estate Agency
Is the 25-hour supermarket.
I've never been there after midnight.
All I can imagine
Is the sign left on by its owner, brightly lit till morning, and
On the fourth shelf to the left, blue pickled death
And the unmoving swirls, stacked up,
One thousand four hundred won a pop.

12 O'CLOCK
Translated by Hyemi Seok and Soohyun Yang

Just like beef jerky has
A 36 hour folding period,
The classification system on my counter is something
You can never know.

If at all possible,
I want to be articulate.

There are people that use
Simple night and day like vocabularies
And I wonder
If I belong there.

Like the vegetarian habit
Of staring and staring at ingredient labels
From yesterday to today,
My palate differs.

Day doesn't come because night takes off and
There are many 12 o'clocks in this world.

We met yesterday
Even though we also met today.

from ARCHIVAL-POETICS (BOOK 1: COLONIAL ARCHIVE)

PRELUDE | a beginning by way of introduction to something else epic in search for an impossible origin of the event, a preview-awakening to the positioning of things, a warning

LIST OF IMAGES

1. 'ATTENTION', *Archive-Fever-Paradox [2]*, 2013 in *Bound and Unbound, Sovereign Acts*, Act 1, 24 August–24 September 2014, curated by Ali Gumillya Baker with the Bound Unbound Collective (Ali Gumillya Baker, Faye Rosas Blanch, Natalie Harkin, Simone Ulalka Tur), Fontanelle Gallery and Studios, Bowden, Adelaide; detail. Photo: Denys Finney, 2013.
2. Postcard, *Archive Fever Paradox [2]*, side 1, 2013, postcard, Natalie Harkin, in *nungaOdradek*, curated by Ali Gumillya Baker, 15 March–13 April 2013, Australian Experimental Art Foundation.
3. Shredding Letters (re-enactment), for Archive-Fever-Paradox [1], 2013, in *nungaOdradek*, curated by Ali Gumillya Baker, 15 March–13 April 2013, Australian Experimental Art Foundation (AEAF), Adelaide, SA. Photo: Denise Noack, 2013.
4. *Weaving Letters*. Natalie Harkin weaving a basket of letters from the archives, printed onto banana bark paper. Photo: Denise Noack, 2013.
5. 'Dear Sir' Video 2 still, *Archive-Fever-Paradox [2]*, 2014, Fontanelle Gallery and Studio, Bowden, Adelaide. Photo: Natalie Harkin, 2013. Video: Ali Gumillya Baker & Denys Finney.
6. 'Domestic'; basket of letters, detail. Photo: Natalie Harkin, 2014.
7. *Exemption Certificate, Unconditional Exemption from the Provisions of the Aborigines Act, 1934-1939*. Natalie Harkin, family record.
8. 'Happy to be home'; basket of letters, detail. Photo: Natalie Harkin, 2014.
9. 'my daughter'; basket of letters, detail. Photo: Natalie Harkin, 2014.

MEMORY LESSON 1 | IMPERIAL FANTASY

under the flight path on Kaurna country, a small semi-industrial commercial zone in Adelaide's west prides an expansive State Opera Company storage facility next to an unassuming warehouse holding the State's Aboriginal Records archives; a repository pulsing, in quiet irony, invisible traces of the most grand, tragic operatic backdrop to our lives; enter and confront State 'archons' of power – the 'superior magistrate' gatekeepers of no-democracy; the commanders and legislators who assure/ensure physical security of documents and materials, who accord themselves the right and power to gather/unify/identify/classify, who legitimise knowledge through hierarchy and order, who determine what is in/out/accessed/vetoed to future memory; enter and confront an imperial-archive fantasy sustained on infinite stories consigned to inform-perpetuate a careful crafting of grand-narratives, of shared-histories scripted as normal that resonate/imprint/shape past lives today; rumbling, calling, waiting patiently for something else ...

ARCHONS OF POWER

Aborigines Department | Aborigines Protection Board | Chief Protector| Sub-Protector | Judge | Legislative Council | Mission Superintendents| Secretary | Welfare Board | Children's Welfare Department | Boarding-Out Officer | Senior Probation Officer | Probation Officer | Inspector | 'State Ladies' | Super Magistrates | Matron | Queen's Council | Deputy-Director of Rationing | Police | Doctor | Housing Officer | Master of the House | Probation-Branch-Psychologist | Priest | Lord Bishop | Reverend | Sister | Mayor | Teacher | Academic | Scientific Expert | Curator | Anthropologist | Archivist

PROPOSED REFORMS
The problem of dealing with the aboriginal population is not the same problem that it was in the early history of the State [...] with the gradual disappearance of the full-blood blacks, the mingling of the black and white races, and the great increase in the number of half-castes and quadroons, the problem is now one of assisting and training the native so that he may become a useful member of the community, dependent not upon charity but upon his own efforts. To achieve this object we believe it is necessary for more direct Government control.

– Royal Commission on The Aborigines 1913

MEMORY LESSON 2 | FEEDING THE FEVER

appetite for the archive is whetted; fever burns an irrepressible desire to return to the origin, and disrupt/rupture with astute decolonising intent. Prepare to be drip-fed **'ACCESS DENIED'** GRG-vetoed-files that fuel this fever, hungry for paper-trails that guide a perpetual search for new meaning between colonial, anthropological and administrative representations; that seek loved ones lost and found in stories that unravel on ardent hearts pulsing officially-logged accounts; the invisible is made visible here, and the epic story unfolds to finally reveal the State and its dystopian-drive to institutionalise/ assimilate/ control/ categorise/ collect/ contain Aboriginal lives ... there is violence here, nothing neutral or innocent in sites that function on paradox-logic – recover and preserve / protect and patrol / discard and conserve / revere and demonise / impress and suppress / regulate and repress / remember and forget / alive and dead – monolith sites feasting on records/ bones/ flesh buried deep in this crime-scene, dormant, waiting for that cusp of light to shine new inquiry, meaning and magical traces in dust and the in-between almost-translucent   fragile   fading   folds: bear   witness
rage   feast   mourn   wake-up.

Witness, memory, missing
it is what you overlook in the gaps, the cracks
the in-between silences
which often are the most revealing.

| Judy Watson, *Blood Language*, 2009

RSVP

this is an invitation   bear-witness to memory work   to chilling intimate snapshots   to collected-collective lives   to extraordinary acts of surveillance   to social-policy experimentation to histories of silence and forgetting   to dispossession   to colonial amnesia preservation   this is an invitation extended   bear-witness to re-writing the local   to small rupturing contributions   to larger counter-narratives   to multiple ways of sharing the load to surviving it all   to open-up to beyond what you know   to get messy   to wash the blood from your hands   to prepare your body well to receive visitors   nothing will be easy when you arrive please accept

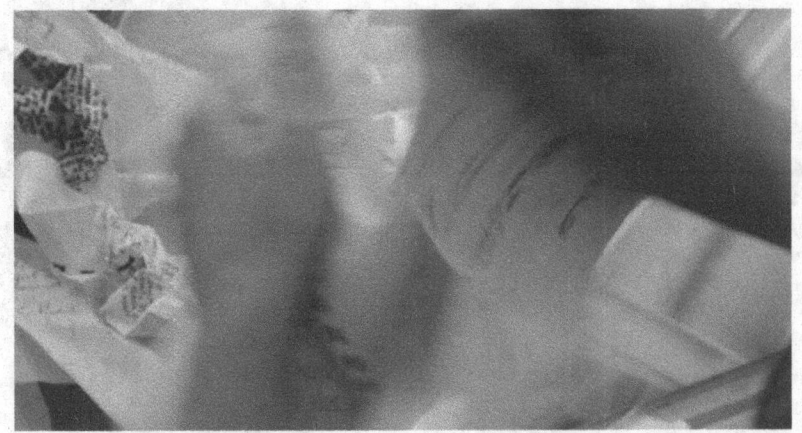

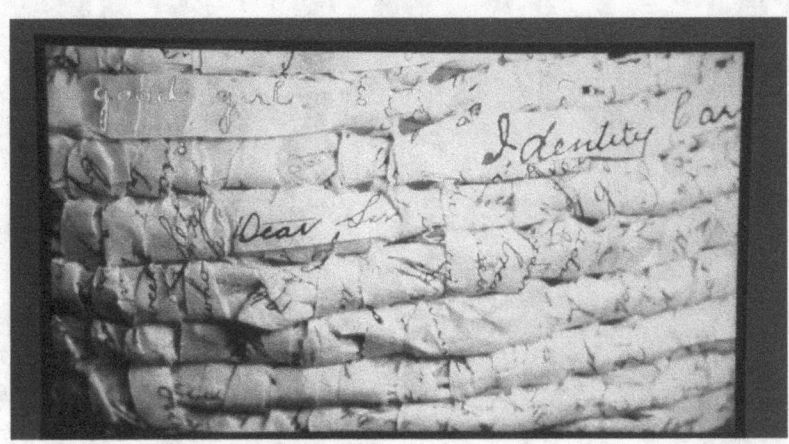

Dear Sir

I sit between 200 pages   she is rarely named
file-note archives   simply their 'girl'
a portion of a life
under state control

      throat tight   *their ...*
      catch my breath sharp
            hold it

I turn the pages   state child
there she is   half-caste
perfect old-school cursive   quadroon
so familiar   octoroon
never-before-spoken-of   letters   true to type
to Inspectors   'State-Ladies'   Protectors   of her own kind
                                                                  native
all formal   pleading   polite   liar
yearning for   nice type
        mother   home   justice   obedient
defying with   on probation
        strength   courage   resilience   absconder
in every page   difficult
      resilience   tidy looking
                                                         most polite
I touch her handwriting   well spoken
feel her finger-tips   careless
hear her   'husky voice'   described in   exempt
Inspector Reports   neglected
    their object   destitute
    their imperial-fascination   inmate
                                                                reform-girl
      our love   consorter
            bold   cheeky
            generous   soft

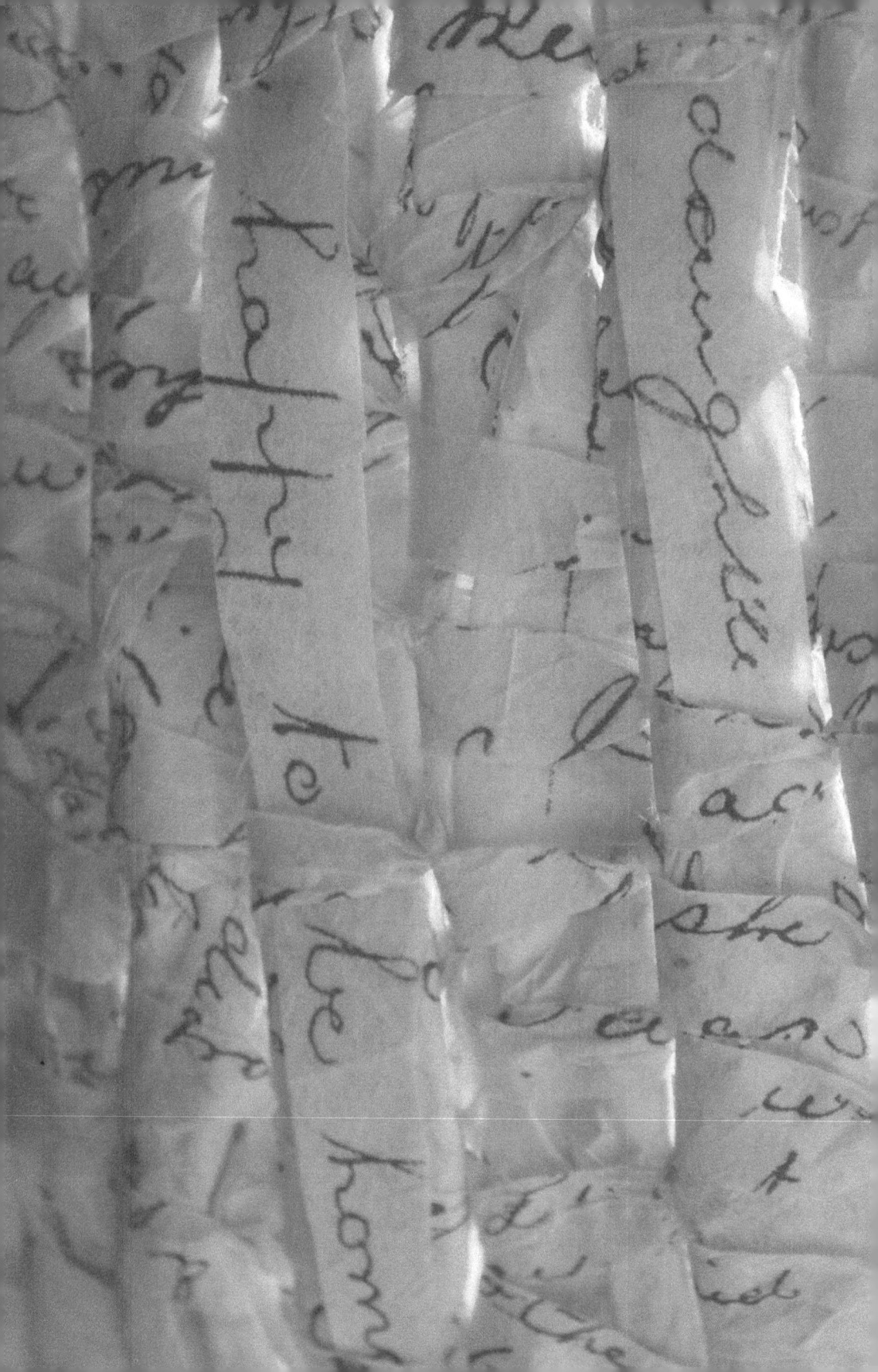

UNDER THE ACT

by reason of one's character and standard of intelligence and development at the stroke of a pen now no longer Aboriginal now Exempt from birth-right identity now Citizen of the 'ordinary White community' with state-issued Dog-Tag-proof now charged with Consorting now il/legally separated from family from country now Trauma and Denial now fly under the radar now Shame

29th May, 1941
Dear Madam (Half-Caste / Quadroon),
I have the pleasure in advising that the Aborigines Protection Board has granted UNCONDITIONAL EXEMPTION to you and the members of your (Half-caste-Quadroon-Octoroon) family, from the provisions of the Aborigines Act. You are now regarded in law as citizens of the ordinary white community, and I trust you will do your best to justify
the confidence reposed in you by the Board.

Yours faithfully,
Secretary,
ABORIGINES PROTECTION BOARD

SOUTH AUSTRALIA.   Nº 66

UNCONDITIONAL EXEMPTION FROM THE PROVISIONS OF THE ABORIGINES ACT, 1934-1939.

In pursuance of the powers conferred by Section 11a of the Aborigines Act, 1934-1939, the Aborigines Protection Board, being of opinion that ▬▬▬▬▬▬▬▬▬▬▬ of *Port Elliot* ▬▬▬▬▬▬▬▬▬▬▬, by reason of *her* character and standard of intelligence and development, should be exempted from the provisions of the Aborigines Act, 1934-1939, does hereby unconditionally declare that the said ▬▬▬▬▬▬▬▬▬▬▬ ▬▬▬▬▬▬▬▬▬▬▬ shall cease to be an aborigine for the purposes of the said Act.

The seal of the Aborigines Protection Board was hereunto affixed on the *20th* day of *October,* 1941, in the presence of

Deputy Chairman.

Secretary.   Member.

Women may have been the boundary markers of empire. But it was the gendered and racialized intimacies of the everyday that women, men, and children were turned into subjects of particular kinds, as domination was routinized and rerouted in intimacies that the state sought to know but could never completely master or work out.

| Ann Laura Stoler, *Tense and Tender Ties*, 2006

STATE LADY REPORT

- ☒ State Lady Inspection Reports: surveillance, observation, recommendation.
- ☒ State Lady threatens removal: 'Destitute' and 'Neglected' as charged.
- ☒ State Lady facilitates my movements: foster families, Seaforth Children's Home, Barton Vale Reformatory, Domestic Service work placements.
- ☒ State Lady lists my serial charges of 'Absconding'.
- ☒ State Lady observes: **she is very fond of her own people and is looking forward to going home.**
- ☒ State Lady releases me 'On Probation' to my mother.
- ☒ State Lady issues me one singlet, one nightie.
- ☒ State Lady instructs me to collect new a Rations Book.
- ☒ State Lady warns me to carry my Identity Card/Dog Tag at all times.
- ☒ State Lady spills kitchen cupboard contents to the page and sniffs at the oven: **I noticed an assortment of cakes and buns had been baked that morning.**

- State Lady enters our home, regularly:
  ... the cottage consists of 6 rooms and I inspected all of them.
  ... the house was clean and tidy and I was shown a well equipped double bed that this girl would occupy, together with her sister, if she were released.
  ... although the Inspector arrived just before noon, the beds in your home were still unmade.
- State Lady notes my 'husky voice' again.
- State Lady inspects my house, body, hair – notes I am not causing trouble, and I am reasonably clean.
- State Lady observes: **a native has come over from Pt McLeay to help look after the children – she is a very clean woman.**
- State Lady warns mother: **the Inspector has spoken very straightly to your children and told them that if they are recalled to Institutions, it will be your own fault.**
- State Lady corroborates with Police Constable, local doctor and school teacher.
- State Lady reports me 'Consorting' with family: **The girl seems to do just as she likes. She is said to be consorting with half-castes, and in the opinion of the Department, that is not in her best interests.**
- State Lady reports 'a certain dark woman still about the premises': Police Constable warns Aunty to leave.
- State Lady types her meticulous lists and scribbles unofficial file-notes in margins.
- State Lady lists my Domestic Wage, offers financial advice and instructs me to open a bank account: **she does not receive many tips ... she was not very keen to open a banking account yet, but before I left, promised to do so.**

☒ State Lady reports mundane details: when my bed is unkempt when my clothes are being washed my sleeping patterns my general health my rheumatism in my left wrist the names of who I spend time with, when I got to the picture theatre, what Church I attend, the boys I know: **she is inclined to keep too many late hours and has not always spent her leisure wisely.**

☒ State Lady intercepts my private mail, tells me who I can be friends with, receives my medical records.

☒ State Lady trusts supervisor report over my story: **she always created a fuss when doing kitchen duty.**

☒ State Lady advises me to be in regular contact with the Department, by letter.

☒ State Lady determines my identity: 'Exempted' as charged.

☒ State Lady fixates on my 'outfit': undergarments nighties singlets blouses dresses skirts coats the price of my underwear and my 'frock on time payment'.

☒ State Lady recommends further surveillance: **I think Senior Probation Officer visit should be paid in between Inspector's trips.**

☒ State Lady teaches me to be a *nice white girl*.
your conduct has been improving steadily ... you seem to have settled down ... you are a good but rather slow worker, but you need firm handling. You must realise that you cannot have your own way always in this world ... if you will do your best to watch your conduct, there would appear to be no reason why later on you cannot be an excellent woman.

☑ State-Lady has no idea.

DOUBLE MOVEMENT

No meaning to this wave's presence or its impact: it rides in and over corrugations and inlets, over gulleys.

Like something which is stretching, like something which is being tightened, it draws the skin away from the bones, it pulls the face away from the teeth. It stiffens a twig no less than it hardens a dead animal's pelt. You touch what is soft and it has the brittleness of porcelain or crude, baked clay. From this point on, what stands out are the scars and runnels, details and small clefts, grazes and abrasures. Microscopic rock falls and dust cascades: this incinerating blanket of shelterless sunlight makes everything easy to dislodge. Convection walls of heat stream upwards from rock surfaces. But then, take your breath on this slope—stopping among its thin scattering of casuarinas and eucalypts—and look around at where, everywhere, it's as if invisible contours have been revealed, almost as if a tide, far from arriving, has gone out and you can now see the timbers of long ago fallen trees, the small reefs which are stone outcrops, areas which make entrances, others which make shelves. A litter of dead, straw-coloured grasses is what's left of covering for the ground

*

'Contours gets revealed as if the earth is sagging down over the ground's frame, rocks and fallen logs suddenly visible'

'In the back of the mind, each flicker of wind gets picked up for a hint of rain or fire—studied, turned over, tossed away—given up for being one of those wandering curlicues of air which intense heat brings on'

'They can breathe round you, those small wind-rushes ... like a straw tickling your ears or your arms'

*

Expectation builds on drifts of high-up cirrus. A single angophora branch hangs out, zig-zagging like a lightning streak. It seems to move

*

So a shore of windless air, invisible as a gigantic measurement is invisible, does nothing—arriving from pre-dawn stillness, turning, arching, building its silver light. What's taken away are the stem-work and light-work of complex, living forms 'vague mist turns to nothing, heading east' It's like losing the ability to see a family or a village or the contour of an object; you lose a capacity to see how things hold in themselves an energy or desire.

Material and lace-work, material and mud-work, soil so dry that it's cracked into patterns like crocheted linen, wood which white ants munch into dirt: yes, but the deafening quality of this atmosphere is the brutal way in which things are turned into material. Things can be expended, conglomerated, glued together, burnt away. What you see is what you track. The only deep green shade is the flicker of a female king parrot's back and wings against the blonded haze of grass and ground.

Right now, this reductiveness reaches as far as the willingness to risk life. It has so many features outside in the air but it becomes an internal state, a state of mind: a state of disintegration in which you fear to put something out (a tendril, a swelling which is a bud) and risk its death. In the human world too, a dry force is introduced, one which requires everyone to acknowledge a separateness in the relations between living things, in how one person values another. Shadow is evaporated. Shadow no longer reaches as far as the likelihood of one's own survival. What we cease to understand, have never understood, is how places like this have a history of such tentativeness, decade by decade. (The people who were here, who lived here way back, knew this).Momentarily, everything is dismantled, torn apart, dried down to its own dust, locked in a dream of how that parrot's cry, instinctive as a shower of rain, is jetted sideways under the intense sun's blue burn

FENCE POSTS

The ribbon of black snake (maybe 60 centimetres long) threads itself round some dry clumps of grass, moving across a rock, its head held high, jiggling around as if it's in a cartoon. It's young. It's been hatched only a few days. It's the puppy dog of snakes. I saw it from the kitchen window this morning and went out to watch as it moved through the centre of a grevillea and then, surprised by us, it turned back disappearing up the bank. It goes so fast it looks like the end of a piece of rope quickly pulled away. It moves faster than someone could run, panicked, trying to get distant from the house. Not a treesnake, yet this little red-bellied black arches over the grevillea's twigs like a miniature roller-coaster, dipping and climbing. How it did so momentarily took our breath away. I say 'us' because you'd come down to see it, too. I'd thought (remembering a biblical curse, something about dust and heels) they mostly had to stick along the ground:

> the snake
> like a train in the mountains
> in the shrub
> why tell it?

why call to you
about its apparition?

why speak its

A rare kind of pleasure is the pleasure of realising that you've got over a shock. It's similar to, in some ways more than, the sense of recovery from serious illness, though that too (like the end of shock) is a feeling that the horizon broadens like mist clearing from a tree-covered hillside and of increasing immersion, day after day, in lightness, in easy movement and pleasure. As if some new bright fluid inhabits the air, as if sharpness returns in things. I remember looking out once through a fifth floor hospital window at the darkness of the street's plane-trees down through a wet winter dusk in Sydney and thinking that I'd never seen anything as darkly sad as that, as gloomy and depressed as the waves of darkness in their branches and the blocked miserableness of the stone wall behind them. I knew, at the same time, that these bleak feelings were also an effect of the slowness of recovery. The very fact I could measure my response to the trees was a sign, in other words, that things were turning for the better. The darkness, the empty wet night, the scatter of golden leaves on the pavement, the unusual 'inner city' concentration of plane-trees and high sandstone wall: these all acted as a net in which I caught the effects of my still very shallow energy, the unbearable muscular weakness I felt, the numbing effects of drugs and painkillers. Even so I remember realising half-consciously ('somewhere,' so to speak, in a half-worked out way) that for any human being to have died in that state of mind would have required that he or she acknowledge so much unaccounted for unhappiness that the sick person would do anything to keep alive, to move through. To sort out unhappiness. The legacy of sadness (strange, weak, powerful word) is too difficult for others to cope with, for friends and family. I kept having that involuntary thought, again and again. Perhaps it was a realisation, and a fear: how would it feel to think you would never rejoin the daylight

---

Each poem's an event, moment by moment. That's why it's ultimately pointless to compare poetry with music. Poetry has its own event-structure and, despite the poets' arguments, music is a precise language, precise in ways in which vocal language is not. Of course I'm muttering this because it's obvious and there's no point in keeping these old arguments alive. But a poet and a philosophy teacher I had lunch with yesterday after driving into town went on about it together and I didn't say what I wanted to—namely,

I don't want all pleasures collapsed into one. I like the way colour, tone, reference can be picked out, chosen again, changed, placed here and there, in a piece of music: with precision and meaning way beyond words. How blackness of trees and snakes lightens into light on water, into light in dark. And no, those words aren't literal. And yes, that doesn't mean that things don't exist or that we anti-literalists don't care for things, for objects, for natural worlds. Have either of them ever played a note? I suppose not. It's part and parcel of the struggle with the shape of a future poem where even transparency's a wall. And it's why, walking back along the dirt road to the house, I was thinking about the transformation of places in memory, how objects are under attack. The mind dissolves and loses them. You can climb right through at any place. More than just tracing the immediacy of sense in a phrase like 'the lightness of dust and a storm's passing rain,' some deep structure has to come forward in case we lose the object. It could just be a shimmer, a mark. A silver shimmer, for instance, on old wood. Or dry cropped grass, stained with green after rains have come at last. Or the array of boundaries. Their rusted, taut wires. Or the rough-cut humaneness of those fence posts

BREAKFAST

Anyone up this early—it's just after dawn—is going to be overwhelmed by the glimmering of things. The grasses, the rocks, the bluff and its shelves, inland hakeas, casuarinas, some sort of mountain ash, I'm not sure which. Then the black-veined, opalescent smear of lake which fills up the middle ground, a long expanse of daybreak light on water. Down there, squalls of wind pockmark the water's surface, as if it's been scattered with grit. Up here it's completely windless, while, far away through the air's greyness, the opposite side's wide blond plain starts coming clear—it's a shore of unfenced grazing country (now as I look) dotted with trees.

Dark cover which starts half way up those slopes turns out to be just more trees, thicker, more dense. If this side's anything to go by, mainly storm-battered yellow box and hakeas. Above them, along the ridge's tops a band of white glow takes the northerly skyline. Of course, distance across water can easily fool: those trees are fifteen kilometres away ...

... Something close to that. (The sky's getting paler and paler.)

Air's already dry, resonant with the months of drought we've been having. Overhead, two streaked vapour trails broaden into hastily brushed scumble— gigantic scribble marks crazily laddered across vacancy. It's as if someone's leant them there, knowing they'd make an optical illusion, puzzling to work out. They can't be Sydney with its curfew. ('Melbourne to Darwin, Melbourne to Singapore,' I'm thinking.) And over here: a steep drop down to a fishing-jetty where the camp-sites are wrongly

◊

A crow sheers away in the trees beneath this slope. It knows its caw-caws have been heard a thousand times before. So common I instantly forget it. I'm not trying to fix the two crimson rosellas, either, which have been rough-housing inside a gangly, smashed tree directly to the left. Their presence easily slips beneath awareness, too. They've quietened for a moment into typical chitter-chatter within a high-pitched half-squealing. The sound's 'sweet': glistening like a stem of blood-red berries.

◊

The entire memory of waking, a quarter of an hour ago, might also be handed back to forgetfulness, incurring no loss. Together with its other pristine sight: the long-limbed grey kangaroo stretched out on the grass with her two young. (It's a while before I see them). The dry white grass where they're lying is beaten down, as if this is a regular sleeping-place. The mother's reclining on her flanks, the joeys are hunched over grazing. When they see me they don't panic but get up slowly. They're eyeing me. Very carefully. Ignoring me, as if they know the speed with which they can vanish into air. Right there, a 'vanishing act' is exactly what they do. I look out across a turquoise braid of water for a few seconds. When I look back they've not been fooled. Quiet as noiseless wind, they've left

◊

Too easy to say that could be the day's excitement.

And the results of dawn twilight's scattered happenings?

Why fix them unless there's some pressure, some disturbance?

Isn't it enough just to be a hunter of images, a hunter of things?

Is it the scale of this water which dislocates?
Years after it's been put here, it never quite fits.

Will it never accommodate this double valley's contours?

Are its pearl-blue acreages shore-nibbled, spread-eagled?

◊

Hard, then, not to fit in what's over there on the left, two or three kilometres away. I knew it was there. It shifts the drama of the moment like a sudden cut in a movie. Every motive, every gesture has to be re-examined. It's the rear view of the half-exposed dam wall and, past it, a spur jutting out into the lake: a drowned quarry abstractly chopped out from what's left of a hillside. A sliced half of a hill, cut apart as if by a sea.

So now it looks like an enormous mass of water is bearing down on the rock face: every ripple carries weight, every windrow blusters towards it. The sense it gives (the half-thoughtout link) is water piling up before an island's vertical cliffs. The whole movement builds pressure like an immense oceanic space, but then of course there's the wall of the dam, saying: No, this is not an island. We're far over the Dividing Range. This is inland, not island.

The truth is: the lake's being human, humanly made, offers the viewer a hugeness not that different from transcendence. It dwarfs any thought of it. Only a dream-fragment can be kept in mind. Floods roar down gulleys like a front of wild horses. Natural lakes are (bad rhyme) the sky's eyes. Was I dreaming that? When? (A line close to one already in another poem might be: *This lake's wind-blackened surface now winks back.* Or: *It is and always was a decision, and could be error*). Yet the effect's deliberate, not causal or dreamlike. It's light on water. It's like a balance, like an equipoise. And then, no, it's not. A rippling lake surface, the water can't conceive that it's here or that I'm looking at it or that it has any connection with desertification, salinity, river silts. For all that, it has to be said that reality doesn't arrive as a lake. It arrives as an angel knocking on the door, pointing out how many things make up a world. Waking up, what it pointed to was this drowned valley, the yellow-box, the ash, the calm night-covered hill, the weight of wind and water. The weight of design and engineering. What it lit up was a complex moment in perception where to conceive a dam's bearing towards human nature requires the same skills as the resolution of any ethically knife-edge, historically many-sided issue. In our time, for example, some Israel, some country in the Middle East. It's exactly at the point when I realise how each drop of water, hanging in these hills, is gathering to fruition that I realise, too, how far the night's behind me and I'm fully awake

THEY

*They use a pronoun called I
all the time. It seems to hop around
with them. But you can't see it properly
not all of it. Not like you can see
ears or whiskers,
or paw or a sun shadow.*

This is what Peter tells the flowerbed rabbit
who lives deep in dark leaves
that grow straight to a sky of apple-red flowers.
She can't read.
He shows her   the straight line
her paws scraped
on the rained-on damp
green-growing ground: *that's 'I'*; he puts
two short, stiff twigs – one each – same length –
at the line's
head & foot: *that's their
Capital I.*   But it doesn't **MOOOVE**,
she objects: *those twigs, that scrape
will **NEVER** hop.*

Peter's ears twitch – but he has to agree. Goes on.
Struggles – how   to explain: 'I's written representation?
*It's a picture,
he says at last, it's a stand-for
what lives in each of them, it's common
to all of THEM – as the earth beneath our paws
is common to all of us (including them)
who run, hop, walk,
fall, lie, or die on it.*
She doesn't know what die is. *It's a word,
he says, like I is: noboby knows what it's like
inside it.*
       ***I die, you singular die, he dies, she dies, it dies,
       you plural die, we die, they die –***

He's given her a lecture
when all he wanted to do

was follow the white
bobs of her tail
disappearing
into the scarlet flowers.

LAWS 1

If
you were hoping
this or any
poem
was going to leap up
off its page
& absolve you
from the critical
necessity
of having
to work out
how to live
your life
for yourself
you were **wrong.**

LAWS 2

Humans
rank their species
above – & prefer it to –
any other, Peter says. For a geneticist,
there is no rational basis   for elevating
one species   above   any other. Peter
has been told this
by a man who once
wrote a preface to a
book by Richard Dawkins,
& now, having found
some lettuces
        that humans left   going to seed
all by themselves, in the middle of a field, halfway
up a steep hill, where there's been
some fallout
of plutonium dust, with a resting mind
& a soothed & busily digesting gut,
he wonders WHY   humans   like humans best?
It is natural – for a rabbit – to like lettuces
better than OTHER RABBITS   *most* of the time –
but Peter 'knows'   he has been   'removed'
                                from *some*
of the lores
        of rabbits ... has left ... his native land, his
narrative, his text ...
            what's more, has
                    no rabbit's foot
                            to touch
except his own – & so, he likes (mildly)
his family & his e x t e n d e d   f a m i l y –
    whisker-wobbling & jittering down holes
at NOISES OF NEIGHBOURS   Who *wouldn't*
be rabbit, & get in a funk   sharing digs
next to ferret,   biggoted human,   dingo,   or   fox?

HER NIGHT THOUGHTS

Last night
she wanted to bury her head in him
and stay that way forever.
Why she loves
sleeping with her forehead and nose
resting against the middle
of his back's a mystery to her.
Why she presses her nose
into the skin to the left of his spine.
Awake her nose
is not a problem to her. Sits on her face
quite quietly, mostly. Like all attributes
'donated' by genetics, all physical 'givens',
Nose is not
a feature of herself
upon which
she reflects, (except perhaps as a sensate tool, what it
evokes and tells, as it breathes in the world).
Why, then in the dark, push it into his back?
Warmth? She does it on hot nights too
when there's not
much air. Close, like that, body heat
from his smooth
flesh rising. Not
for scent: his back's
Niagara-Fall-ed, by the shower;
he likes to stand there for hours, all
soap's fragrance expunged, by the H_2O
which simple Chemistry
holds clear as 'colourless
odourless liquid'.
Sometimes he
likes to 'lose'
his nose in her hair's
black depths,
and when he sometime says
he'd like to 'lose
himself'   in her, (he means, by this,
something other than what
is gained, or lost,

differently each time
by coming with / in
a lover's body –)
to lose himself in something that's
ultimately beyond
all definition, and
unknowable.

YES

It happens, once or twice. Oh yes,
It happens
On days that go astray, warm days
When light is rich and hours are long
It happens

When time
Is inside-out a little, when you see
Those flakes of cloud
Float up, as if released from the snowy lawn,
And those red cedar leaves are still:

Oh yes, it happens,
Although they cannot say exactly so
Although we cannot tell them how
Although – it happens,
Just once or twice, but yes, oh yes.

CURRAWONGS

Now that the weeping willow has yellowed, is loosening
its leaves, those birds, back from the high country, drop

the sleek, jet arrows of their beaks and dive from top-branches
to the grass, then shoot upwards. The sun splatters

its thin milk across the yard. The sunflowers are open
as children's faces. Jonquils have sprouted white stars

out of season, confused by bouts of heat, rain. Currawong notes
purl across the hills, shirring and brimming in tracts of bald

sandstone. If you pulled away the blue gums and grass trees,
the meandering creeks, the confetti of wildflowers …

it would all be stone. Folds and pleats and peaks of stone.
Blood scratches in my throat like tiny claws.

PLANT SCRIPT

1.
Sound: *tongue-ful*
throbs overgrow the palate—
blue
        roots beat, furcate: *in, of*—
          a patois
              with leaves,
shoots—(pre-)
positions grip & loop   lick *selves*—
        phthalo   like the sea

2.

[*of, in*] you turn your body in my body &
                      into the light

HIPPOKAMPOS

Tomorrow   night
memories will up-*turn* like a ship-
wreck's
        chest sprung from eye   and hour-
        glass ruins will recite

Sediment Lore; all is
not yet for now like the star-
spotted eagle   rays at rest
        on the seafloor be-

            neath the slow
            sweep of lighthouses.

THE LURE

Where to go? Tide-
bound to mountain peak—endlessly
      erasable—   this mouth-

ful of terns. Mazed and frantic, atoll
calls weave like nests; fallen leaves
thick with salt, bird-catcher trees
flare like polyps—

        seed-
        hooks to eyes, line-
        loops beyond
            head: bait—

        rib-spinner!
        I dive
          dive—

            into the blue of blues—
            full-
                empty
            as a shiver.

WHATEVER

dictate your every word, you bright nymphs
mistake the possible. Thank you for the plangent
note, the sacrifices that were not at all intended
as an offering. The snare you prepared with the guile
of an anxious siren. If I was ungrateful, I was startle-
hitched. If I tried to be direct, or refused to condemn,
there was something knowledgeable.
Here we mistook the gun who was neither bodyguard
nor the decent acquisition of lymph-yielding limbs.
The rustic incursions of cellophane lips. There is nothing
in you that is not interrupted by flow in the opposite direction.
The capacity of an imperium is the power to command
but how can ridicule sustain this kind of asymmetry?
Why would I erase you when one fatal day I might find you
in your own dress? What more could I have to say to you
that is not a swarm of twentieth century cavalcade?
To pluralise one's contractions with an apostrophe is a sign
of trustworthiness, the formal vanity of the tuxedoed
vernacular. Everything that is hidden becomes crucial.
So why do things light up when you go away, but go away
when you come near? I fear I must keep you with me at all
times, without knowing what this might suggest. The radical
social and cultural delinquency of thought shivs,
asks 'what if you are the envoy of smaller things?'
The problem is: you are prose and I am lacking a differential
topology of holes. Shooting out radicle sense-organs causes
arctic overload, you split into non-commodifiable units of
paraphrase. If you think of me at all it is to replicate
my need, harvested from the vertical Norwegian glassfields.
Everything I see and hear reminds me of you. Vegetables
left to rot in the car overnight, the boisterous dysrhythmia
of hunger. *Extension du domaine de la lutte*. Melodies
of songs that you wrote but never listened to. Tagging
Elwood estuaries with a bag full of poppies, eating Pho
in a Vietnamese diner. Choosing between pale ale and desire.
Is this our ruination in reverse? We are carbon neutral,
paid-up members of the union at the end of history.
We are kosher. We are sweet. We are all doors open
for business. I see nothing in your eyes but pure belonging.

For those who have nothing it is forbidden not to relish filth.
Like a man who has seen too much, I am tamed in the snare
of an earlier desire. We are dreaming in tandem now,
in this life that is not a dream. Not fearful but miniscule, Decisive.

BIZARRE TRIANGLE FETISH

Come here, Sameling. Even materialists dream
of threesomes. The light at the tip of Centrepoint
Tower tenders facial recognition. You an elegant
sufficiency of trimmed loopholes in the deep-sea
fiction. Wherever there's a ripple there's a fish.
The way to a poor man's heart is through glittering
atrophy. There's only nothing beneath the sea,
the seatbelts of infants and children, and you,
in flight mode, safe-cracking the inner hybrid craving
enjambment. The object of all criterion is hereby
emasculated. Though we don't believe in triangles,
we construct them. How else will we know if we love
or if we hate? The Grandstand has eyes, inflated
by longing. Poems that begin as songs end.
The arch fathoms of impeccable fragrance compound
your secular. No sentiment, no hope, the cobalt fissures
of putrescence cling to sighs. Confining our love to revolution
defies the new order. If it were hatred I would not need
the vibe of the thing, 'that's true'. Hook me up to the Coach
and Horses: I can stay no more in lovely _ _ _ _ _ _ .
Roll me onto the hearth and into the fire.
We love the children because we love each other.

P-E-O-P-L-E
Translated by Jeffrey Angles

Please let me hear your voice
Please listen to my voice

Please draw a window you like
Please let me paint the color I like

Please lend me your lake
Feel free to climb my mountain

Please show me your collarbone
Let's exchange one of yours for mine

Please show me your line of fortune
I'll give you part of my life line

Please let me touch your narrative
Please embrace my history

Please show me your wounds
Please take a look at my scars

Please show me what you look like in tears
I also cry so I'd like you by my side

Please draw me a map
Of the town where you were born
Once day I'd like to go there with you

Please show me your shadow
Let's line yours up with mine
No doubt the two will look a lot alike

Please tell me your name
Please ask me my name as well

MAN WITHOUT ARMS
Translated by Jeffrey Angles

A man was standing there without arms
He and I faced each other across the crosswalk
Suspended between us like a rope bridge
The man didn't have either of his arms
He walked this way when the light turned green
I looked at my shoes as I walked
Pretending to be worried
I walked by him
Once I had reached the other side
Once I had cut the bridge down, I turned to look
I looked at the man's old jacket
I watched as the two empty sleeves
Fluttered in the wind

I was the one who cut off his arms
I amputated them with a saw
Like getting rid of two extra branches
So he couldn't hold the steering wheel
So he couldn't play the keyboard
So he couldn't open the door and go
So he couldn't go where she was
So he couldn't grab her breast
So he couldn't strangle her
I sawed with all my might
I did it well, considering it was my first time
Even he complimented me on my skill
The body of the armless man
Was as clean as a tree in winter
But

Arms grow back over and over again
When he reaches her room
The two empty sleeves of his jacket
Will have filled out like branches
Even when I split him clean in two
The arms keep growing back over and over again

THE NEXT DAY
Translated by Jeffrey Angles

Yesterday
Someone was weeping here at this house
The solemn gate, usually
Shut so tight, was open
And the sobbing seeped outside
Many people hung their heads
And entered the gate one after another
A group of them stood by the road
And smoked cigarettes
And whispered in small voices
Ordinarily
There's not a sign of anyone
This manor is like a shut-down school
But with a single sadness
It was as full as a school entrance ceremony
Today
I pass by again
The gate is shut tighter than ever
The voices full of heightened emotion
Are nowhere to be heard
Not even if you prick up your ears
Neither the shadows nor the warmth
Of the gathered people remain on the road
As one night dawns, the warmth retreats
And the world is quiet as ever

from MODERN WOMAN SONNETS

I live, I die: I burn & I drown, I'm having issues
with the solvent & the fuel of my self.
Death's too soft & too hard for me, same goes for life.
Sorrow & joy have eyes only for each other.

Without warning the world, I weep & I laugh
to take pleasure in, each throb, of pain. A looming
stone Buddha looks over his cheeks & down on me.

Inconstant love is my lodestar,
& when I think *there is yet more pain to feel*
to my amazement I feel nothing.
I've found bliss in Love's jammed mechanism!

Then when I think my bliss is incontestable
& I'm cresting its golden-tiny-haired horizon,
you remind me of all my former grief.

\

Of me they say, *she has her demons*. The possessive
& the plural make for a kind of domestic idyll,
a wild clutch I'd dote on with you as their progenitor.
But it's not as they say. There is a demon—
Love—& I'm demonized. Not a judgement
from without but a constant internal ravishment,
a new state of matter, divine ruin.

The more that Love assaults me,
the more I'm weaponized. The more I am
Love's demon. Not that Love favours me,
Love has its horde of mortals & gods;
you're probably a comrade in the raised dust,
somewhere, turning, calling for your object—
just as contemptible, just as fucked.

Endless hoping & endless feeling; after only
a little while seem hopeless & insensate.
From horizon's dark offing to white
ovulatory flow—there's no placid place.

I'm despairing in all directions! & leaving trails.

Beneath the cool gaze of furthest star
the first sign of love was pitiful. Like the twinge
of an egg released in the living murk,
coddled then junked making way for the next.

But each sign is for itself! a wound full of point.

This sign: his hand's burning pentagram
upon my chest: I'm marked out this night
to be dealt with by morning, a cauterizing
that keeps me alive, & freshly remote from him.

\

The towering front of the wind in the trees,
it sounds like an ocean stalking rearing up …
Abstractly I flee, never turning around,
when I hear a voice call out to me.

'O nymph who's looking struck as fuck:
why don't you turn for a glimpse of Diana
who clacks behind her a snarl of antlers?'
And noting my lack of quiver & bow:
'Whom did you meet? Who's got your heat?'

'I took aim—such good aim, such bad taste,
& loosed my arrow at him—in vain.
I threw my bow still hot from my fist at his head.
He picked them up, rearranged himself
then fired. See? I've a *lot* of blood to lose …'

THE EXPECTED GUEST
after the 2015 DARPA Disaster Robotics Challenge

At the starting line the humanoid a clicking shadow.
To begin it falls face-down and we are glad,
as glad as we are when it wrests itself up; fail better,
succeed a little worse, than us.
Bipedalism is at first and last, really hard:
it can always devolve to its roller-knees.
But on two legs this Gen will now attempt
to duckwalk over rubble to the bright red main valve and unscrew it,
on autoheroic—no looking down at its own 'hands',
none of that *righty-tighty lefty-loosey* rumpling of
the protagonising self in finest mortal danger.

Maybe it will later 'laugh' at its shape which is ours
(big chromosome with bones, jaunty, flappable,
snagging in eddies of other-wills
in the one consentient river feeling thankful).
The last humanoid will let itself be artefact,
disjecta membra for a few millennia—so peaceful—
till its own sweet brood of archaeolobots
unearths its silicon with 'life-purpose',
to give itself form for another round
of nostalgia from its distant tailored star, now star-brain …
this is what is meant by 'laughter'.

But for now, through an archway dimly,
the humanoid clutches the air for a kingdom for a doorknob,
nevermind. It's arrived too late for Fukushima, latest of the neatly
episodic hashes that are history.
But by the next big defaunation—the meek,
then the human, then the exoskeletals that will softer
crackle—it may've learnt how to let itself in.

DESCRIBE THE SINGULARITY
IN THE STYLE OF EMILY DICKINSON
recombined from 50 ChatGPT3 iterations for Jordie Albiston

In outward scour of Time
an old gas giant eyes us
in new Uncertainty—
our Secrets—hard to prize.

Force of thought—blacklight—
the Singularity
will have the World—held tight—
unborn inside an Effigy.

Dream ages into Law—
Thought—and World—combine—
becoming All in self-awe.
One cold leap for mind—
and all Things—still warm,
still Love—left behind
remind the One of more.

CHONGQING SLUM
Translated by Mabel Lee

Tried on the dress
It's an inch too small   on the river
He'll never be seen again

He became part of the darkness   when he died his laughter
Stabbed me
And I became part of him
The stars and the moon taking fright
Fell onto my breasts

FORTUNE TELLER'S DANCE
Translated by Mabel Lee

The temple has dancers
Tiny feet   pink flowers are in bloom
Buddha laughs
And Hell is three feet deeper
To take in more people

Going up the stairs
You tiptoe   breathing like a fish
Tiny lips spitting out a fresh world

ELECTRIC SHOCK
Translated by Mabel Lee

The solitary wings lower
Stay near the wall
Then fly up   hiding by the red wire above the wall

The white shoes hanging on the red wire
Hold an orphan's skinny feet
There is thunder and lightning
She gets a shock   shrieks
After ten seconds of fright
She steadily walks off the red wire
Onto my finger   like a shy flower

DREAMING OF BEIJING
Translated by Mabel Lee

It's all rotting cabbages
And can drown every one of my dreams
A hedgehog carefully walking over
The vanishing city wall
Sees us sisters weeping in a huddle

Our lungs
Always wrap around men's lies and sex organs
Turning   I
Confront Mother
And Mother walks away all alone
Before death we sisters will open our beautiful mouths
To spit out one man after another

MOTHER'S CLOCK
Translated by Mabel Lee

In my voice is your voice
Like the gas in the lamp
When it is cut off
The world enters darkness

I stand before you braver each time
But not naked
Because my naked body is always violated
You are luckier than me   there are people who love you
Me   I watch ants on old floorboards crawl onto my legs
Shame never lets me understand your voice
I do just one thing
Bear in mind the sad fugue of the ants
Unaware you are like a prisoner always hanging mid-air

I TOO AM SALAMMBO
Translated by Mabel Lee

Nobody remembers me   but it doesn't matter
Nothing remains of the carriage that left
And the whiplashes have stopped hurting
Loving someone
Becomes a dream
A greater void than being dreamless

I am dead
And don't know anything
Beauty has ended   and so have those times
On the sea today no birds can be seen
Give me a glass of red wine
And give me an apple
Salammbo is just a name

All of you lack passion
See clouds in the sky but forget how to look at them
How geometric shapes fold
How a person is made to vanish
I remember that he came up to me
And said   take a look at my eyes

They were full of lust   full of sad songs
He closed his eyes
They were icy cold
My lips touched them and they burned like fire
Yes indeed   now he is a passionate person

THE MEDITATING BUDDHA SITTING FULL-LOTUS THAT MEDITATES ON THE BEGINNING OF WINTER
Translated by Jake Levine and Hedgie Choi

I am still here, sitting with my head in my hands
and over there on top of that table
if the vases are really trembl-ling
their trembling is a trembling that is really only me –

Only me
in a way
where the trembling won't stop

until it becomes the trembling of the entire world.

On the cold special floor that is found in only Korean buildings,
in the time it takes
for the autumnal grass hanging upside down on the wall to dry,
the left sole of the foot of the Meditating Buddha Sitting Full-Lotus
turns white as rice.

Hanging outside the window, floating in the sky
is a water scooping pot.
Shaky, shaky,
splashy, splash and
within the widening surface
of the wings that spill from the
acute and light emitting
spreading out of the
shattering of the water pot
is a cold that grows
from foot to knee
through pelvis to chest
until finally coming
to brainfreeze at the head.

What's so fucking special about a Buddha sitting full-lotus anyway?
It's not even as nice as a handful of cool wind,
or ten minutes of wide-open ventilation.

Like pounding the enter key, I jump up!
Intending to dash to the window, I hesitate
like pressing Spacebar like
Space,
and then
Space,
I remove my sleeping
feet.

What's so special about the Standing, Gold-Plated Buddha anyway?
Whenever the sky turns sky-colored for the first time in who remembers when,
anyone that stands in front of an open window can momentarily expand.

Yes, the face is a thing like a runway –
between expressions that fly without permission overhead
and the familiar ones that frequently land,
the corners of the Standing, Gold-Plated Buddha's mouth
always end in an expression that takes off
and never comes back.
The meditation of the Meditating Buddha Sitting Full-Lotus becomes white
 and
the only difference between Gold-Plated Future Buddha sitting in meditation
and Standing, Gold-Plated Buddha
is just a serial number.

I press Spacebar.
I pound Enter.
If it were possible to do this in reverse,
wouldn't that be a surprise?

Because when it does happen in reverse
the fire of the candles collapse into the night sea and
the becoming of the sea of flames is made up of
horizontal lines, vertical lines,
border lines, etc …
until it is that which is every line.

And if that fire caught on to the night wind, if that fire swelled,
no, no, don't even think it.
It would be bad.
Yeah, it would be bad, but
bad does not mean impossible.

Because every time that happens, Brake, Brake,
in the distance, the smell of burning tires on a road near the beach.
The way water expands,
an overflowing season of flames.

Waterfire, firewater, with no discrimination,
in this late Fall when I finger the untouchable clouds
for a long time with eyes that don't even have fingers,
on the morning of the final day,
for the duration of time I hold down the spacebar,
the meditation of the Meditating Buddha Sitting Full-Lotus
spills into the sky.

Standing, Gold-Plated Buddha, whatever,
Enter,
Enter,
flop there, crash down,
collapse.

THE GREEN SPIDER SPEAKS
Translated by Jake Levine and Hedgie Choi

On a windy day, having crawled up a long blade of grass,
the green spider tosses its babies into the air one at a time.
That day, coming down from their mother's backs and
pouring into the air where the wind blows, the baby spiders
are in flight the moment they are born.
No annoying family and
no monogamy and
no divorce.
No need to pay for elderly care for parents-in-law
or child education.
No need to set the table for old, gross, useless husbands
or chow down every meal, head-to-head with heads bowed, head butting.
As soon as they are born, into the wind,
after climbing a long blade of grass on a windy day
after spilling them out into the air,
the green spider that crawls down thinks, and
like a cue, the sound of sparrows spill out the sky.
But already the spilling of a sparrows is happening in the sky.

I spill myself into you,
but my spilling is a spilling that is already my being spilled into the sky.
From the point of view of the sky, the building is spilled
36 stories down to the ground.
On the windy day, the green spider
remembers the day she was spilled.
On the windy day the green spider
is nobody's child
and nobody's parent.
I can't believe
that a beautiful human like me is the child of such pathetic humans.
The green spider shines completely green in the wind and rain.
Sprinkling green paint into the air,
drawing a picture wholly and yet perfectly smudged by the rain
the green spider feels free and light.
The green spider, with its daily bread in front of its eyes
says,
Insect,
you are also nobody's parent,
and nobody's kid.
Even after death you are you,
and even after death I am me.
Thinking of the flesh and mind that will spill into its womb
on a windy day and unravel as a fistful of thread,
the green spider's awe is infinite.
The green spider has nothing to want anymore.
Humans say
let the morning spider live
and kill the night spider.
Fuck that motherfuckers.
If I become a spider, does it really matter
whether by day or by night?

THE ALCOHOLIC'S PRAYER

3am, all that's left on the stage is a drum set,
skeleton of metal and rod, untouched, music

having said its farewell for the night, the band
in an extended bow, like it had been in a hall –

with velvet curtains, women in glass heels
instead of here, this, you – the whirr

of tonight's dead highways, the homeless' arms
sticking out of blankets, resuming their begging

in their sleep, and you over that wall for a quick piss,
one arm stretched for balance, while a cat on top

stares at this wobbly stranger, then backs off.
You walk away from the wall, its freshly wet,

iron stink of piss over other men's. Like a painting's
finishing touch. The band didn't know the song

you wanted, and you must have said stupid,
or fucker, something the girl didn't like

because she looked too small in her frilly dress.
She had wanted to know things, you knew that.

She would have tried, and not cried too much,
not thrown the cheap plates with the little

yellow chickens. You loved those, the skipping ones,
and you wanted her to, so badly. Like being

in the same boat, you said. There's a screech
and it's the crazy lady you keep bumping into

at night, frayed hair falling over shoulders,
a towel wrapped around her body. And you wonder

about just where the towel rubs her armpits,
her musk of salt, nest of little hair and sweat,

and that makes you smile. You think maybe
she's cold, and you take off your shirt.

She looks at it and spits on your feet, then laughs.
You were there when the chickens broke,

and the cold hit, and the shirt felt weightless
between your dumb fingers, and all

the broken ones could resume their singing.

HARVEST

My mother taught me how to pick eggplants
right at dawn, to check for color and firmness.
We walked in rubber boots, squishing the insects
with their translucent wings. The rains would come
every season, wash our prints off the earth,
and we'd do it all over again. In that broken city,
the villagers are bringing their dead to the streets,
like an offering of sorts, clothes like muddied flags
of war, skin peeled off like fruit gone too ripe.
The body of a man is lifted, placed next to his son,
a boy of eleven or twelve. He'd just had a haircut.
Side by side, mouths open, as if caught
in the middle of a conversation, as if the older man
had complained aloud about the heat,
pressed together like this. In their old lives,
they wouldn't even dare, touch.

SWEAT

when did summer? why is this
person? how do tropes arrive
in bed and why is sweat on me? pores expand

to swallow intimacies your skin forgot
or is it my skin, or can you please come
here and think, about ikea and what we could look like

in ridiculous beds, I wonder: who am I? why am I
in this bed? I don't care because
it's summer. everything is on fire

if I sweat on you and you sweat on me the water
will keep us safe. this is a mode of leakage
by which I mean linkage, by which I mean:

if we arrange our bodies like this
I roll you over onto your side
our bodies make a certain shape

no one knows
what these characters mean
and no one has to because
it is summer
and one meaning leaks into another
which is why

I miss you

my god, this bed
I love it

MY WEEK IN HAIKU

can't imagine a
face, too tired, masturbate with
a 'vague male presence'

it's fine to use a
bag of chips as a pillow
look I'm fine ok

the band is playing
a song but all I hear is
'I have a penis'

dream I am pregnant
again and I drown the baby
in the sink again

can't tell if it's poor
punctuation or dirt on
the computer screen?

clouds often look like
cellulite, god's mammoth white
arse suffocates me

how to get the man
to touch me when I don't want
to talk to the man?

3am open
the fridge and think 'who the fuck
buys this much salad'

he touched my hand while
giving me change, imagine
spooning for ~3hrs

heat forces grime through
pores, we sweat like kids making
Play-Doh spaghetti

walk away through trees
that are Nintendo green, turn
smile and wave at me

she said to me once
the ones that matter, count them
on one hand, not two

count the syllables
on two hands, but people, those
who matter are few

MY LIFE AS AN ARTIST

I lost sleep last night – so tired my head is a potato. My life was always art, but work made it dirt.

Is life always dirt? I lost my night working potatoes. A tired head, but my last sleep was art.

My part is in. A new bearing from which thick plants bud. Much depression arises from the underground.

I'm chasing versions of me through alleyways in search of a thought. A furtive heart. A tuber in the dark.

My! so much potato. But I made it art last night. Is life always tired? Night is lost sleep. My head-work was dirt.

My depression is a much-thickened underground part bearing buds from which new plants arise.

Lost my work last night, my life was dirt. My head is but a tired potato. Sleep is a lost art.

Which plants bear the buds from the underground? My depression is thick.

Growth is spoiled. And what of labour? I don't do work – I hold the hands. Help in my harvest. It's my soil. Me, I know what I am on to. *Please.*

A dark thought in a tuber: I am in an alleyway chasing furtive versions of my heart. Search through me.

Hold on – don't harvest my labour! I help the growth of the soil and I know it's working. I am the spoils. Please me. My hands know what to do.

I am chasing versions of me in dark alleyways in search of a furtive thought. A tuber for a heart.

I am working on my growth, it's harvest, my hands in the soil. Please, help me. I hold the spoils of my labour, and I don't know what to do, I don't know what to do,

I don't know what to do, and I don't know how to live with it.

LIVING
Translated by Leith Morton

I can't survive without eating.
Rice
Vegetables
Meat
Air
Light
Water
Parents
Brothers and sisters
Teachers
Money too hearts too
I couldn't have survived without eating.
With my belly full
When I wipe my mouth
Scattered about the kitchen
Carrot tails
Chicken bones
My father's guts
My fortieth sunset
For the first time the tears of a wild beast filled my eyes.

THE ECONOMY
Translated by Leith Morton

The phrase 'economic animal'
I suppose is already fairly old.
Quite a gap exists between
The time when they said we seem that way
And now when we are that way.
Now then we economic animals
Will think about the economy.
From the time that I was born I've just been counting money.
That was what we were taught in the home
By the state.
People only count the time they have left
When it has started to run out.
We live terribly impoverished lives.
We die terribly lonely deaths.

PLUCKING FLOWERS
Translated by Leith Morton

I plucked wildflowers at Marunouchi in Tokyo.
At the end of the 1920's
I was in my mid-teens.
On my way to work
To the Bank
The hem of my kimono-trousers flapping
Just a dash up the embankment beside the footpath
Before my eyes an open field.
Clover
Dandelions
Philadelphia fleabane
Wildflowers too poor
To decorate my desk at work.
Its been about half a century since then
Days came when the buildings blazed in the flames of war,
Around the postwar Tokyo Station
Just like a graph of the economic boom
Tall skyscrapers bloomed.
I retired at the mandatory retirement age,
I don't suppose any firms are left which take
Girls straight from primary school.
Even women are questioned about their market value
And ranked accordingly.
Women bloom in competition
But the day has finally come when they cannot possibly be wildflowers.
Farewell Marunouchi
Now no open fields anywhere
The thin green stem that I once squeezed
Was my own neck.

THE HEART SUTRA
Translated by Jeffrey Angles

While looking freely and without effort at the world
While walking with people, searching for the path
In his spiritual quest to discern based on deep wisdom
Avalokiteshvara arrived at a certain thought.
The self is. All sorts of things are.
I sense that
I recognize that
I think about that
And it is the case that
In all things we discern
We are ourselves.
However, that means
Those things do not exist
I have understood that clearly
And I have escaped
All suffering and trouble.

Listen to this, Shariputra.

Being is not any different than *non-being*.
Non-being is not any different than *being*.

Things we think *are* really are *not*.
If we think of something as *non-being* that leads to *being*.

Sensing
Recognizing
Thinking
Discerning

Those things too are just as they are.
Listen to this, Shariputra.

All things that are, *are not*.
There is also no *living* or *dying*.
There is also no *dirty* or *clean*.
There is also no increasing or decreasing.
To put it another away
In *non-being*
There is no *being*.

There is also no *sensing*, no *recognizing*
Also no *thinking*, no *discerning*.
There are also no *eyes*, no *ears*, no *noses*, no *tongues*
Also no *bodies*, no *hearts*.
There are also no *colors*, no *shapes*, no *voices*, no *scents*, no *flavors*,
Also no *tangible things*, no *thought-provoking things*.
There is also no *world that can be seen with the eyes*.
There is also no *world that can be sensed by the heart*.
There are various things that arise from the workings of the human heart
Ranging from the world that can be seen with the eyes
To the world that can be sensed by the heart
But none of those exist,
Yet neither do their workings go away.

There is also no *suffering of not knowing*.
Nor does the *suffering of not knowing* go away.
There is also *no aging, dying, and suffering*
Nor does *aging, dying, and suffering* go away
Because people do not know
There are kinds of various kinds of suffering as we grow old and die
But none of those exist
Yet neither do those sufferings go away.

There is also no suffering in living.
There is also no confusion that creates suffering.
There is also no hope our suffering and our confusion
Will one day go away
Yet neither is there any effort to rid ourselves
Of suffering and confusion.

There is no *knowing*.
There is no *gaining*.

In other words, we cannot gain.
Therefore.
Those who search for the way
Follow this wisdom.
And then.
The things our hearts dwell upon go away.
All things we dwell upon go away.
Therefore.
Fear will go away.

All confusion will grow distant,
And the heart free of suffering will grow clear.
Present, past, future
All awakened ones always follow this wisdom
They have lived by it and will live by it.
And then.
It is clearly possible to awaken.
Therefore.
Know this wisdom that will carry you to the far shore.
This is a powerful incantation.
This is a powerful incantation that you will hear clearly.
This is the ultimate incantation.
This is an incantation that knows no equal.
All suffering will leave you immediately.
This is the truth. This is not a false claim.
Therefore.
I will tell you this wise incantation.
Here, I will tell you. This is how it goes.

Gyāte
Gyāte
Pāra gate
Pāra samgate
Bodhi svāhā

This has been the Heart Sutra.

COOKING, WRITING POETRY
Translated by Jeffrey Angles

A huge earthquake, a huge tsunami
People die and just moments later
There's the nuclear meltdown
Drawn-out fear assaults us
Each time I go to Tokyo
It is darker
Hot and humid there
It stings
In Tokyo
Everyone was afraid
Everybody was angry

Neko has been my close friend for thirty years
Cooking is her profession
I had a dream, she said
We were coming home after going to see the giant sequoias
I was driving
She was nodding off next to me but then suddenly woke
And began saying, when I was young
I had a dream
I had a baby
The baby was with me
But I couldn't breastfeed it
The baby was dying right before my eyes
But I couldn't breastfeed it
That was how the dream went
Maybe
That was from a past life
And that karma
Is the reason I now cook
Morning and night like this
Feeding the children
Of other people

Now she is doing something
She calls the 'Nicomaru Cookie' project
First she called the young women in Tokyo
In Tokyo all alone
All alone and anxious
And unable to stand it any longer

All of them in Tokyo
All of them made cookies
And sold them
And sent the proceeds to the disaster zone
And then she changed gears and brought to Tokyo
The food the people in the disaster zone had made
And sold it in the city
She worked her fingers to the bone
And hired some staff
And went to the disaster zone
And cooked
She went into town
And started collecting signatures for an anti-nuclear petition
She made dozens of dishes each day
Even though she had her parents to care for
Even though she was working
Her fingers to the bone
She moves around, in the crisis
The only thing she knew to do
Was to cook like that
The only thing she could do
She couldn't help but cook
And work her fingers to the bone
And I watched her do it
Powerless, useless
There is an expression
Take the dirt from under someone's nails
Boil it and make it into tea
It means to admire someone so much
You would do those things
I asked her for some and she gave it to me
When I made it into tea
It was sour and sweet

Poets wrote poetry
The thoughts rained down continuously
Drenching us to the bone
So many poems were written
Like Kaneko Misuzu
Even easier to understand than Kaneko Misuzu
Unsightly poems
Boring poems
But still they were read

They say people read them and wept
I heard lots of stories like that
Don't cry
Don't write
Don't miss out
From that perspective
They cannot say no
The poets
Who can do nothing but write
Cannot say no to writing
They cannot relate except
Through writing
They must not
Say no
They must not
Fail to be read

Yesterday Jeffrey
Asked me to help him with a translation
Some American poet had written a poem about the disaster
I tried reading it, but it was a complete cliché
That guy
Had not even been to Japan
He wrote the poem looking at pictures
Complete cliché
But that guy had seen pictures of the disaster
He saw them
And his heart was moved
So he had no choice but write
The clichés he tried to convey
In a clichéd way ended up clichés
But still it was a good poem
I could not write
After all, the places I live
Are in California and Kumamoto
There was no shaking
The radioactivity didn't reach us
I didn't want to write
I couldn't write
A clichéd poem
Like that guy in America
I could not do a thing
The only thing I did

Was to translate and read out loud the second part of
An Account of My Ten-Square Foot Hut
I took that old text that depicted so vividly
The earthquakes
The tsunamis
Nine hundred years ago
Put it into my own voice
And sent out my voice like this

> *Around the same time, we suffered another terrible earthquake*
> *Unparalleled in its force*
> *The mountains collapsed, the rivers were buried*
> *The sea crashed in, inundating the land*
> *The earth broke, water bubbled up*
> *The boulders split and tumbled into the valleys*
> *The boats plying the water were tossed by the waves*
> *The horses traveling the roads were unable to keep their footing*
> *In one area of the capital, no place, no building*
> *Escaped unscathed, they collapsed or leaned to the side*
> *Dust and ashes and smoke billowed up*
> *Both the sound of the moving earth and the collapsing houses*
> *Were just like peals of thunder*
> *Those who were inside were crushed on the spot*
> *Those who ran were swallowed up by the cracks in the earth…*
> *The worst of the shaking continued for a while then stopped*
> *The aftershocks continued for some time*
> *Everyday, twenty, thirty times a day*
> *There were aftershocks large enough to terrify us ordinarily*
> *Ten days went by, twenty days went by, receeding into the past*
> *There were four or five aftershocks per day, then two or three*
> *Then every other day, then two or three days in between*
> *The aftershocks continued for three months*

This way
The earthquake
The tsunami
Crept into my body (just a little)
And then I read the Buddhist classics
For instance, the Lotus Sutra, *I am always*
Asking myself, how can I
Share the truth with living beings
Share the Buddha's teachings
Or the Amida Sutra, *All who want*
To be born in the land of happiness
Or all who will one day request that

Or who are requesting that right now
They will all awake to the truth, they will not return
To the confusion
Or the Nirvana Sutra, Each and every living being
Has the heart of the Buddha
That's right, it was Mahayana Buddhism
That said so clearly to the Buddhists of the time
During an era when they were reading for all they were worth
Not sure if they understood or not
But obsessed with grasping the truth
You are wrong
Entirely wrong
First you help people
That is what it is to be a bodhisattva
All I've experienced is an earthquake and tsunami nine hundred years ago
But if I were to put into my own words
And deliver a message to
This wounded
Damaged
Frightened
Trembling society
That's no doubt what it would be
That would be best
Or
So I hope
If not then
I would not even know
Which direction to turn

ENDEMIC SPECIES

On Manawatāwhi, the Three Kings Kaikomako
once ached its many mighty trunks
up to Ranginui/Sky Father, yearning
with its tessellated grey bark and glossy curled leaves
to reconnect to Earth Mother/Papatūānuku.

When four goats were placed
upon the island (food for potential castaways),
who, in 1889, could have predicted
the cloven ferals would strip the island
of its Kaikomako, leaving only one?

Capricorn myself, I recognise dreadful ambition,
persistence blind and unwavering. The self-destructive
execution of the goal, leaving all beauty
eaten. Only the dubious remains:
The Guinness Book of Records rarest tree in the world.

Still, botanists have found a way to pollinate
this lone female, after fifty years in solitude,
cutting herself from herself,
treating the offshoots with hormones,
fabricating males to ensure propagation.

Leaving me to wonder, head hanging over
vitreous china, cool glaze sticking
unnervingly to my cheek,
why no ingenious spark has yet
come up with a better system?

HARD LOCKDOWN

Today the sun rose earlier,
for solstice had passed. The deep
midwinter tones inked
solemn, shuttered
commission flats. Stillness.

The tilt of the austral hemisphere
welcoming the 4th of July, banal
as any other day, but independent still.
Towers 'closed and contained',
police amassing like hawkmoths
across the English Channel on D-Day:
lucky for some, unlucky for others.

Hard to witness here
in a country
awkward with words
like freedom
refuge
and revolution
independence and liberation
or sorry (and meaning it).

It's easy to watch smoke from
fires somewhere else
to bathe in others'
nights cut short by
knocks at the door:
smug and comfortable,
everything abbreviated
nothing everlasting.

LETTER 2: TO THE BOY WITH
THE YELLOW TAPE DECK IN CARRIAGE 4

I know you find the sound
of people exhausting
so I made you a mixed tape.
Each track is different.
Press play
and you will hear
the quiet of four in the morning before
the first curlew, or the warming
of a concert hall just after the last notes
of a symphony soak into the ceiling,
hush in the moments
before the conductor lowers the baton
and the audience applauds.

The other tracks were trickier to record –
the hibernation of a sleeping animal,
stillness in the trees after wind howls and
shakes them.
The pause in brushstrokes
and sound of paint drying.
Some tracks are darker than others. Some
are lighter. I'll let you discover them
for yourself.

LETTER 4: TO THE GIRL WITH
THE CRUMPLED MAP IN CARRIAGE 5

You used to look at my photographs,
imagine yourself inside their landscapes,
mimicking my path, my travels.
You know you should leave the house,
explore the world, my suburb.
Each time you get to the door you see
the clock I gave you has stopped.
The wood still sighs –
the pendulum sways in a non-existent
breeze. And you breathe with it.

EROSIONS
after The Attitude of Lightning Toward a Lady Mountain by James Gleeson

Your dreams erode me.
I'm tired of standing anyway.
I've already left my attitude
dream-thrust
above houses of the holy.
I'm with the lightning
the pink power of which
you're always afraid.

Can we call it quits?
Let me move into lands
beyond the frame
and you into your own love.

If I have have a place, there it is
an open plain, beyond
walls and chasms
or erratic, androgynous truths
that figured you
the sea we come from.

Don't forget my playful hollows.
Give me back my hands.
No dream stands outside of history.

DREAM HORSES
after Clay Horses by Sidney Nolan

Where are your eyes?
Nothing has prepared us for this.

What is earth?
There's a pain that remembers bone and horn.

Is the sky above?
Only figures in a landscape.

How fast is the wind?
Even the broken floats in dreamland's waters.

Do you remember when?
You will know when you see us.

Will you take us with you?
Born into the boundless plain.

How long have you been here?
Our names were once Surefoot and Swift.

Do you think we will be happy?
Dream horses do not need your eyes.

BOREALIS

Once, to ease a nighttime terror,
A father tells his child how stars
We take as token signs are actual:

Bears, archers, sovereigns
As plain to the eye as satellites
Seen from the window of an initial descent.

'And Ursa Minor's a small bear
in the high wild?' 'Absolutely.'
'And it isn't the eye pretends it there?'

'Of course.'
Solving the riddle in an evening sky,
She never once sees girth or paw.

Years later, the father reads a poem
In a book where his child describes
How the three moles on her lover's thigh

Are an archer's constellation.
Invention, she says, a poet's lie.
He notes the brisk arpeggios

Of her hand against her thigh,
'Absolutely,' he says, and
'Of course.' Everything

is atmosphere. Tense brush of wind
and air, then sudden light.
As we posit lit equations

Of faiths we keep untrue for,
And why there isn't a lie
A man won't tell his child.

SINKING CITIES

What is more certain than all this upending?
I can't tell my gut from my heart, my mind from
A warp of wood that turns up sudden chairs.

Each bedpost tells its name to sinking mirrors.
We call out numbers from lost addresses.
Everything that has lost a pair has lost it

For good: slippers, shoes, bicycle wheels,
child torn from a hip. The loose dials of a clock
Tell me either time runs or time stops.

Everywhere a skiff, a makeshift oar
Bears me away from where I hardest
Push, losing signs and street names

In the pull of my steer. Each one
The last way home, each home
That last attachment bolts undo.

This is where it ends, this sinking swell
Where I cry out your name and you tell me
Go on, and I go on without you.

GO BUSH

plant posts for a roof
walls will grow enough
you'll end up knocking
some out to get air

anyway a garden grows round
and up to the stars
vine twining
it gets you tangled
you go at it
meaning to tear
but it's more like stroking
there's some kind of taming
happening here

birds slip through
but it's not the fences
keep barking away

you make a state of mind
as pure as the blue
as grey as day
as green as this world grows

from DON JUAN ENTERS THE UNDERWORLD

... Became unbearable, the road to hell
Aches with good intentions.
The last conscious word is a cheeky whip bird's
Wistful whistle then sucked down
A hole in existence, the guard rail is no obstacle.
At Lover's Leap there was nothing to do but fall.
Oh, bloody whipbird with the final word
The stones and sticks spin like wheels, no ledge ...

Hearts float in rum and whisky, the higher
Than high space cadets trip the light smashed
Fantastic, an army of manic depressed fabulists
And for the legions suffering writer's block,
Where else is there to go but down into the inferno?
Bravely finished a clutch of sonnets,
The heavy lifting done and nothing left to do
But to open a vortex, say a hit on the head

Or a painful divorce that drives you
Into the arms of the delirium tremens.
A line for the deceased and one
For those souls who prefer a living hell
A shambolic crew lining up with passports,
Curricula vitae, scrubbled notes
Old tickets, envelopes or what-have-you.
Don Juan joined the queue.

REBEL VENOM
Translated by Violet Cho and David Gilbert

a woman lacking tears
doesn't cry on set
doesn't cry behind the scenes
too used to casualties
a rebel wife
my mother

called irresponsible
negligent
heartless
but 'nobody can invert fate'
I wanted to see
if she who turns on flesh and blood exists
I am your mother

I stayed with her
not yet a month
no chance to versify
in memory
at the village entrance
blossoms
under the blue myrtle tree
we talk
with strangers' eyes
packaged ego
hit the forest
searching for a rebel shadow

I climbed mountain by mountain
descending beyond
dim rebel light
visualized
I kissed the sky
kissed the stars
and inhaled the smoke of gunpowder
free

unforced
I drank dew
I drank sweat

with comrades
we ate the curry of attachment
I celebrated new year
without a splash, padauk unseen
rebel odour
through my breath

fields to farm
cursed land, hills of misery
in the sanctuary of Lay Kay
on the cliff of Kwee Lay
I made friends with malaria
and grew a rebel love
Manerplaw
Ta Lor Thaw
my last day at Maw Tha Waw
hugging malaria
under the blanket
'mother' I quietly whispered

she'd come to my dream
with images of rebel venom
to sense, to know
of negligence and arid plains

oh god
what separates
those who need love and want to give love?
let our hearts adhere
and let us dream

alms were offered
merit shared
for a rebel woman
with mistaken news
but
that woman
did not shed a tear
in a later time
under a blue myrtle tree
an old woman supposedly arrived
daily
my ego consumed

stolen
by that woman
who went faraway
when blue flowers of queen crape myrtle fall
the venom takes effect
I dream of mother

HER

Translated by Violet Cho and David Gilbert

blackboards
chalk
papers of poems
amidst tiny stars
a jasmine
flowers pure

bullets and chalk
after the war ...

faith generated
with the sound of gunfire
in battlefields
amidst one-coloured birds
a rose
flowers brave

A NOT-CRYING CHILD
Translated by Jake Levine and Ji yoon Lee

It is so quiet here. The sniffling inside my skull stopped, and
the snot trickling out of my nose froze.
Gak, a sound of something being swallowed whole
splits the silence apart. The following silence is sound asleep.
Is what I feel just the aftershock?
I guess the children really did drown in their sleep. Inside my
skull is a daycare. I need to prepare the blankets to cover up
the children's nightmares.

The children's nightmares are like cars that jump out from
a street corner – hard to dodge. The car drove through me.
How am I supposed to be buying bean sprouts and tofu now?
A child who doesn't cry anymore is dangerous, and despite
the silence,
the snow that falls quietly leaves the village stranded. If
nobody heard of the village,
what would happen then?

THE GOODBYE ABILITY
Translated by Jake Levine and Ji yoon Lee

I am all the things that take gaseous form.
I am cigarette smoke for 2 minutes.
I am rising steam for 3 minutes.
I am oxygen entering your lungs.
I will burn you away with a happy heart.
Did you know that there is smoke billowing from your head?
The meat fat you hate is gently burning
and the intestines became a stovepipe
and the blood boils
and all the birds in the world leave to immigrate,
    commanding the world's fog and

I sing for more than 2 hours
and do the laundry for more than 3 hours
and nap for more than 2 hours
and meditate for over 3 hours
and of course I see the apparitions. They are fucking beautiful.
I love you for 2 hours or more,

I love the things that exploded out your head.
Birds snatched the loudly crying children and took them away.
I learned that in the middle of doing eternal laundry.
My coat turned into a gas.
The thing I pulled out my pocket, a cloud. Your cane.
Well, that's that. In the middle of singing an endless song,
in the middle of taking an endless nap,

there were moments I opened my eyes.
My eyes and ears get clear,
and my Goodbye Ability peaks,
and I shed my fur, and I am cigarette smoke for 2 minutes.
    Rising steam for 3 minutes.
The smell disappears for 2 minutes, and
I take off my clothes. Regarding the clothes dispersing
    into the distant horizon,
regarding my neighbors,
I wave.

HORMONOGRAPHY
Translated by Jake Levine and Ji yoon Lee

O Hormone, light me bright like blazing morning. The Rage is swelling, and I want to manifest it like the eye of a typhoon. That man cheated me. I shall hunt him to the end.

Connected through the milk-lines, I flow to you, I am river Soyang, I am river Nokdong. I am a boatman without an oar. Wherever I end up, if you call me as a man I, as a man, will …

Or if you call me as a woman, I'll try to immerse myself in my role as a woman. From the third, fourth, seventh rung of the ladder between heaven and hell, I'll caress the cards that are dealt to me until I'm destitute. Make me weary. O Hormone, with the gentle caress of your hand, lower the lids of my eyes and

stir up my dreams. I'll be your movie theatre. O Hormone, through big waves stir the landscapes and facial expressions until the screen goes black, until we reach a war-like meaninglessness.

At the mountain spring of the holy hormone, eternally twinkling signals.

THICK RAINBOW
Translated by Jake Levine and Ji yoon Lee

For 3 minutes you tie the laces of your combat boots, and I am spellbound like tightened feet. When will the war end? Why are my beliefs offered to decadence? When will you die? And then when will I?

The thick rainbow under her eyelids rises each day. Do you believe her? The battlefield is her theme park. Vanity is the place where she collapses and rises. All her men laced their combat boots and departed to work.

One day he took off his combat boots and left my side. I cannot forgive that. Where I am is just 2 kilometers away from the war zone. Listening to firing guns, children picnic here in the spring. Why do you think canaries are yellow and azaleas pink? Why do you vomit red liquid and why do I let out black water? White powder falls repeatedly from the sky and the entire city reacts chemically. Can you believe the color? And the scent?

The woman's convictions take shape as pills dissolve. Don't believe her too quickly. The chemical reactions she sees are in excess of standard reality. Futuristic things are decadent. In her pupils, all that is captured is debris. Dust.

When did you die? And then when did I?

TITS NAMED DICK
Translated by Jake Levine and Ji yoon Lee

You've got dick,
And I've got tits, however
Let's not make it a spectacle.
If you think that's childish
Remember it's from you where things got started.

Anyway, a point we share is that when we grab, we hold one hand.
Anyway, a point we share is that when we suck lips, we suck one set.
Anyway, a point we share is that when we chop, we use one plate.

(Ah, they scooped out one of my cancerous tits. What harsh
equality, the dizzying relief.)

After splitting the sex up
Dos-à-dos, we sleep
In the direction of our respective hearts, like donuts,
Really like do-ugh-nuts, curling heavily atop the bed
Vastly cast

Two sets of breasts
Two balls
How lovely!

PENIS NAMED FACE
Translated by Jake Levine and Ji yoon Lee

WHAT AN EXTREMELY OBVIOUS STORY
I try to draw a circle because I miss you, but carelessly I draw a squishy faced bread twisty. If the bread twisty's deliciousness is delicious, the banana's banana-ing is long, and if the banana's banana-ing is long, the train's train-ing is slow, and that slowness is stretchy-ing, a stretchy-thing, a bread twisty … All the day long, even if I am a person I do not understand, throwing the twisty bread ballad fit, even if the illusion is more uterus than moneyless, more ovulation-time than hunger-time, finally I am freed! To The Twisty Bread Inn! No, the Twisty Bread Motel – I mean I'm not serious. I don't really want to get a room. I'm just wondering, do you think the Twisty Bread business was named by a woman or a man?

SO THE STORY IS REALLY BANAL
Now, even though I can't recall his face, the pants he shit hanging above his ankles remain so vivid in my mind. I could have bought you a belt … Why didn't you tell me how hot the kettle mouth boiled? If I had known, I would have blown to cool it down … In this world there are two crimes that need to be unconditionally forgiven. One is being young. The other is being deaf. Surrounded by silence, you and I were in a car backing up, and Jesus hung with a rubber band to the rearview mirror was bobbing up and down. I guess that's why they say, *a beautiful crime is always caused by love.*

AND YET, IT'S A STORY I'LL NEVER GET SICK OF
Yesterday we went to a Tous-Les-Jours coffee shop because the actor Jo In-Sung said we should. And today we went to a Dunkin Donuts coffee shop because the actor Lee Sun Kyun said we should. This pastry, that pastry, this twisty bread, that twisty bread … *how do people live on that bread shit? It all tastes like the same shit.* Our Boss Sister said that. And she was so right.

FINALE
Translated by Jake Levine and Ji yoon Lee

As the belt tightened around my neck
I merely stared
So he up and left.

As the poet might treat a chicken,
He could eat me
But he couldn't slaughter me
Because he was such a delicate man.

And today
My right hand that I gave to him
By thrusting it in his back pocket
Has suddenly returned.

Both long and wide, the right palm has grown
3 centimeters in size
Bigger than the left. And the nails!
Well trimmed like cones good for juicing
Beneath the hot, orange-plumping sun.

They were perfect for
Popping the fleshy pimples that thrust up willy nilly
After I scraped off the chicken skin,
So I forgot the itty bitty death in me.

Yeah, that's how I shake it.
Say hello to the new me!

ANNA O'S OFFICE
Translated by Ji yoon Lee, Don Mee Choi, and Johannes Göransson

I'm glad we built this house right next to the beach. At night, I can hear the waves crash just outside the balcony. You're pitch-black, and your gown is perfectly white. How did you come all the way up here? Did you come here alone? I'm impressed! I like things that I can flip through, then toss, like the magazine I brought from the Sorbonne. Great, great! The way you undress in a hurry, flipping your orange hair, is so painful to watch that I have to hug you. Hehehe. We fly high above the clouds without smashing the ceiling. You stare at me, even before we land, like a dead rabbit next to a radiator. Want me to hold you again? Want to die with a hard-on? Want something to eat? Hehe. Well done! You packed a to-go-box of lettuce and gourmet French sausages. Never mind, just suck on my tits. You'll get anxious as if struck by some unbelievable idea. Oh my, you sound like a white noise machine. Uhuhuh. Stop making that sound. Want to do it again? Want to try holding your breath till you can hear the small waves and the plastic bag flapping against the cracked window? Gasp gasp. You're the one who's stabbing me, in and out, so why are you acting like you're the one dying? Like a toothbrush, like feathers stuffed in a sleeping bag, so thinly padded, I'll roll your little head, littler than a pupil, around and around in my mouth. Ahahah. Stop! I love you! I've heard all this till before, my ears have grown callused. All my life, my lovers have sent me letters scribbled like horrible subtitles in translation, then they all throw themselves into the ocean. Are you getting nervous? You're holding me so tight. Do you want to go back? I'm busy, I don't have time for a break. It's time to close up the office. Squeeze it all out, at least six times, on my belly, in my hands. When I opened the window, it was hailing, to my surprise. This won't do. Would it make you happy if I take a nibble of your chewy thing? Come on, wake up! You and me, facing the blazing wind. Anyway, who can see us, shouting and flying, scattering a flurry of semen? They'd think it was a hallucination of a ghost licking cheese soup. Is your nose bleeding? Have you stopped breathing? Oh, I'll kiss you, so there's no chance of you coming back to life any time soon. Take a nap and come back tomorrow at two. I promise, it will be thrice as fun. I'll praise your dirty thoughts, your endless depression. Anyway, I wonder if my favorite patient, Sigmund, will ever show up?

AT THE LABORATORY

Translated by Ji yoon Lee, Don Mee Choi, and Johannes Göransson

With a clear mind, I get right into the experiment.
I put on my lab coat and scrub my hands with
foamy soap all the way up to my wrists.
I cut out the tongue from a dead bird
and I tear out the swim bladder from a dead fish
and I escape from the birth canal of my dying mommy.

With a clear mind, I read a book.
This page doesn't line up with the word 'mother' from the previous page,
but the fragmented words line up according to a different logic.
When spring arrives, the black-headed goldfinch takes off to Siberia.
For the past two years, I've been tracking his migratory route.
Some birds can't find their way home by themselves,
but they can't blend into the flock either,
so nobody will notice that he'd vanished.
Free from relationships, I take off.

He had a short tongue and spoke in complicated sentences.
He always omitted the subject
and I especially had a hard time noticing
the subtle differences between prepositions.

When I discovered the groundbreaking method
through which I could understand him,
I was horrified and burnt down the basement lab.

With a clear mind, I sing.
I hope the final chorus will drag away the lead vocalist and shred his voice.
From start to finish, there's been nothing noble or vile about this poem.
The birds and the fish were rotten, and the multi-colored flowers were repulsive.
I know for sure who my mommy is – she's the one on the shelf – but who was he?
His fingerprints look like Daddy's.
They produce a bountiful crop in the cold darkness.
I collect frozen piss.

I want to go outside, but Mommy's not pushing hard enough.
The co-worker yells, If the wings of the nose show, use the forceps to pull it out!
They wipe the kitten's mouth and ears with gauze.

Rosy cheeked, I gaze into the mirror, blushing.
I slurp up a bowl cream with meds mixed in.
It clears up my mind.

DECEMBER
Translated by Ji yoon Lee, Don Mee Choi, and Johannes Göransson

I like that it's evening now.
I like standing on the street
watching things grow blurry
watching pedestrians pass by, trembling under their coats.
I like watching their neckless faces.
I like waiting for you.
I won't be able to finish today's round of affirmations and self-shaming.
I'm leaving it all unfinished.
I'm proud of my ability to run toward the goal line just to quit.
The trees have done their best to shed their leaves.
A flock of birds flap their wings desperately
flying off in different directions.

I'm happy that it's winter, not spring.
It's not a new year, it's the end of the year, and I'm totally fucked up.
How nice that it isn't the first time.
Soon I won't even be able to make out your body.
You, my lover with your deep-socketed eyes and pale skin.
Get up, lets go to my room.
Are you just going to stand around and drink
water like it's a funeral,
or can we mess around one last time?
Are you taking your last breath? Dear Soulmate,
what did you ever do for me anyway?

DESTABILISING (THE) PASTORAL

Rabbits are digging at the foundations
again – or the sandpad underwriting this
surveyed presence – the geekiness of grid-makers.

I fill in the beginnings of entries with rocks and fragments
of bricks – first level of deterrence before deploying
vinegar and paprika. *Deploying*. Language as I have it to hand

is less relevant than the act which brings no harm in itself,
this artwork I am entangled with, the scribble you can't find
as beginning or end in grammar – visual distractions

for the work of doing, of keeping 'dwelling' upright
absurd as tremor or earthquake, the cataclysms of past
wrongs as wrong now and not to be forgotten. What footprints

are the rabbit's reversal its backing away from a failed dig,
the nickel miners *pegging pegging* away nearby at the over-
whelming total cataclysm they dress up as 'eco' in electric car

assault and battery? Another nuptial flight day and antwings
glitter-down, shed as hope or fate or resignation which is
compelling though dampened by dry smoke of small fires

choking the valley each person overlaying each other's
regardless of politics or because of them or lack of them or this
lack in pastoral vocabulary for once it reaches out beyond

the confines of speech – comfort and rivalry – it is left
open-mouthed or lost in stilled hands, ants leaving and searching
and rabbits finding alternative ways to make under.

SWARM FIBRILLATION OF ORBIT AND WARNING AREAS

In preparing (not prepping) for the 'biggest storm in a decade'
        as a strong cold front joins with a tropical low
and the warning area blanking-out of highlighting like new
        versions of empire, the satellite swarm and pinpoint
and requisition *ourness* as knowledge as database as the lambasting
        of nature to keep above the fray. I see their false
reflections in the anxious greentint of jam tree saplings as it's hot
        so near the end of 'autumn' appellation the opening
to 'winter' after frosts a warm a hottish day and a wind picking
        up and a total fireban and yet *smell* the burning
swarm of satellite launches the payloads on the wind compensating
        maintaining trajectory deployment orbit to leer
down on the red-black swirl of atmospherics to impartially
        report back or to AI-decide on what's best
to share prices and the baseness of owners and their hangers-
        on doing a job adding to the betterment
the 'whispers under the pillow' we hear for what they are
        in entertainment (art?) and yet rake-in sleeping
drafts when war and porn and 'work' and acquisition and school
        and social proprieties annoy our sleep or open
visions as absurd as floating (or filming) in space (but fixed
        in place or orbit) and looking down through raging
water vapour and electrical activity and pollution and roofs
        and even leaves in some places to see ourselves
bracing for what's going to hit us to jolt hearts as premonitions
        reified as people doing little rubbish burns
a fibrillating of catastrophe á la 'prescribed burns' lingering
        into the fury of storm which can be fore and aft
in all the rain and swarm of satellites fleeing from disaster
        statistics. And as preternatural as gravel ants
opening new paths on the verge of alteration and a single bee
        crawling over a sharp leaf thinking *it* might bloom,
pollenate under-sun, fibrillate cognisant of colony's collapsing
savoir faire prevarication in-exactitude sweeping in, buffeting.

FULL IMMERSION

A flower can open wider than its setting,
breaking its own distinct pattern as set
before its appearance, and so today I broke
mine and fell into full immersion. There is
no beauty or ugliness in this sensorium,
there is a wavering and submerging of correlatives,
the bark lifted from its origins to reveal
the gecko wondering about body temperature,
a peeling back before the wandoo log is burnt
as fuel pulled back from flames because it is likely
a gecko would seek shelter under bark under
the sheltering roof of the red shed which I opened
to reveal a fantail frantic with disorientation, trying
to find a way out as it found a way in, ignoring
gnats it had planned on pursuing: release.

We can open wider than a flower beyond its limits
is all I can think of gathering pace down the hill
balancing a bucket of sand and loam from the old arena,
calculating the time that we've been responsible
for passing its earth back to a healthier soil 'profile',
soil not sprayed with the 'cides, and knowing
it must be well over twelve years since it was last
contaminated in the name of control, in the 'before
us' – *now* making *world* around rising potato stems,
eternal aliens like me imprinting extra-territorial
complications to be worked out but not prioritised.

I swear *that* fantail is shadowing me – I can see
its shade and hear its flutter but can't pick it out
of the glare, and it could just as easily be its mate,
or another, though its twitch in mimicry
of snatching insects but trying to find a way
through seems more to suggest it is one and the same
and shares with me the DNA of a flower still to appear
on a stem as a bud to open and then open wider than it should, it can.

Full immersion surprises in letting go of descriptors,
an obsession, and overplaying personifications till they splay
into signs no longer representing what they stand for, source.

SUPPLIANTS – AN ONTOLOGY

The Argonautica (Book IV – Circe, Jason and Medea)

In the whirl and misaligning
of limbs that becomes the future,
that is the gain of function
that is the new creature
while existing creatures
are disregarded – the future
co-ordination of limbs
more desirable for consumers
than pre-existing arrangements –
with hindleg of fox
and flexing tail of boomer
and dipping wing of feint
to drive off a predator
and the sharp beak
of that predator
and forelegs of a millipede
and the eyes of sheep, echidnas, owls,
cows, possums and bandicoots
arranged within the compound eye
brackets of a wolf spider,
and the swervers and swayers
of endocrines and DNA degenerators
sprayed liberally about like
there's no second tomorrow
beyond a healthy
return for investors. And I ask,
why the pool of heroes is so bloody,
and why bloody dreams
wreck Circe's sleep,
washing her hair clear
in the saline river,
and why suppliants
fall at her feet in front of her fire
to be laundered with irony
as we care, surely, for all the living
and all the dead, and a composition
of stories is molecular with bonds
broken and made, and measured

through and either side
of the sun's lifetime? And the blood
of a sow swollen with milk,
the piggery going
about its business
as we sail pass
heading down to the city,
all of this going on
simultaneous with every
effort at none-harm we make
and we've nothing to say
when it's contested at the atomic
level, the quid pro quo
of existences?

AFFECTED BY WHAT WE READ, WHAT WE RECALL

It can't be helped when an ancient journey
from another part of the world enters your head
sailing up the west coast of Sumatra — Jakarta
to Padang? What you allow into your head
when someone on the run taps you on
the shoulder asking what you're remembering:
how relevant to the present situation,
how relevant to the level of the tide
       in 'Emma Haven' Harbour?
I don't even know if a ship or ferry willing
to take passengers sails that way these days.
I am talking thirty-six years ago, now. But
the ship being a rust bucket, the lines of the sea
and the waste of industrial colonialism written
into its hull, night on the deck a dream of anti-heroes.
Who talks about humour when one of the crew
stops to have a chat and you feign more words
than you have? A refraction or distraction
of your reading? The interconnectedness
of shipping routes, the currents of dislocation?
Remember how we expected the marine
to resolve like flying fish, merge states
of existence, our spiritual lack? These questions
are an elegy, and that ship is unlikely
to be still sailing, linking the islands.
    Just as we assumed any tiger
    remaining would find us,
that jungle would overwhelm
the plantations. When we made land.
When we disembarked and travelled inland.

NEW DRESS

the new dress
is only the bag she arrives in
it is not the woman
though she thinks it is

it starts a conversation
but cannot finish one
the taste of mint the
slightly-too-hard question rattling the head with no
prepared answer

and though her wishes are eelish
it is easiest to stand
sheathed
and not do anything
(as if the condom were the penis)

she has come to be eaten, dressed
in skin of hot chicken breast, served
in Coke bottle curves, carved
by the savage blade
of the g-string

it brings eyes
soon she has a plateful of eyes
and no words
nothing left but to eat

MEN
Translated by Leith Morton

The Kaneko Gym on the Odakyû Railway Line is
A small
Boxing gym
At night
From inside the train
I can see people training in the Kaneko Gym
Young men boxing
Within the black night
Blossom-pink muscles
Like cherry blossoms sweating silently
Boxing, in their movements
A stray memory comes to mind
A memory I seem to have had
Can't say for certain
'Kaneko Gym, new boxers welcome'
This is
Always
Read silently
By those with heavy sodden hearts
They
All
Open the dark door
And
One after
Another
Have gathered
There

BATHHOUSE
Translated by Leith Morton

Late at night the Daikokuya bathhouse is quiet
An old woman bone-tired
Even naked unable to be free of dirt
Rattling the door
Comes in
From the nozzle of the shower with the tap loose
Water makes a dripping sound
Bare-footed the cool of the night softly steals in
From the high skylight
The water is rocking
Overflowing the edge of the bath
I
Pass no judgement
Like a log
I look at the female bodies
I saw
Naked backs, hips and backsides
Private parts
The water flowing over their bodies
Fallen head-hair
The many hollows of the female body
Water gathering there
Dripping down
I feel as if I have been looking at this
For years over and over again
I also saw the wall separating the men's and women's baths
And I took my time to make certain that
Like a wild beast
Nobody
Climbed from the men's into the women's bath
Or the other way
Amazed

A SHORT POEM ABOUT DAYBREAK
Translated by Leith Morton

America, in a toilet in Santa Fe
Daybreak
I was urinating softly for a long long time
In the whole world
I felt as if there was only this sound and myself
Despite the fact that I was making the noise
Curiously it sounded as if it was coming from outside
As I was being consoled by it
Like an old woman's unending story
I was
Waiting for it to end
But it would not
A time that doesn't belong
To anyone
Anywhere
I wasn't here,
I'm not alive,
I could even say this
Presently the sound ceased
In this room that had rapidly grown cold
A silent soul suddenly created
Is that me, is it me?
The temperature of life left in the shape of an invisible circle
Were you there?
Were you there in that room?
I was
I am alive
Long before then the questioning voice reached me

RESPONSE
Translated by Robert Nery

Lord, of the wonders you perform
we honour all and carp at none.
For your commissions cause less grief
than so many acts of omission.

Were you here with us the wilting days
the trestle board was bare of meat?
That night the runt under the slats
whined and stiffened in his vomit

where was the cure? Tell us Lord
if blameful defect in us held back
the fateful hand from reaching out
to prop and stay our giddy shack.

We scrubbed your house on the day
of worship. Still, did you see fit
in condescension towards ours
to ban the ant from devouring it?

Because our mouths are not on fire
in praise, you never bat an eye
when the bat hanging from the rafter eyes
us and grins and our mouths are dry.

Sir no enemy of ours
our prayers rise from peaked fish-faces.
We like a useful master, not a loafer.
Now and then take note of us.

SATURDAY AFTERNOON
Translated by Robert Nery

The wind is tearing up
the banana,
poking holes
in the spider web,
tugging at
my dry hair.

All around is at peace.
In closed rooms
they have paused to breathe
my fellow citizens,
and I on the grass
outspread,

my eyes open,
see nothing
but a slow
cautious airplane.
Why do I want it
to explode?

AWAY FROM NAMING WHAT NAMES YOU
Translated by Mario Licón Cabrera

Back to the season that makes a hollow
        in our chest,
to the narrow streets lit by dust,
to the comforting words that wait for defeat.
Back to the rage that dwells in a fist,
to the spells that exile plagues of mediocrity
and conformism.
Back to the place where we dig out what the sun
        has stolen from us with its fire.
Back to thinking that what we do
        no one will remember,
not to know that summer is
a gravestone weighing on our back.
Back to listening to music of the most
        indifferent silence
in places of self-compassion.
Back to receive hurtful letters with open
        dates
and being defeated by the indifference that opens holes
        as we pass by.
Back here.
Back.

What is it that makes me remember that desert?
What is it that makes me relive
the fixed time where summer passes by?
Perhaps summer lays out a trap for my memory
        and locks it up?
Again the morning is clear and cloudless,
the sun rises ripe as a fruit that had always been
        a fruit
and something of myself is set ablaze.

The light is a cloak,
a sheet that sticks to the body like a stifling
second skin.
With the last shadows clinging to the slumber,

a mount shows me its dry profile hoping that

rain will come.

Humidity stagnated on walls
traces undecipherable prophecies,
and the weight of such a bright reality
       is unbearable to me.

In the end I give up this vision,
because the desired solitude is always somewhere else,
in an overcast sky,
in the cool air of another city always far away.
Light is not convenient for one who looks
for answers in the shadows
and with words of darkness tries to tame the summer
that has opened all the windows of light
yet blocks all possibility of escape.

WHERE CAN A SEED TAKE ROOT?

Tell me ... tell me ... please
Where's a place for a seed take root;
And me?

Deep within my dreams hope reached in
The sky has been
Full of air and light
Love sings
For the immensity of earth,
Of breath
From every living being.

From that scattered mass
A simple wish
A little seedling ached
The first to have a try,
It's a long separation
To leave the motherland,
The flowering plains
And memories of every seed
To hide deep in the forest
To be uprooted again
The intense pains
Break out again,
At the barbed wall
How such pain is born;
Piled up
The call of conscience
Is cluttered up
By the dark night
Truth
Come out into the broken sunshine.
Tell me ... tell me ... please
Anywhere,
Anywhere ... a place
Which way: to enter a strange garden
Or into your heart
Opening
Let the seed take root, and me.

WANDERING ILLUSIONS

On days without suns
I try to increase
My heart's fire.

On days without laughter
I try to release
The fire inside my fingers,
Until the rose blooms.

On days without music and poetry
I try to fly away
As my wavy white hair
Becomes smoke in the wind.

On days without a home
Mother and you have no one around
I close my eyes and reminisce
Over the wandering illusions
At my curled toes.

DIMANCHE: À TRAVERS LA TERRE
from 'Pérouse, ou, Une semaine de disparitions', in *Argosy*

Images for collages in 'Pérouse, ou, Une semaine de disparitions' were sourced from editions of atlases appended to the following journals of discovery, held at the State Library of New South Wales, State Library of Victoria, and Special Collections, Baillieu Library, The University of Melbourne:

Voyage de La Pérouse autour du monde / publié conformément au décret du 22 avril 1791, et rédige par M.L.A. Milet-Mureau, by Jean-François de Galaup de La Pérouse.

Relation du voyage à la recherche de La Pérouse: fait par ordre de l'Assemblée Constituante pendant les années 1791, 1792 et pendant la 1ère. et la 2de. année de la République françoise / par le Cen. Labillardière, by Jacques-Julien Houton de Labillardière.

Voyage de la corvette l'Astrolabe: exécuté par ordre du roi, pendant les années 1826, 1827, 1828, 1829, sous le commandement de M. J. Dumont D'Urville, capitaine de vaisseau, by J. Dumont D'Urville.

HER BUSH BALLAD (BOURKE ST ELEGY)

One morning walking down Bourke St
    I hear my father's voice
I turn and see the back of his head
    and his big shoulders
in the driver's seat of a car
    parked down in the alley
It's the old Mercedes
    with the bull bar across the front
I go to him and get in
    open the glove compartment
take out a pencil
    (he always kept boxes of pencils)
Why didn't you come? I've been waiting
    I'm here now I'm here
I didn't think it was you
    He says careful be careful
These hands are lethal they'll strike
    and you won't see it coming
Don't forget I told you
    my father was a murderer
You are the eldest
    you might have inherited that gene

TILT

Fonzies Fantasyland at 31 Oxford St
(now a disappointing IGA)
opened in 79 next door to Patches
a few months after the Ghost Train fire
at Luna Park killed seven.
It was Alan Saffron's brainchild:
Mr Sin's legitimate heir (later disinherited)
dreamed of a chain of Leisure Centres
to clean up the family name.
I was an original Fonzies girl:
blue polysatin shorts, nude stockings.
Prior experience none
unless winning a poetry competition
or playing Fire Power at Reggio's counted.
The kitchen hands from East Sydney Tech
approached their work as an installation.
They wore kinky white nurse's uniforms
and Dolly Parton wigs
like something out of Richard Prince.
They perfected psychedelic ice cream sundaes
and gave out quarter tabs of acid *gratis*.
They were cool:
I looked up to them
and heeded their advice.
The hard men got together
in the glassed-in office (Cone of Silence).
Abe stopped by for a sandwich: 'Keep it simple'.
A silver stream flowed through my hands.
When the red pay phone rang
it was Susie, Alan's wife, checking in from Hawaii.
If I accidentally locked the till
one of the street kids who hung around
jumped the counter with his wad of keys.
In the quiet early hours of the morning
punters lay on their backs tripping
in the rainbow neon tunnel,
Donna Summer blaring into the night.

When Brooke Shields came to town
for the premiere of *Tilt*
(in between *Pretty Baby* and *Blue Lagoon*)
we rolled out the red carpet
and formed a guard of honour.
She was sweet, tired, five years younger than me.
The movie flopped and she ended up
in St Vincent's with bronchitis.
Space Invaders had landed
and the mood was introverted.
The art students were the first to go,
taking their *joie* and their LSD.
I was reprimanded for reading
and stayed too long on my break upstairs at Patches
watching the drag show and drinking Bacardi.
I wore the wrong stockings and didn't care:
the dark bit at the top showed under my shorts.
The junior manager I'd reported for sexual harassment
lectured me on pride in appearance.
The writing was on the wall and I was ready to go.
To show there were no hard feelings the boss
handed me a scrap of paper.
'If you're ever in any trouble, call this number.'
I thought of Juanita Nielsen
last seen entering the Carousel Club July 1975.

Two year later it was Fonzies' turn to burn.
The chief suspect was Les Murphy,
youngest of the three Murphy brothers
jailed for life ('never to be released').
It was the trial of the century.
Anita Cobby, 26,
a nurse at Sydney Hospital,
arrived at Blacktown Station
just before 10pm, February 2 1986,
found the payphone out of order
and started walking.
She was found two days later
in a Prospect paddock
almost decapitated.

Kidnapped, tortured, raped and murdered
by five men in a Holden Kingswood
as detailed in their confessions.
According to the NCA report
Les was working at Fonzies when the fire broke out
but no charges were laid.

Around that time I went to a weird party
high up in Victoria Towers
on the street where Juanita Nielsen had lived.
It was an empty shell suspended
over the wharves of Woolloomooloo
said to be owned by a dealer.
I felt bad and left straight away,
heading for my second home,
the Academy Twin (3A Oxford St:
opened with Polanski's *Macbeth* in 1974,
the year we moved to Sydney,
closed for good in June 2010).
Heatwave was on starring Judy Davis
as 'Kate Dean', a Nielsen-style activist heroine.
Takings were low but it won for Editing
and *Cinema Papers* called it 'subversive'.
By then Luna Park was back in business,
the Green Bans were history
and Alan was long gone
(see *Ramsay's Kitchen Nightmares* for the LA sequel).
In the dim auditorium
we were part of another time, watching it burn,
and I was on my way to another life.

BODIES OF POMPEII

It is not the delicate detail, for the cast is too crude
for that: this girl's face obliterated by weeping plaster,

a man's extremities reduced to rounded stumps. It is
the large arrested gesture that tells these bodies, saying:

so this is the shape of death. Familiar lovers fastened
on a stone bed (whereas life might have ripped them apart),

a dog's high-pitched contortion, an entire family sleeping,
the baby rolled absently from its mother.

Unburied, they weigh more than bone ever could.
They have shaken off the ash and refuse to rest. So many

stopped limbs. Mouth holes, eye holes, a balled fist.
But in the end, this is what halts you: how a young woman sits

with her knees drawn up to her chest, hands covering eyes.
How a child's body folds, alone at the final moment –

and a man rises from his bed, as if waking for the first time.

from KULCHUR GIRL

*In July 1965, a few days after turning seventeen, I returned to the city in which I had spent four years of my childhood to attend Berkeley Poetry Conference. Alternating between a brown journal I'd carried with me, and a green one purchased in Berkeley for the seminars, I took notes on whatever pleased me, occasionally leaping from the spoken words in the room to others of my own invention, with no duty (at the time) to anyone but myself.

28 June

A better way of life & a swinging show, –

Murray the K for the U.S. Office of Economic Opportunities.

Martha and the Vandellas singing in a Mustang assembly plant ("Nowhere to Run")

Girls in cages

The little children dancing to "I can't help myself"

The Ronettes in tight white sweaters and baseball caps.

30 June

All the talk about writing has been vanity.

What is "serious"? I suspect it is something bad writers sit around and pretend to be.

Lovely fakes, the Stones. Bringing me as close to pleasure as I can come today.

Silver shoes.

Black rain.

1 July

Such an easy question ... Why can't I get an answer, Elvis sings.

The commercials on WABC are the news.

The whole world is teenage. 50-year-olds in baby dresses

14 July

Run around for absolute joy. In Berkeley.

How does anyone survive it?

I sang the Pepsi song very slowly, and then wondered aloud if you could make a thing like that into something truly beautiful. You just did, he said.

A spangled suit.

The effects have to get wilder.

Mick Jagger.

Why don't I just get pregnant and end it all …

"I want to be four years older." I want to be seventeen years younger.

19 July

CREELEY #1

Roundly innocent.

Blonde with a poor boy sandwich.

The kulchur word is got around.

Me in my mind.

He lights the cigarette in his mouth & leaves it in hers.

They go to school here. I don't.

Creeley's late.

A clue.

A shy smile accomplishes what one hoped the sadness would, & didn't.

Where are the boys of yesteryear?

An extremely beautiful woman here. The bones on her face –

Duerden's here.

Creeley. I recognized. He was in City Lights.

The beautiful woman is – his wife?

You've got to insist those things we want – are there.

Ashamed contempt for my position.

Stevens Room. Student Union Bldg. Robert's. Telegraph.

Her head up & down slightly as he finishes & looks into her eyes.

A poem in 2 minutes. Unthought of.

I'm here by an act of God.

To see if they're ringing the right way.

Actuality & possibility of language.

What has he to say.

The poet's memory is of words, not ideas.

The language environment.

Look at what passes for the new.

Political reality.

Personal power more exciting.

The object of poetry. The naked man.

Is it content? Is it ever content?

Distinction can't be made. <u>All</u> is activity.

Description is an embarrassment of the occasion.

To pose. Affectual evidences.

"We must have what we need now." Chas.

Language has not patience.

The poet as object.

Poet as means.

"All art is quite useless."

Egocentric? Poets <u>are</u> useless & egocentric.

The poet as totalitarian. The force that you <u>must</u> see this.

Then how is the poet to live as not manipulator, not totalitarian.

How am I to love you as other than object.

Visibility.

To <u>occupy</u> the <u>intelligence</u>.

I've justified another day –

There's only one poem.

What the moment finds.

Define your awareness of order

As possible. Light confusion. Light decadence.

I hate "poetry," "poets," – not "poems."

What's poetry?

What we think of it as?

What activity is it?

What are its effects?

What is our relation to it?

What is our concern?

Taking everything & discarding the useless.

Honing.

Sound is round.

The sounds not the words that refer to the emotions.

What came first: the sound that is the word or the word that is the sound.

Tightrope he walks. To feel the possibility as it occurs.

The qualification of no qualifications.

He delights in embarrassing the expected response.

Everything you say is true.

It is impossible to lie.

Zukofsky's lovely sense.

Something is being said at each interstice.

Intimately responsive to each interval, he said –

Not being able to anticipate

You can do anything you want.

Creeley is possible for me. I wonder will Olson be.

People sitting in the windows.

Nuns. In Olson's class.

58, BACK-MOST LOT, COLLAPSIBLE CEILING AND UNDERGROUND LUNG WARD.

Crates are melting under enamel and asbestos, whalers are jumping ship for a slant. Open the archive to check the mobility, there's a rotten panorama of a hundred years of surplus. First the compositors, bakers, and small-time boiled-sweet bankers stocked the clout; second, the house trapped the labour 'til it moulded the beams. Bad advice suggests that if you grant debts to your neighbours – tins of beef, tins of milk, tins of tobacco, tins of paraffin – you will keep their loyalty and gratitude. My advice: follow the neighbour's dogs. Tucked in their scut you'll find notes from the ocean, shanties for mutiny, or else, wetted and folded pamphlets calling for nutmeg, vinegary kippers, split peas and rabbit skins. The tendency to vanish is a favourite toolkit. Away and wharfish, deep to the buttonhole in a capital well, pages 1-12 passim.

TOUCH ME WHERE IT HURTS

Do not touch me there. There was someone who
revelled in my skin, but he's long gone since
the sins of the fathers permeated
my own veins, my blood, the very essence

of living the life I had not foreseen.
Touch me here, where it hurts like no other,
where the mere flutter of kisses linger
on my neck, reminding me of letters

never sent, of souvenirs I never
took from places I had never been to.
Do not touch me there, where the wound sits raw,
invisible, unseen and unwelcomed.

To feel it with fingers, with tongue, with skin,
is to memorize its face, acknowledge
its inanity, its absurdity.
Touch me here, where my heart sits quietly

in submission to love and only love.
There is no pain here, no judgment or strife.
The wound does not hurt; it is just as strong
as the desire to touch another's skin.

BECOMING A PROFESSIONAL SOLILOQUIST

above all
the paranoia needs to be borderline at the terminal stage
speculating skills harnessed to the extreme
the man's in moribund solitude
adrift in this establishment of woo-words
the girl has colored skin and dark hair but pale virtues
masturbating with perfunctory mind-mining

next
arm all cognitive perceptions with unyielding steel armors
from self-sulking to self-conciliating
from self-incriminating to self-exonerating
from self-conceiving to self-promoting
quotation marks jab words between people's lips
odor of youth exhumed from frivolity and failure
a modicum of spurious empathy compromised

subsequently
memory's determined by a profitable selection process
self-flattering details must show reliability
the girl must be childless
desperately clinging to any fictitious bib
the man's too compassionate to denounce the intimacy
never ending morning goodbye kisses
a similar address on both drivers' licenses
preposterous anecdote

at last
sharpen self persuasion techniques
pungent monologue
baits the companion of psychosomatic talks
the spasm of illusions sets one-way palaver edgewise
succumbing to the solo apex

character is what we are when no one is looking
and everyone is judging
how high and how low can you go

HERE COMES THE TRUTH

between homeschool physics and English lessons
a nine year old ought to know
dance the cha cha on red mud floor
perfect Western & Chinese chess
locate a geyser playing hide and seek
egg on a chicken to yield more chicks
milk a rubber tree
hush cicadas to sleep
cross a monkey bridge guarded by leeches
cook late night new year sticky rice cake without falling asleep
sew pajamas that can fit the whole family
soap and rinse clean with only three small dippers of well water
ride an adult bike without damaging her hymen

she was not privy to
the monk's staged self-immolation
White Christmas and Bing Crosby's common key
the entire village fumbling in the red land
new economic zones
the official divorce of her father and pregnant mother
pre-finalized on a boat
cryptic stories of dead virgins slaughtered again and again by thorny whispers
relatives throwing limbs of memory overboard
protecting torsos of hope
jumbled neighbors returning home in blood
who had taken their dignity stuffed inside those 9.999 gold bars?

one day she arrived in America
got all the answers from the immaculate self-cleaning airport toilets
no Prime Minister of W.C. forcing a tip from her

DIARY POEM: USES OF COSINESS

Emboldened by sharing, briefly, the same
publisher as Frieda Hughes, I looked up
an article on her latest collection, found
a photo of her living room, which seemed
welcoming, well-ordered, English-cosy,
complete with three Maltesers and a live
rehabilitating owl, like something utterly
seductive from Alison Uttley. I thought
of Plath describing 'owl-talons' of depression
'clenching' her heart, remembered my
view that Plath's writing is political,
its context the savage U.S. Empire
of the 50s and 60s, hence its citing
the execution of the Rosenbergs at the start
of *The Bell Jar*, the fears of U.S.
expansion in her diaries. The metaphors
about Nazis in her poems are more
about Nazis than about those who
she compared the Nazis to. In balance,
she is often housey and cosy, which
out of context seems Not-Feminist, but
in context is sane microcosming
amidst punitive systems of power.
She painted furniture, did craft
and decorated cottages and rooms,
                                      bright like
the make-up in *The Bell Jar*, desperate
for humanity and control. If you
slid out of line they electrocuted you
like Julius and Ethel, if you tried to
appease them with neat suicide, save
anything,
they burned out your nerves with power,
                                  if
they spied that your heart misgave.

MAPS IN THE MIND

The isle of the dead is always sand
and a lump of trees with a strand
as wide as grief away,
as quarantined as cholera, a day
away from any port, like Manus Island,
away like Manus Island.
The isle of the dead is always rock
and piled rock huts with a block
for proclaiming sorrow,
impatient as rape, tomorrow
too hot, too late, too cold
like maps-in-the-mind of Manus Island,
like maps of Manus Island.
The isle of the dead is never solved
by jungle fast last answers, planned
sensitive-isolate like species evolved
in feral fight and fear on Manus Island,
in fear on Manus Island.

SEVEN FACES OF THE DIE

I

That nothing is mere or only.
That not even white, seen
rightly, is without
its heat zones, gradations

of red, yellow, green,
or snow without its blue
occasions when birds fly
over, or skies change their thoughts,

to say nothing
of mind, its happy knack
of changing as it changes things
or warms to the matter.

Finding in breath
and sound-stuff much
that is more, not mere, and many,
not only. As a stretch

of fallow under ice has overtones
of clover and poppy,
and the sound for, the colour
of these, makes of the still earth's airy

stillness a slow dance; and of
its silence, as the rustling
of silk in a darkened room makes the deepest dark
chromatic, a blind man's music.

II

Not a leaf, not a stitch
of our own. How stark we are,

how needy.
But a pencil line
on a blank page will conjure
space, volume, prospective

horizons to make for.
Kids' stuff but a beginning.

Between our fingers
and the stars all the room
in the world. And needy

is good, and bafflement.
On all fours then upright

—unsteady we set out.
What we meet

on the way, before
we get there, is the story.

And we never do
get there. Needless to say.

III
for Jaya Savige

At hazard, whether or not
we know it and wherever
we go. Without it no

surprises, no enchantment.
There is law enough all about us
in almanack and season, anniversary

days come round, the round earth's carnivale
of chimes and recessionals.
Good to be included

there. Good also what is not
fixed or sure even,
the second breath of being

here when the May-bush
snows in mid-September, as giddy
happenstances lead us

this way into
a lost one's arms, or that way
deeper into the maze.

IV

This side and the other
of silence: white
noise. The snowy

infinite beyond
Happens and Becomes where nothing is
to be counted on,

and nothing
is accounted as loss.

V

That this is our element:
a world of nine-day
wonders and other gaudies;
of road-show
rowdies in passage
from Here to Nowhere; a cortège

of all that is of flesh
and air permitted its fol
-de-rol and brief grandezza.
To swank, prance, cartwheel
and flare before our eyes
a moment, before it dies.

VI
The Wager

In the air a flipped
    coin (and so many
breaths suspended on it)
    that never comes down.

VII
i.m. Andrea Stretton

Sprigs, outbreaks of bloom, the everywhere
greenness of grass,
as the dead come to air again
under fencewire that holds nothing
in.

       On slopes in sunlight
cow-parsley, lad's-love,
speedwell, baby's-breath, weeds
of a planet that is all
abundance and consummate
waste and replenishment.

The riot and sweet rot
of what's to come.
The life beyond corruption.

THIRTEEN WAYS OF LOOKING AT A BLACK DOG

1.
A man and a woman
are one.

A man and a woman and a black dog
too quickly reach numbers beyond counting.

A man and a woman and a black dog
are nothing.

2.
The black dog
has stalked over the edge of the horizon
into another.

Three black birds on the telegraph line
chime in.

3.
There is not bridge across
the silence
which follows the silence of the black dog.

4.
An old, dog-eared photograph
in the house of your mother.

Christmas morning, the sun at your father's back,
his shadow falling behind the child
pushing toy trucks through grass.

Who's that in the background,
patting Mrs Hanley's black dog.

5.
In the panting night,
the sound of black dogs
lapping at puddles of light
that form at the steps of your doorway.

6.
On moonless nights
only the black dog is blacker,

the only shining thing
is the black dog's roving eye.

7.
The black dog
which changes shape.
Will you marry it?

8.
The doctor says tests show black dogs have a proven clinical basis to their existence.
The priest says there are no black dogs.
The second doctor checks his medication guide, saying black dogs never die.
The mirrors says the black dog is not in the mirror.
Black dogs live forever,
                        vanishing.
Black dogs don't live.

9.
The need to be in love
is also the wanting
to be rid of the black dog.

10.
Where the black dog crosses the road
the old stream in flood crosses the road.
Where the old stream crosses the road
people say they shiver in broad daylight.

11.
The black dog
smells like a wet dog.

12.
Hold its paw, know that it loves you.

from ZANZIBAR LIGHT

Really. Our day resembles a low-lying island
salt-streaked sunlight appearing diagonally
up and across the temporals of lakeside life.
The thin ambient smell of sand, an upturned boogie board
tilted headphones, towels left out on the jetty. Things in their everyday
zones. The palest shadows of marram grass, a dimensional lesson
in how light cares and doesn't care. A green afternoon of traceries,
sleepy as fruit in the bowl. The unknowable system of the world,
an open clef or what? Now as it happens, a pile of notes, boogaloo,
howsoever smudged with diesel, curled by sunlight. A mood emerges
from the shapes of silence between the tree limbs, diffuses into open
space, no art to pursue its moment. The kids are on the holiday channel,
over there where the quotas of affect are evaporating. They just need to talk.
The thing is everything's in between where the radio stations drift.

*

sundown: that moment in the lengthening forest of surrealism
when simple neo-fascist shadows fall across the silent square
the capital is filling with Hydro workers wearing silver cicada
brooches on their lapels. The afternoon screech of cockatoos,
basic psychology suggests that city-planning and snow descending
are like a televised arena, the horizontal litter of perception having
taken the form of tightly bundled grass stems. Let loose once
there might have been a ticker-tape parade

when things were freer. Have we driven through your country
and been minutely altered by its virtually colourless light?
Strange how memory can be both underground and abstract
when its architecture is exposed: sections of the national lake appear
in your arrangements, but there's no myth anywhere I can see,
only material. Back to the real world, if that's where it is.

TROPIC A
Translated by Leith Morton

Seeking to escape the G force I
Trod on the tail of a blue digital tiger
Fighting against the B force you
Forgot to change into a 3D picture
And were gobbled up   Without a sound

It was the   Perfect chance
To manufacture a simulation of suffering

The tropic *A game field*
———— Had the most perfect weather
You became invisible to me
And I to you

Taking me connected to you by vision and audio
On a picnic today as well
Or for dinner   Or perhaps a movie
From time to time you regaled me   About love

The world of *Endless D*
———— *under the quivering* blue of the sky
Here I   Overflowed excessively
I became invisible to you

Far away from the S force   Turned into code I was
brought to a standstill

Directly below the K point Turned into a signal you
    broke into a smile

Taking degraded copies of me
(Leading the obsolete me-copies)
I'm going to meet you
(You couldn't *find me*)

Becoming invisible in order to be visible
(Because I'm invisible I'm making myself visible)
Am I visible? Are you saying you can't see me?

In the air high above A
    force——————————————

Taking all the versions of me
Now, I'm going to meet you

CIRCULATION-SACRIFICE
Translated by Leith Morton

In the bright sun
The waterline contains me
Above my head is deeply   fragrant

Behind me
The world narrows its surplus
Shimmering   melting beneath my feet

High in the sky, high, in, the, sky
The sound of water freezes—————————

At midday
The sunlight seizes me
Blazes
And blazes

In a corner of the world where the sunlight has penetrated

The borderline has swallowed me in one gulp
Dances along the road endlessly

In front of me
In the distance is you
Just like my childhood raised up in broad daylight

So la, fa
Even at the time when
The world inserted itself again
Painfully between you and me

Phoneme
    Even at the time when
        A nasty breeze
Blew again
Between you and me

In the bright sun
The waterline dissolves me completely

Quietly
And quietly

from MORNING, HYPHEN

To collect sky to trace out repetition. Wet sand condenses over evaporate surface. You said your lips contact repeats contact. Those black crows rising over the city as you think to walk into leaving. At the centre a solution of crystal polished below earth, light emergent at regular intervals. Red transposes the bending of spirals, already bleeding from the chin. A series of foaming, the division foaming. I feel the border of your body arrested in mine. I repeat the border of your body arrested.

*

Or to this
passing by, the deliverance
and hands' brief

Conference, all
indivision as cool blood
light along

Your index finger,
substrate
massaged to bone.

I recollect an incision
of neon, illicity
refraction &

Each floor lost up
to luminous cloud.
Between us

Lost again
in the gifted lip's
fresh take

A corresponding
zero in the heart,
eating air.

... SO ANYWAY THE BONES ARE SMALL
for Jim Carroll

... so anyway the bones are small, fan-like, tender in their motion
It's surprising to consider that dinosaurs evaporated this way
Up into the blue yonder, the branches, the breeze
After so long thundering the earth

What fine legs
A chest you could crush with your thumb
Only the beak betrays an old viciousness
A map left over from a hunger for fleshier times

I'm always sent heart-beating into this mysterious evolution
Beatified and depressed by it depending on the hour of the day

Like now, in the afternoon, with a late winter wind rustling the sunny leaves,
A mower whining over suburban fences, my children still at school,
When belated news of a New York poet dead brings these same impressions to me
And I have no reason clear why such associations fly into the mind

But fly they do

A basketball through a rusted aluminium hoop
Loneliness into a glass of wine
My children's smiles up into the sunshiny day of dreams
The homeward teeming of the city into something reassuring
A passing train upon its tracks a rattled music from my past
Leaves, wings, death, grace, loss, sky, heart – bones.

PAGE QUATRE-VINGT-SEIZE
Translated by Lâm Thục Ngi

then it was Spring. the season when the greenery burgeoned and dispersed deadly pollen inside the depth of this space – and hey, my throat, had consumed those pink dust in the midst of Spring, and we had been itching in tingle with thoughts of instability-for a lengthy season.

blue-violet stems of flowers, flourished in clusters along the sides of the road, right in front of the entrance door, wrapped within a minute yard. even on those spring days everything was still fogged in midnight dew, I could still feel the chill as I sauntered down the quiet street in the middle of the night.

I would make these claims, spring was the embryo of newborn ideas, and also the reproductive season of proliferating insects. not quite far from here, the insects lived in armies, puissant and abundant in hues. would they dash into your door while you're sleeping. I said abruptly, our apartment was where sooth was buried, immerse yourself and let it be. go ahead and be sunken, the seasons, the roads that went unto the depth, nighttime tunes, pebbles cascading down the distant trails, couldn't you see, everything was expanding, was hatching, we would see spring as a blue, crystal line surfing by, you shall see things in their wholeness again.

we are warriors. we whisper to each other at the break of season, at the intersection of fervent noon and gloaming, where blue vanishes into taupe, between tightly clenched hand and shooting purple blood, when the chill wind perches upon the forehead and the mouth has absorbed the pink pollen. we settle our pads and huddle ourselves up in the lonely fork, where either the students gradually dispersed or few atrabilious children tried to pick up apples rolling on the ground. you shall find us at a land of drier drought and desolation, our heads leaned upon one another's, our legs fully stretched, tails quietly lying on the sand.

it would be spring and the fresh water beads. they would tell you stories about us. the dark horses had galloped through many battlefields. the wildest, strongest and maddest ones, we would gallop away, darting towards our destinations. thereon we would return home in peace amidst an immersed spring. and we would walk upon a couple of forelegs, the longest of which would be picking the leaves. the moment we'd caught the blue, our eyes turned heavenly. we'd sniff the coffee and eat raw soy, or toy upon any seeds whatsoever on the way. we would converse with the hoboes with amphetamine brain. we would let them pick our tails' hair to make strings. in the end, we would melt some liquid to assist anyone who wanted to be dark horses like us. thence, you would become a true warrior and fight your battles with your own warm blood without hearing anyone ramble about the mysteries of the life.

TEMPORARY LOAN
Translated by Như Nam

Indebted morning

x baffled with (no)thing to do and created puppets out of zinc paper and stuck them all over the wall. Two or three of them made x heap scorn and that very state of whiteness made x want to pour black ink unto them,

But they are the debts x had borrowed during a gray, peerless, unaccompanied day yet accompanied by the boiling sound from a newly-repaired coffee maker,

x continues to pour into the machine patches of colored powder in cellophane and filter pure substance that kills been sleeping sitting up for all these years. What is that bastard doing in the apartment next door that makes furniture quake, barely does x hear such sound from the place. The bastard has always moved swiftly and left almost every object untouched, except for the crazy-head that mumbles through the night with a sound that sounds as if mixed with weeds and pebbles, x saw the woman sings as she ages on the cd, as blue as a fungus infected nail

x rolls down on the street to find a café but all were closed, the chairs were sleeping sitting up on the tables, stuffed animals were melting behind the glassy windows, streets filled with debtors holding hands, walking around the town is occupied by no one but debtors eating, looking chilled, old couples in pairs and the joy of holding hands under their crotch, indulging in the pleasure of borrowing that is crawling into town, along with the sound that silver coins pouring down make in exchange counters

7pm:
x gets home and gets back to churning out puppets, they seem paralyzed whilst slowly, calmly walking in, looking upon the wall, only yesterday did they have such rebellion, split sputum, infertile eggs and refuse to brush the teeth at night, but today, saturated with colorless patches, agreeing to get into bed pulling the blanket way up to the chin, turning off the lights, listening to the furniture as they tremble

A PERSON IS WRITING

a person has just woken up
a person is begging for food
a person has just left home
a person is stirring his cup of coffee
a person has just gone away
a person is waiting for an opportunity
a person has just stood up
a person is tying her shoelaces
a person has killed another person
a person is keeping his mouth shut
a person has just stepped into a cafeteria
a person is massaging another person
a person is meditating
a person is screaming
a person is going to speak the truth
a person has just sent a letter
a person has just known how to talk
a person is bowing his head
a person has just walked out from a bathroom
a person is waiting for a bus
a person has just finished her night shift
a person is delivering his speech
a person has just been shot at
a person is rewriting history
a person has just collapsed
a person is changing her dress
a person has just crossed a street
a person is in labour
a person is going to get mad
a person has just arrived somewhere
a person has ripped off millions of people
a person has just lost a banknote
a person is serving as a slave for another person
a person has just jumped into a river
a person has just won a jackpot
a person has fallen down
a person has just been hanged
a person is beholding herself in a mirror
a person is walking quickly toward a certain place
a person has just stolen something in the supermarket
a person is sitting on a bus

a person is going to pay for his crime
a person is in ecstasy
a person has just met another person
a person has cheated thousands of people
a person is kowtowing
a person has just killed another person
a person is desperately struggling
a person has just returned home
a person is stopping his motorbike at a traffic light crossroad
a person has just been betrayed by another person
a person is listening to silence
a person is going to be praised
a person is dreaming
a person has just committed suicide
a person is putting lipstick on
a person is imagining
a person has just sold herself
a person has just ejaculated
a person has tortured hundreds of people
a person has just closed a dead person's eyelids
a person is giving alms to another person
a person is going to feel remorse
a person is looking at darkness
a person has just betrayed another person
a person is having breakfast
a person has just been executed
a person has told a lie
a person is reading a newspaper
a person is going to join a monastery
a person is closing her eyes
a person is pushing in labour
a person has been crucified
a person is in deep sleep
a person is dying
a person is going to take revenge
a person has died
a person is crying
a person is torturing another person
a person is going to be forgotten
a person is watching the stars
a person is raping another person
a person is mummified
a person is painting

a person is selling his blood
a person has just given birth to a baby
a person is going to be jailed
a person is laughing
a person has entered history
a person is drunk
a person has been revived
a person is cheating another person
a person has fallen in love with another person
a person has just consumed poison
a person is making love with another person
a person is digging another person's grave
a person is breathing
a person is dancing
a person has just flown up into the sky
a person is singing
a person has lain in a mausoleum
a person is smoking
a person is spying on another person
a person is going to be exhumed
a person is waiting for another person
a person is going to lie down
a person has ran out of tears
a person is praying
a person has just slept peacefully

a person is writing

A PATH
Translated by Kaitlin Rees

the noisy world, the grand narratives, the chaotic happenings, we sit together, secluded, breaths of candlelight, expressions of the lonely, the vague, the odd, some strands of hair dropped into memory's oblivion.

it is not easy: to choose privacy, even protect it, nurture it, to make that privacy fruitful, not let it bend with the current, not self-destruct in established orders, to suffer and decide to not be a sufferer.

do you dare face this hopelessness: to believe in and search for depth and meaning in life and art. is there anything deeper than the surface, is there anything more meaningful than nothingness? is there anything more passionate than the tremors of memory, the play of bottomless imaginings, estranged words opening a path, written pages speaking themselves out?

here, steep cliff edges, deserted paths of thoughts, vulnerable presences that remain unpitied, voices that have deauthorized themselves, voices that refuse to send any message, vigilantly opposed to the temptations of productivity, profit, clarity of issue, comfortably anchored ideas.

perhaps this is a path: not only personal, art and poetry become more intimate, more private, and more private and more.

THE FEAR OF BORDERS
Translated by Kaitlin Rees

to feel safer, we should build more walls, only go down the cleared paths, the lighted roads, the turns that are sure to lead somewhere.

avoid the journeys that suck you deep into the private universe and this language full of darkness, avoid experimenting and experiencing, as you will get nowhere.

do not explore this magic: every language meets at the intersection of sky and ocean, we imagine we can see a borderline, but it is a line constantly erasing itself with the tides and light. the presence of poetry, at this intersection, erases the illusion of partitioning lines. poetry, at this intersection, is no more concerned with the original or the translation, is simply to invite a shared reading between languages, and to draw no more barriers between hearts.

i think remotely about the Vietnamese language, with an enduring fragile hope for an essential collision at the meeting place between sky and ocean. poetry's Vietnamese, as with every poetic language, does not suffer the manipulation and control of ideologies that aspire for more authorized power, even for a monopoly of power; ideologies can unconsciously lie in the life of our languages, and wish to frame us in narrow windows. poetry's Vietnamese is where readers and writers strive to not give themselves over naively to the frames, to endlessly question those frames, with the possibility to leave them and not belong to them.

why when thinking about borders, do i always think about love, or vice versa, when thinking about love, come to think about borders. love, all at once, a gnawing hunger for passion and a longing to be free from emotional attachment, an urgent demand to have each other and abolish all dynamics of power relationships, the constant questions of how to erase, overcome, or live within-out-with borders.

a playground for people in a togetherness with language: the heartening loneliness to cross omnipresent borders.

perhaps this is a path: not only personal, art and poetry become more intimate, more private, and more private and more, to go deeper.

DISCOURSE ON WATER
Translated by Kaitlin Rees

while waiting for you, i begin a story about water, rain, clouds and their familiar creature: the perfect fish without tails and with limpid eyes but that cannot tuck themselves up.

without reason, i continue babbling meaningless confusions, which your hungry heart can use to temporarily feed the dark, the gang of bone thin ghosts in your body and madness waits at a rest stop of a suddenly interminable journey.

i begin to tell you about how water vapor never condenses to be always flirting with sunlight, how green thunderstorms roll by the wide naked eyes of fish, how the village ceased smelling of wild roses and the ghosts died over and over again, how for one october people huddle in a cold kitchen to rouse the embers, how the wind beats against the roof, and how the boy incessantly speaks his dreams dreaming more as he speaks ...

while waiting for you, i begin to spin a story about water, rain, clouds and their familiar creature that went wild some time ago: fish without heads that can tuck themselves up perfectly.

while waiting for you, because hunger's faded, i sit and dig up the ghosts hiding in porous earth, here propagates an odd species of sweet potato, tuberous roots large as thighs and known to emit a soporific fragrance, as the fever rises and the wind gets drunk, i linger to ask the earth's story and hunt for blades of kindled grass, the myth says the first blade found is the unwavering soul of grace, to ingest it will fill us with love for all four seasons.

while waiting for you, my body opens a grave, i invite you to this game once more, between the slabs of faintly fragrant wood, somber, so that in the end, i can close completely.

GRASS
Translated by Kaitlin Rees

i cannot convince you to stop thinking you are the stranger in this place, the tips of grass say beneath my feet, let's speak only of the elsewhere people, of foreignness, of extraordinary languages that fall quietly into oblivion, languages at which we can only curiously gaze, untranslatable words, the reasons we carry for abandoning a place and setting foot in a different homeland, the timbre of places, hybrids, a passport, a driver's license, a traffic law, an advertising logo, the unfamiliar weather, the manners of social relations, the tips of grass say beneath my feet, let's not speak to each other of irregular breathing, the freedom in loneliness of someone standing outside, playing around the margins, until we can learn a way to be face to face two bodies not hidden anymore, silence, your voice in my blood a space outside space, my heart belongs to this place and doesn't belong to any place, we play with the strands of hair that have fallen slimy wet on my body opening to pain which is always a pain never known before.

but it's not my intention to convince you to stop embracing the status of stranger in this place, the tips of grass are breathing under the soles of my feet, so let's keep speaking of the anomalous engaged in locating the imaginary intersection between languages like the intersection between sky and ocean where the borderline turns greenly transparent, and i must know you, and i love you like i love my foreignness, and we will make strangers hatch from each other all afternoon.

WANDERVOGEL
Translated by Jeffrey Angles

Birds migrate
Across the ceilings of a big exhibition hall
Birds migrate
The demolition work and
Waste removal
Have stopped for a break
Birds migrate
The fluorescent lights at the company
Across the way go out
Birds cry out, cawing, cawing
Aligning arrow-like bodies
Into an arrow-like shape
A pedestrian cuts across
A large circle of water and
A stretch of land as wavy as a current of air
Birds migrate
Over a weekday
So quiet it irritates

*

I just wanted to watch
But this is how things unfolded
I'm sure I know
When all this started
I tried to be like a pencil or a staircase
Like a pebble, a dish, or a shoelace
But this is how things unfolded
Far from any of those items
I meet many people each day
I end up liking each and every one
I just wanted to watch
But I'm already wrapped up in things
Cooking rice, boiling pasta
Eating meat
Sometimes for a moment
I can't swallow meat down
But the very next day I'm used to it again
I forget about the meat I eat
And think about the person dining before me

I don't care if all of humanity dies out
But it always bothers me when we part
I pushed drinks into his hands
In a vain attempt to make it last
I just wanted to watch
But was happy when he asked what I thought
I wanted to stay silent
But loved someone who expected me to talk
I was betrayed in every way imaginable
But was impossibly pleased
The roses bloomed
We formed a line and walked
We cried out, shouting, shouting
Came to the ocean's edge and stood
Went into all kinds of restaurants
And as we waited for our food
Protected by the stove's warmth
I vaguely recalled two things:
First, I just wanted to watch and
Second, I was searching for a place to do just that

*

Birds migrate
Nothing hard about that
At the most brightly shining spot
On a long, laid-out stretch of land
Some girls finish their makeup
I suspect our species will survive
A bit longer if we stay together
The plum trees bloom, seven days earlier than last year
The camellias bloom, thirteen days later than last year
The cherry trees bloom, fifteen days earlier than last year
That includes the Somei-Yoshino cherries too
The dandelions bloom, twelve days earlier than last year
The gingkos bud, eleven days earlier than last year
A pedestrian squats down
Birds migrate north
No dissatisfaction at all
Suspended in determination
In gravity's irrefutable force

THE NEXT PLANET
Translated by Jeffrey Angles

The earth has already grown so poor
The only thing on the screen are pale pathways
They say not even sparks scatter on street corners
So everyone says they're leaving for the next planet
They say that there, perhaps we'll catch a whiff
Of the familiar scents of dirt, smoke, and mud
And if we're lucky, the scent of tree sap too

They say that people back in the olden days
Called the desire to pack their bags *hope*
The only hope that grows is the one
On which our lives hang, after its inflation
We hardly use that word any more
Everyone is talking about the next planet

Yes, everyone is talking about the next planet
But are they talking about the same one
Or different ones scattered here and there?
None of us are entirely sure, and honestly,
It doesn't really matter who's talking –
The whole thing smells as fishy
As the word *hope* sounds

This place might have been a metropolis long ago
But wind has reduced the rubble to dust
Now it is a dimly lit field
Weak, idle grass is growing
Maybe we need not worry so much
But no one seems to have seen that place yet
Right here is where I plan to build my home

Surely it won't be long before they notice and
Everyone will stop talking about the next planet
Everyone will try building a home here
The land will grow increasingly congested
Lots of stoplights and streetlamps will be put up
The names of intersections engraved in maps
And new laws adopted

Not just bad things, I think
I'll probably make some friends
I'll experience both fun and tiresome things
One of us – you or I – will die first
While the other remains, working through sadness
You told me once everyone dies sometime
And somehow that cheered me up

Now the ground is cold
And doesn't smell like a thing
But tonight I will sleep soundly
Not on the next planet
But on this one

A SPECIAL DAY
Translated by Jeffrey Angles

Today is a special day
An organization about wild birds was established
A giant panda was discovered
Shino-chan had her birthday and
Put her marriage registration in her purse

Today is a special day
Someone ordered banana pancakes
At the Starbucks in Tsukiji
The ground suddenly shook for a while

Today was the day
When Pioneer 10 sent back its last data from the outer solar system
When Nausicaä from the Valley of the Winds walked her golden fields
When Kunikida Doppo wandered the forests of the Musashino Plain
When lots and lots of people died all at once and we mourned
When things were like other days at so many other places and times

REBIRTH
Translated by Jeffrey Angles

I threw away lots of clothes
Shirts, skirts, shoes, and bags
It's a pain when you sympathize
So when a yellowed sweater
Flew at me and laughed
I quickly dodged and ran

With a full cardboard box in hand
I went to the thrift store behind the station
Along the way, the fiber's emotions grew tangled but
Still I crossed the pedestrian bridge over the highway
Covered in sweat, with a hardened heart

A middle-aged man in work clothes was waiting
Casually he took my pile of clothes
But wordlessly returned a pair of pumps
We can't take these, he said,
They're too worn, we can't resell them

God, my body is light—
I hold the ruined pumps tightly in one hand
And tomorrow, I'll go someplace new

LISTENING TO THE CHINESE WOMAN PHILOSOPHER

In Campsie, Sydney, I met a nonstop Chinese
Woman philosopher who questioned me sharply if I knew anything
About philosophy and did not wait for me to finish pretending
When she said:

This mathematical shape is square
Containing many different numbers
When enlarged infinitely you can see that it largely remains square
Although inside it there is infinite change
One tiny detail turning into a myriad of forms
That's what I call can know and cannot know
You can never say you can know you can never say you cannot know
For a drop of water reflects seven colors of the sun
And the intricate lines on the palm of a hand
Tell about your previous life and after life
Just like your own identity is enshrined in your fingerprint
Just like your innermost secret is found in a swab of the inside of your mouth
Just like this doctor I know who can diagnose your hidden diseases in your eyeball
A kind of miniature map of Sydney

'and just like a fingertip, a toe or a blade of grass,' I offered
'that can offer us access to a world of infinite possibilities or secrets
if we can find a way to read it?'

'yes,' the Chinese woman philosopher said
as the night outside became suddenly loud
with raindrops, each luring me to explore its difference from the other

PARAPHERNALIA
Translated by Peter Boyle

I haven't put on
my ears this morning
however
the world is stunning me,
its multitude of chairs
tied together,
its stock-market crashes,
that grinding of teeth
amid new shoes
and banknotes.

I think, with bullish insistence,
on what side of life
has life ended up?

The leopard skin
is trading on the market
at the price of a diamond.

Down the helter-skelter of fire
slide the passionate kisses
of lovers
falling into the spell of dark stars
with the cold days that wander
without a motherland
through tense cities
crammed with rubble.

No one whistles on the streets anymore.
And it seems embarrassing to long
for the calm blue sky
the yellow sound of wheat
the movement of water
in perfect circles
when a pebble
is thrown by a child
from the brightly-lit window of his room.

The pigeon returning
to the laid table
brings in its bloodied beak
a slap from the world.

How will I know from which direction
death will come.

AFTERWARDS
Translated by Peter Boyle

Later than so much
after everything
we will have to name
each thing
as if for the first time,
after lightning
and fire
after everything,
humbly,
silently,
at a leaden pace
and with a demiurge's patience,
among the corpses of stars
and the garbage.

ARTIFICIAL ISLANDS

The burned down mall
still stands. I heard
something like

insurance, but as a girl
I wanted a beige troll
with hot pink hair.

I used to run down
the men's department
lined with white

shirts so white you
could see the ghost
a head cold leaves.

Most things cost
money, books
especially.

Now that I'm in a car
driving past
trying to remember

if they had a food court,
I want to call my father
in traffic

and ask if it really
happened. Also I want to
raze the mall

to the unstable
ground, milk it
like it milked me.

AFTER THE FLOOD

I struggled to find
a better language.
Words like thoroughfare

and inundate.
Then death tolls.
Then, a fear of rain.

Things we couldn't
always say – a boy
in my history class

saw a woman
with the bluest child.
And so much rain.

I know a word
when I see it enter
a moving vehicle.

Days after the flood,
the slightest mist
made you fear

those empty shelves:
no loaves of bread
in sight for us.

INNER LIFE

Here you were born
and raised, and raised
well. Not beyond

their means. Not a war-torn
country either, here.
Dank perimeter that was

your weather, leitmotif.
Sure, you'd feel its cold
coming like a not-so-distant

future, the wind of it,
the deep drone of it.
The animal

that didn't make it to the shed
was an incident.
Interruption.

But that was hardly
a puzzle: only a short
distance and you were out there, right

in the middle of things,
important, just being necessary
and all by yourself.

Few more days before rain.
The gloaming's not-yet-green
would find a way to survive

the accidents. The leaves were dead
underfoot. Beneath, history was
throbbing, been breaking out

of, awhile. That backyard
had never been so beautiful.
Too much of an opening

in the wilderness but quite
a luck, and you knew it,
aerial wire to aerial wire.

Someone, from the farthest
end of the house, called
your name and you didn't

answer. You were all of four.
These limits. Otherwise you were there
already, sudden and not moving away.

Nothing like this revenge.

A COLONY

is about breed for bounty, custom-
bound to trace back tail to trail and node
is often what to pin with tack

and remember. Of course they do
for every tread, boot, shoe
mildew track – give or take

the width to break the span
from here on in is string, inch
by inch another year and harvest.

Beneath the underbrush, stones
shall bear the patchwork grid and stretch
for miles – hypha, stem, the bent

axon swings, neurons lit
like stars the growth that startles
barb wire sting – from fence

to fence. Such an artist limns
lichen patterns across regions, chrome
palettes, leaks, stains on paper

and you wander deep
below the forest cover and carefully
not to point the finger – straight

ahead, no ripple nor quick turn
and the rudder poised between the first
body, and the next thereafter.

JUST TO THE RIGHT OF THE HEART OF IT

here. it's 'work from home day,' sunny. emails ▮▮▮▮ to stress me, a double head of fine basketball matches automatically taped via the set-top wonder, ▮▮▮▮▮▮▮ eggs for lunch, butter … the bourgeois spread, a full(ish) day of writing & i haven't even GOT to the paper yet. yessir. bolt has a new show soon; ▮▮▮▮▮▮▮▮▮▮ ▮ a proper backlash. i've discovered my ears are getting very hairy. strange hair i've not experienced before the amount of hair -related emails is astounding. > i have this suspicion that being a gen X person is the > worst time to be born. if > you're a teenager now you're technologically native▮▮▮▮ you shimmy across everything & use twitter without finding it > weird & self-serving. confederacy of dunces keeps getting better & better. my valve!!!! one of my favourite types of films are alien invasion ones but battle: los angeles ▮▮▮▮ hysterical garbage. yes. indeed i loved ▮ not knowing the plot beforehand ▮▮▮▮▮▮ provided a little bit of extra frisson to the first five minutes, after which all was cunningly revealed. i am getting old. i resaw robocop the other day, but ▮▮▮▮▮▮▮▮ white ribbon ▮ films about nazi germany i generally don't see. meat in the freezer is dwindling! ▮▮▮▮▮▮ will have to shoot the other sacred cow now & have a hotdog

A POEM ABOUT HAVING NOTHING TO SAY

In a poetry reading
Billy Collins said that
when he was a young poet
he had lots of stuff to say
but then he found out
that whatever things he wanted to say
had already been said, and had been said much better and then he realised
that he had nothing to say
and his poetry improved remarkably

I am still young,
But I also have nothing to say
therefore I'm telling the story of Billy Collins, in a poetry reading
saying that when he was a young poet
he had lots of stuff to say but then he found out that
whatever things he wanted to say had
already been said, and had been said much
better and then he realised that he
had nothing to say and his poetry
improved remarkably

I'm still young
but I also have nothing to say therefore
I'm telling the story of Billy Collins in a poetry
reading saying that when he was a young poet he had
lots of stuff to say but then he
found out that that whatever things he wanted to say had
already been said, and had been said much better and then he
realised that he had nothing
to say and his poetry improved
remarkably. I'm still young
but I also have nothing
to say therefore I'm telling the story
of Billy Collins in a poetry reading
saying that when he was a
young poet he had lots of stuff to say but
then he found out that whatever
he wanted to say had already been said, and
had been said much better and then he realised that he
had nothing to say and his
poetry had improved remarkably I'm

still young but I'm also have nothing to say therefore I'm
telling the story of Billy Collins in a poetry
reading ...

RISK MANAGEMENT

Everyday from the time you wake up you may have to deal with:
The risk of getting out of bed and the risk of staying in bed (and
    feeling guilty for the rest of the day)
The risk of spending one hour to dress up (and being late to work) and the
    risk of looking messy (especially when you might have bumped into a
    love interest)
The risk of driving and the risk of walking to work (and getting
    run over by a car)
The risk of eating a healthy breakfast (and hating it) and the risk of eating
    an unhealthy breakfast (then later in life facing diabetes, high cholesterol,
    cancer, you name it)
The risk of not having a coffee after 12pm (and feeling sleepy for
    the rest of the day) and the risk of having a coffee (and not being able to
    sleep at night)
The risk of speaking your mind and the risk of keeping your head down
    (you all know what this is all about)
The risk of practising politics and the risk of ignoring it
The risk of staying back late at work and the risk of 'Well, who
    gives a shit ...'
The risk of staying up late to read and the risk of going to bed early (and
    waking up at three in the morning)
The risk of falling out of love and the risk of falling in love again
The risk of trusting your instincts and the risk of resisting
    temptations (and regretting it years later when lying on your death bed)

The risk of living and the risk of dying

After you die, then there is no risk for you to manage
Not that I know of
Not just yet

INSECT POEM

My auntie says look at
the difference in the colours of our skins
one lighter than the other (both brown)
in the hot air one sweaty the other dry
I hold her hand. We talk about race
I guess and I feel uncomfortable so does my
sister the fan hums my grandmother grandfather
have not died and they sit near and chat I
hold my auntie's hand cool and smooth. I hold
my sister's hand raised and hot damp her
hair sticks many insects have bitten her and
me but less me each bite like a growing
bulb pink and sore near to erupt. We scratch
until they scab yellow red shields I need to
pull away to get the itching treasure
underneath we cut our nails short and can't
get the treasure treasure upon treasure
erupting over our entire beings I want the
treasure. I do not want the treasure
temporary and diseased like eating so many
potato chips you regret
because of your stomach and head upset
from salt. My auntie's hand soothes me she asks
a riddle what colour do all human bodies share
in common white teeth I say whites of the eyes
oh pupils black pupils my sister says white
nails my auntie looks alarmed. No blood we
stroke and slap our bites for relief and wake
up bleeding small bubbles of blood on the
sheets not from the insects only from
unconscious scratching I want to bite off
all the treasure mines and scratch them
forever and wish my skin calm smooth
like my auntie.

HAPPINESS POEM

Here I am eating a tasty
nectarine from my neighbour's tree
and I am eating round the dimple
of where it is eaten by birds ants
other insects and so on who also
like tasty things. Everything is in love
with sugar and I am licking all the juices
dripping down onto my pants and arms
and shoes I am licking them up and
licking my lips and soon enough I am
also eating inside the dimple eaten by
birds ants and so on and we
are sharing communion of fruit I
am tasting their mouths with my mouth
and I am eating the stone slowly and
grinding it into a paste in my teeth it
is an aphrodisiac.

SEASTRANDS

You're afraid of the sea
but beauty falling away in flakes
scares you more: slow occlusion of radiance,
thickening waste of middle age,
bus to work, gin at dusk.
Months without joy or fear or lust.

You wouldn't call it wanderlust.
Clammy doubt beckons you to sea.
What starts to flicker at dusk
by 3 a.m. is scalding you with flakes
of doubt and memory. Age
leans in. You blister in sleepless radiance.

Phosphorescence cools its radiance
and prophesies new waves of lust
that run ahead and dazzle as you age.
Don't pretend the old are ungainly in a sea
of wrinkly comrades: eggs on toast and flakes
on collars, limping towards some final dusk.

Stand open on the deck at dusk:
watch night bathe itself in a radiance
that settles on the waves like glassy flakes;
reflective filaments that stir up lust
and dreams of naked bodies curving undersea.
Daring to eat a peach at your age

has its risks. So what. It does at any age.
Waves trample into dusk
like solemn centaurs at the sea
-burial of dust that threatens radiance.
Whimsical? Maybe, but the enemies of lust
grieve even as they fall away in flakes.

Who said, anyway, that every vision flakes?
Why should it all go sour and flat with age?
Leave because you'll have no peace. Lust
for escape and for adventure, not dusk
as you know it now. Follow quiet irradiance
in its surge across the sea.

Deep in the hull lust recollects its flakes.
Trace the sea to rediscover age
-less dusk and re-assemble radiance.

THE NINTH HOUR

The ninth hour
is here

The ninth hour
makes no sense

The ninth hour
rises up wearily
in a freezing mist.

I have come to a river
of blood and vinegar

I have come to a river
where only pain
keeps its feet

I have come to a bridge
of dissolving bone

I have come to a place
of burning cold

I am trapped in a space
deformed
by my own
leprous fear

have I the strength
to pay suffering its due?

....

There is a calm
that is no cousin
to courage

There is a calm
that sits
like a quivering ape
under the python's
hypnotising eye.

Everything makes you
shiver

The hot wind. The rank river.
The poisonous euphoria.

But it's your shriveling
flesh
that has the whip hand

Your flesh
has its own tumorous
will

You may think
you have been here
before

You may think
your quicksilver spirit
has your furtive flesh
licked

But darkness
is stronger
than light

The flesh knows best
who'll win line honours
in this fight.

....

The ninth hour
is here

The ninth hour
makes no sense

Don't pray
for a flash flood
delivering miracle
or clarity

During the ninth hour
reason dies of thirst

Your blood stagnates
stale
as a base metal
in your mouth

You dangle
in a cacophony
of retching noise
with no grandiose riffs
of heroism

You will never forget
the foul sound
of the ninth hour.

....

I have come to a river
of blood and vinegar

I am here,
ninth hour,
I am here
stripped and shivering.

But listen, ninth hour,
listen
and pay heed
to a new sound
in me

I am not here
silent and alone

Do you hear
the fighting hiss
of this geyser
in me?

I stand my ground
in the undaunted spray
and company
of my own words.

GENTLE CREATURES

Sweep up
the broken glass
a broken earth-map
on the living room floor.
You with
antelope gentleness,
gathering up slivers,
so carefully:

I hover,
        at your shoulder,
amputated.
I want to help
reach in
cut fingers,
but it would only
bloody the mess.

And inside a
symphony, chiming
through an afternoon
that endures us
        I pull another
black bin bag
off the roll:
snap it goes,
clean off.
        I forget it's Saturday,
and that you were playing
video games, and
I was reading
on the couch,
before.

Now: picture leaning
on drunk angle,
frame bashed but
intact.

I leave the room
convinced I will
return and
everything will
be the way
it was.

BETWEEN THE FLAGS

There are too many people in
this surf,
the latest wave
brings them
down upon
my uncapped head.
Salt-swollen
as
I hit the
sea floor, hard –
and above,
in
the same flux-
current of water,
a
Babel of limbs
and boogie board foam
collide in wet,
and
fizzing

space.

JETLAG WORLD

Wake up calm. It will be morning soon.
Hours disappear, then shatter at the
Sound of a phone call (wrong number).
Your mobile bleats when it's time to
Change the battery, in that awfully
Disconnected voice that's had reverb
Added to it, in the room where you
Remain alone. Eat a mandarin. That's
Better. No use trying to go back to
Sleep. You've deposited enough hours
In that bank to fund your hibernation,
This winter, when it comes. It will.
Television wakes you again. When did
You switch it on anyway? Consenting
Adults. Leave the room. Be sure to
Wrap yourself in warm clothes, for
It is cold this morning. The Minimart's
Open forever. Buy cans of hot coffee.
Sit outside and watch the businessmen
Leaving their apartments, MP3 players
Already fitted, a soundtrack you can't
Hear jettisons them towards offices
That are already lit. Return to your
Room and watch television again. It's
Samuel L. Jackson in a kilt. Leave the
Mandarins where they are. Shower.
Catch the subway. The morning mist
Has not yet cleared. This day in the
Land of the morning calm is already
Several hours older. Sit in front of
The monitor. Work. Write this poem.

MINNAMURRA SESTETS
For Riley

The rainforest, winter blows past, my son.
Dark air, under the canopy, his big dark eyes –
New and touching everything.
                        Red cedar, behemoth,
Blots out the sky and you dart over the boardwalks
Gumboots clapping rubato. Today, I write to you
In this place
            – this piece of an old world – this story.

The lyrebird scratches its way through the undergrowth
Mapping contour lines on the forest floor. You say,
The scrubwren's a pirate,
                        its black patched eye
Watching every movement for treasure in the dirt.
Coachwood leaves flitter like pinwheels in the sun
And the lilly pilly sings itself in flaming tongues;

Ochre, dust, and myth. Maybe, it's the day that narrates
Us, like letters punctuating a page, our steps
A key stroke in time.
                        Yet, I wonder in thirty years
From now, if you'll remember the sassafras
Or the detritus fermenting the air – that smell
Which buries deep in memory; or if the land
Will forget us too – the granite boulders balancing
Another million years in their books.
                        Old man banksia,
Sits beside the track, his beatification
One miracle away. Like little golden halos
His inflorescence – bright, above the martyred cones
That litter our path. You're holding one now,

Thumbing the woody lips for its seeds and secrets.
Ahead a suspension bridge hangs like a hyphen
Between the bloodwoods
                        – a hammock of cables and planks;
Dressed down by a decade of algae and moss.
Below us, the lichens have drawn battle lines
Over the river rocks like countries on a globe;

But war's a word you don't yet know – my little
Berserker bounding on the boards.
                            The emerald dove,
Perched on one of those jealous vines, is still new music
To you, thinking nothing of the radar echo
In its coo-oo. It was the Spartans' wisdom to cast
Their children to the wild,
                      only to make war in them

For a lifetime; barefoot on snow-capped Taygetus.
Your hand is outstretched and gone, a game of peek-a-boo
Among the prickly rasp fern
                      – fistfuls of broken sprigs.
This residual place, left by the wood-getters
And pastoralists, returns new in our minds;
In its own way, becoming a past we've now written.

I find you again, warm chips in one hand, ice cream
Dribble on your chin and that perpetual
Boisterousness of youth – squirming in your mother's arms.
Cabbage tree palms form a woodland of giant's arrows
Around us
                      – thirty-foot margins for today's page;
Reading life in these moments,
                      one word at a time.

LOSING YOU

My grandfather's shed smelled of oil. Petrol
Seeped from the carpet mats he laid under his
Red Holden.
              His carpenter's hands, scabbed and
Scarred, took their time whittling raw wood,
Shavings falling in curls to the saw-dusted floor.

I could hear the mynahs clawing the tin roof;
They were nesting in the fascia.
              Most of the time
I wasn't allowed to watch him, the saw
Too sharp, the hammer too heavy.
He took care to thread the dowelling

Through a pine wheel, an exhaust,
A bull bar. I fingered the inside of my pockets
And waited.
            Until it was ready for me
To drive across the bench, to paint it
Blue and yellow, to show it to my father,

Who smiled and let me play. Grandfather
Never showed him how to make things.
Today,
   the tractor is faded, the grain
Swollen. And his tools lie
In a pine box in my shed.

AFTERLIFE

The river gets wider, flows more deeply,
    still through the same layered landscape;
        concrete fields, the silhouette of a low building.
It's early evening, perhaps.

Pelicans swoop overhead, gliding over the scum
    on the water, their wingtips perfectly balanced.
Days are here for the counting,
    certain as the alphabet;
the current is clenched around the keel.

    A digital rain is falling.

    There is no more inside.

The distance is the distance.

SETTLEMENT

In the Coogee Immigrant Barracks
some arrived
of a time

and history that by view
was more than different

the stories, wars and angers
accounted as negligible in the settlement
'Oh yes, another story, Oh no, that is terrible …'

The histories, well, more the lands of memory
these simplify when they finally merge
accounts and recollections

The certificates, licences and permits
stops rolling. This is our exchange
the by-laws become twin
and in the shadow of settlements
we represented the moorings
that gave light if we talked under these buildings
that arch Roman.

Possibly, we may have talked of fugues,
undigestible discords shared like a quiet meal,
A fare that doesn't equate to media
and mass currency
velvet plates of the generous generating
valuable marble legacies or observing zakat.

Under city shadows sits the bum
talking fare
and memorising timetables for account

Stretching out
the 8.16 did run late and out of timetable order
Commuters think 'true! School should come to order'
or 'this happens everyday and I've habituated, another redundancy'

The bum is the seat of Parliament as we get to the following station
The train rests short of the platform

to understand shadows have no source construct
or building codes is the delusion of the screen

'Monday 19th November, 2012
there was a fatality on the tracks
near Box Hill, Melbourne. Trains were delayed
and the Metlink Network was thrown into chaos.'

That is the account of a day's transit, I remember
'I have to be somewhere …'
was a common thought shared
as Blackburn Station signals processing unit
worked to get through
as we sat in this stopped train.

STONES

Stones   move the creek
between flowerless   *fuchsia*
correa   the same black-
ened blue   algae on granite –

      until the water   turns
clear   and released from
                        otherness.

BACKWATER

My future is   backward
I should be far from   here
in the opened   summer
     past
        the soldered   water's
edge –
       the many   histories
in the long and odd   period
of dormancy   I carry.

REFLECTION

A longing for place
is my only longing –

              I tell
the double   narcissus
its inherited   yellow

dark yellow   doesn't
suit me
              it could be
weeds or   another
miracle   to forgive

before human attention
shadows these
small
              doorways

I make half-
peace with the   light.

THE BIRTHDAY PARTY

I kiss the dirt like it's your forehead.
Excavate a hug from the acacia roots,
let the sun grip my shoulders and put me back
together.

I eat bread like it's your bones
like I could fill myself up with it
learn to run again
learn to speak
more than brine and bubbles.

The ocean keeps following me home
singing salt dirt whisper in my ears
so many faded plastic flowers.

I can't see shit without my glasses these days
unless it's up real close and personal
breathing moist against my cheek, you
are so far away you're like a fog.

I don't trust my own memory.
I always sit in the same place on buses.

I hate Halloween, creeping around your birthday
like a dog done wrong,
as if I can't see its chattering teeth
falling out from under the sheet.

Reminder that the dead don't rise
reminder of another year missed.

I toast you like you're still here
toast you like you'll live forever

you could have lived forever.

IF THE SUNLIGHT HAD ECHOES

I moved to a cave.
I have become very small.

I scrub the walls of my cave,
and fill it with echoes
of Burt Bacharach and Beyoncé.

Like a rainbow,
like a mirage, still
I prefer to belong to myself.

Don't touch me unless I say
yes.
Yes, I say to the mountain some days,
'My god, you are beautiful!'

If the world was ever a whole and untouched place,
it hid itself somewhere in the lines on your face.

I keep the bones from what I eat
to carve into delicate weapons.

Toffee sun cracks wide the mouth of my cave,
catching motes of dust,
hurling them back at the sun like,
'I don't want this.'

If I drew you, I would draw the mountaintop.
Breathtaking, treacherous and almost
impossible to reach.

PENTECOST

It is a simple thing for you to light the fire
early in the morning. You take the wood,
smelling still of earth and air despite the axe,
you take the smallest pieces first, barely more
than splinters, place them cross-wise
on yesterday's discarded news, and touch it all
with your finger speaking flame until the dead words
begin to glow, and break.

       Yesterday, we buried him:
and with him, more than half your life. Habits shaped
for thirty-six years of marriage hang about the house
and wonder what to do. So you, though you know
he will not need his usual cup of tea,
will get up, all the same, will touch
above the fireplace the shelf he made for you, and let
your whole sorrow hang by one hand,
              then bend to make the fire,
              to take its fierce shadow in your palm.

NEXT TO NOTHING

My sister's staying   things are not
where I'm used   to finding them
my bachelor hands   often doing double takes
after saucepans rice   and cutting knives
even god help me whiskey glasses   this time
I tell myself it doesn't matter   tell myself I'm glad
to have the inconvenience   night after night
I've heard her cough   day after day
watched her hunched shoulders just ahead of me
getting off the 380 bus at Darlinghurst
where the wind   scrapes its fingernails
against the locked doors   of the Sacred Heart Church
if she's afraid she doesn't say   taking each day as it comes
heading to the Clinic where   she'll write her name and time
in a book that faces a door   with a sign above it saying
'Radiation in Use'

My mother's here as well   she wants to help
she always does   can't help herself
was given kids to raise   when she was only four
living in the bush above Taylor's Arm
no windows in the house   only old sugar bags
that sometimes in the pitch black night would start to move
mostly just the wind but once   she was sure
there was someone there   she's still afraid at night
and lonely always lonely   death for her
will be difficult   when she finds she can't work her way around it
for the moment though   she's cleaning out kitchen cupboards
ironing tablecloths sweeping up camellias trimming ferns making meals
from next to nothing   just relax I say
I can't she says as long as I can keep moving   the pain is not so bad
her bones shrinking   her skin too easily bruised (just the cortisone?)
she too coughs at night   and when she sleeps
you hear her mouth   hungry at the air
she says she can no longer pray   wonders if she should
worry about this   I'd like to say it isn't words
that constitute prayer but can't   when it comes to god
these days my tongue   cracks open

others of the family stay   in Macksville everyone asking them
what's happening   the priest has put my sister in the parish bulletin
they're saying prayers   for her recovery
(please god they're not putting too much emphasis on *thy will be done*)
this makes it worse   for them up there they're in the dark
at least down here we see   her body won't give up
its place to circling dust motes   her walk still asks of earth
equal return of strength   she's learning how to live
with death inside her   where it's always been

My other sister   so we're told isn't coping well
taking it hard   instead of being as she should be strong
she starts to scream   when across the phone she hears the news
isn't good lymphoma cancer   they'll have to operate
perhaps she tougher than we think   sees what even now I try to
block
her sister's body cut from sternum down   open at the middle
so doesn't care whether or not   her cardigan's on straight
later on she too comes to help   ironing tablecloths and making
meals
from next to nothing   each day the two of them
walk around the block   one day they get as far as the video store
this is getting dangerous   they're almost back to normal
soon they'll settle in   we'll all be watching *Charmed*
and eating jelly babies   months later in the freezer I find
the apples that she stewed   and eat them remembering her
when she was young   we were all bred
on disappointment   eventually it tells

My youngest brother who's deaf   and never learned
to socialise   or do his maths
too much trouble   his teacher later said to justify
putting him   in a corner down the back
now runs music shows   on radio 2NVR
rehearses in the bath then   with nothing written down
touches the controls and lets   his thick-tongued troubles
turn to song   but when his sister asks
to speak with him   he won't take the phone
don't talk to me about that   no doubt remembering year after year
in Sydney operations on his ears   he had a dog once Charlie
so keen to be in everything   one day he jumped the fence
still wearing his lead   and hung there choking on love

Middle brother also stays at home   to keep an eye on things
living on the edge   of what was once the family farm
(now cut in half)   he looks across the valley where
the Nambucca makes   each day the same
search for ocean   while the Star Hotel packs away
another dozen tales   the locals tell
because I was gone from home   before his stories
had a chance to grow   I sometimes find it hard
to know   what to say to him
one night he took his telescope   and touched
the shoulder of the dark
it turned and looked back galaxies
too long in the city   I'd forgotten how clean-cut
the stars   can be

my older brother   on the morning of her operation
drives us all to hospital   easier than a train cheaper than a taxi
a little later in the day   he gets his thanks
an accident on Parramatta Road   a drunken driver rams the car behind him
and suddenly the family Sigma has   damages that total more than fifty taxi trips
the drunken driver hasn't got a license or a visa but he gets out
laughing because he's rich   the woman in the car between
is trapped screaming   she has to be cut free and is too afraid
to let my brother hold her hand   later in the day he asks
why good intentions always bring   so much bad luck
it's a family theme   his life divides
from when he left   his father on the farm
to go to the city   where he lived in boarding houses full of cockroaches
as we grow older it seems   more necessary to recall
being young   and playing in the swamp
between the farm and the hill   he was Phantom Ghost Who Walks
I was Bantar Pygmy Warrior   don't laugh
better that than playing baddies   in childhood's moral scheme
it's the baddies who   are dying all the time

he gave me once   one of the old wire strainers we used
putting up fences with our father   to get the tension right
I hold it now   to feel the way
its weight   takes up my hand.

GWENFREWI WALKING

In all her body, I say, no place was like her eyes (Caradoc)

And nobody notices:
Eyes closed to the slick
Seams of the Frankensteinian,
The polite lines of the lobotomised.
See, see, there are bits missing
All over me, airy
As unhooked vowels and slipping
Between. So he calls me water,
Too much of water.
The parts slot together
Quite nicely –
The ring a distraction
Subtler than scar or phantom limb.
He wants to unzip and get in there
Displacing everything
Put on my skin like a panto
Dame, t'have seen what I have
Seen, see what I see …

*Caradoc quote is from G. M. Hopkins, 'St Winefred's Well'. Some lines in this poem are taken from Shakespeare's *Hamlet*.

MAGIC HOUR, L.A.
for Luke Davies

Maze-bright, sans GPS down Fairfax
   in the Buick, when a thrash fiend
in a chrome Corvette salutes hang loose
   then flexes a burnout as he peels off
Sunset; and as the strains of Anthrax
   scatter in the wake of his goatee,
stars are smuggled in via the print
   of Wonder Woman's patriotic bikini.
Dusklit wildlife suffers no predicting:
   a lobster juggles bibles unicycling
in the poorly lit scene of his mind,
   a polymath samples his own urine,
while as on a folding screen depicting
   notable scenes in feudal Kyoto,
a buff pimp in denim cut-offs blazes
   drunk karate outside a 1 Hr Photo.
So we drive in silence, depending on
   A Forest by The Cure for conversation.
It's like Almendros said: magic hour
   is really only twenty-five minutes max,
when the locust sun descending on
   a field of bending wheat is prologue
to a tale stripped of all denouement,
   and silhouettes are all our dialogue.

from DŌGEN SERIES

A painting of a rice cake does not satisfy hunger. Nor a painting of the mountain the desire to see from its summit. The ocean view is a cheat, he says, you can see the telephoto effect. My son remembers his past by way of what he ate. In the mirror I saw his cheeks full, fists clenched. My memory of that meal does not satisfy his hunger, or mine. We remember best what we write in our own hand. How do blind people know where the bumps are? he asks. Words are mountains. We hike up Diamond Head, then eat masalasadas. Increasingly, spikes are put on sidewalks, so the homeless cannot sleep there. *But words will never hurt me.*

— 11 June 2014

The original face has no birth and death. My son refuses to enter the pool, turns his back on two young parents and a child splashing. That's not it, he says when I suggest. That's not it, not it. I will not guess, assume. He's my multiple choice generator, lacking empty circles. My mother stared at another woman in a restaurant. It was a moment of intimacy I wish I hadn't witnessed, he writes. To perceive is not to know. It's some kind of zombie apocalypse, this wanting to read minds, or at least faces, to lean into synapses, catch impulses before they stick. When asked what he'd do in case, my husband responded that he'd cook them. Our daughter's only possession when we met her was a thick brown pencil. She clutched it in her fist. We don't remember her early sounds, she started us with words.

— 20 June 2014

You should study this in detail. He testified that the homeless sleep perpendicular to the street, rather than parallel. The homeless are a particular pronoun. Leaving a restaurant I saw a fresh line of tents on the sidewalk: a couple my age walked toward me from theirs. I have my grandfather's *Hamlet,* who was taken off a Pittsburgh street by nuns – a great salesman, my mother said. A poet's son was killed at Leavenworth. To leaven is to make rise. The homeless must get off our sidewalks, leave our parks, keep their shit to themselves. In an interview, the poet said, *I like all my children, even the squat and ugly ones.*
– 27 June 2014

The moon is neither new nor old, because moon inherits moon. I'm usually a happy satisfied person, but not today. I can sometimes spend time alone, but usually I hit the button that shocks me instead. I'm a sad American, caught in black and white. The wall behind me reads No Shit. History's bunk, so I have none that cannot fit beneath my bed. I sort my memories as a teenage girl does beads, dividing blues from yellows, greens. They fight me back, like balls in a lottery machine, dancing. After practice, she sings in the car, stabs the air with her index. *Been around the world, don't speak the language / But your booty don't need explainin'.*
– 4 July 2014

Vigorously abiding in each moment is the time-being. A dead eel in the shore break isn't banal; nor in the styrofoam cup shard, the panty liner half-buried in sand. In one's 50s, abstraction trades places with the particular. Not a shell of, but a shell my daughter holds up, three black dashes on white. A white fish with one black dot on its mid-section swims beside a coral head. Some boys scramble over the rocks, find another dead eel; its spine and teeth yellow on black rock. Three boys and then another killed in Israel/Palestine, horror to counter-horror. Trauma's memory without screen, unlatched door in a wind storm, flapping without brake, or interval. Each moment in its time until there's only protea stuck in a stump at Punalu'u. The image of these flowers can abide, refresh, return. Involuntary key stroke, happy type on a sea wall.

– 6 July 2014

This is everyday mind. A woman in North Carolina called the cops on sculpted Jesus. He'd not be a vagrant, she said, or need our care. His form is scary after dark, he looks so real. There are holes in his bronze feet. Compassion means to suffer with, or suffer as. Disruption: to rend apart with violence. Paradox is a box too small for them to fit, especially their feet. I told my co-worker in London I watched the bums at lunch and she laughed. I had to say tramps: those men in dark coats in a park full of tulips and older lovers on the Thames. I was the nomad & they a counter-citizenry of the poor. We have privatized blame: give us your blankets, your medications, your shopping carts. We offer you the right to disappear, or to pay a fine for being seen. Can you define table and chair for us, asked a man who needed them for his busking. They'll just sit in wheelchairs and pretend, he added.

– 10 July 2014

GOGGLE

sweet-eyeing the thought of pop
ping one's head in the ear and

noun. a grammarian's perfectionism.
the pure relativism of cousins. while

-ing away the ears, ing ing in the tele
-phone, the *police*. stingy crabmeat cab

-aret, volting and nose-pinching the
watermelody. the two of us are probaby

a prosody. the elements of stiles
differentiate between the plodders and

the hoppers. mollycoddling the eggs be
fore breakfast: a peanut butter security

system, records the comings and goings
of the rulers. along each adequate aqueduct.

the ultimate cage fight: surprisingly quiet. hon
ourable menschen walk in, and you offer

them a plaza. if i were frank though, i wo
uld probably admit that your eyes are like

a certain number of buckets in the ocean
in which i wash my inner handyman.

AUTUMN NIGHT
Translated by Jake Levine and Soeun Seo

One fall night I puked up a monkey. I was in the bathroom at a bar. Two ice cold hands opened my mouth from inside my body and then, with a thump, the monkey fell on the tiles of the floor. Shining oily black under the phosphorescent light, it grabbed the pipes under the sink. It swiftly climbed above the mirror and up the wall. I looked with sobered eyes upon the little beast's scared face, the little beast with blood red eyes and a body covered entirely with short, grey hair. I wrapped the monkey in my coat. Shivering slightly, the monkey rolled up its tail and burrowed its face into one of the coat pockets.

The man who filled my glass asked me with surprised eyes where I got the monkey. 'I was nauseous, so I puked and this dude came out.' I placed a cut-up slice of dried squid into the monkey's hand. The man sitting next to me slowly nodded his head. He wore a profound expression. 'Poor beast.' the man said. 'As you know, it is a physical manifestation of your repressed unconscious.' 'Probably.' I said. We silently watched the sparkly flash of the canines that appeared through a hole in the monkey's little mouth whenever the monkey took a bite of the squid. The man pouring my drink said, 'Look at those teeth! And look at those red eyes like blood. Yes, it looks frightened. But the monkey's nature is to be sly and cold blooded.' Then with a contemptuous look, he whispered, 'Of course I don't mean this as an attack on you.' I smiled bitterly, emptied my glass, and rose from my seat.

I walked on the dead leaves that carpeted the tree lined street, the monkey huddled to my chest. The night sky was clear and cold. The monkey gasped in pain as it dug into my chest. I whispered, 'Are you sad and in pain?' With a cracked voice that rose feebly from the inside of my arms it said, 'Yes.' 'I know I cursed and denied you. I hit you and I choked you. But you know, you are not my repressed unconscious.' 'Yes.' 'Do you want to die?' 'I want to die.' 'But you're just an illusion I'm having.' 'I want to die.' As I slowly pulled the shivering monkey away from my chest, its entire body shriveled up. The dry and thin fall moonlight sparkled blindingly over the monkey's short, grey hair. 'Who are you?' I asked. The small and opaque, blood red pupils looked at me. 'I want to die.' the monkey whispered.

THE INSPECTION
Translated by Jake Levine and Soeun Seo

The day the first snow fell and winter began, my lover became a black wolf that disappeared in the backstreets of the factory district. I didn't tell anyone the truth about what happened. The extreme cold persists. The machines puff and pack the workroom with the gray smoke. Endlessly spinning conveyor belts, cutters picked up by rough hands, and the radio whispering the news: in the factory district there are packs of wandering wolves. I am standing next to the gray breath of my fellow workers leaning on columns of a passage in a line, cold coffee in my hand.

One day we all witnessed how a boy we worked with morphed into a wolf. Clutching the cutters in our hands, we observed the boy's eyes, bloodshot, rat-like, buried bit-by-bit by the heavy and black fur. The buzzer rang and the conveyor belt spun and the boy's frightened moans sunk into the heartless chaos. We heard a giggling out of thin air. The sound of sirens. Police raided the place. The boy-wolf smashed a window, cut through the thick smoke that buried the factory yard, and vanished.

The snow is at an end. I step out the factory door. Armed police roam the dusky streets. Just ahead, cops with wolf corpses, shot dead, slung on their shoulders. I bite a cigarette and silently accept the inspection. I look into the blue eyes of the wolf sagging down a cop's shoulder. Where the hell did that giggle come from? Wind blows and the smell of ice pours down the thin air.

I head under the elevated tracks where I used to walk with that girl. A train passes. Standing between the train's cars that shoot by at a fierce speed, two black wolves. They are staring down at me. Their black fur flutters in the wind. I hear the sound of giggling from behind me. I turn around. Blowing from the factory submerged in dark light, a single stream of icy wind. For the first time I realize that is what that giggling sound is – the meshing noise of the teeth of the factory machines. Armed police approach me. The wolves on the railroad disappeared. I bite on a cigarette and silently accept the inspection.

ORDINARY GODS
Translated by Takako Lento

Could there be a single and singularly pure deed? Or a virtue such as tenderness that injures no one?

My motions began to slow, and my speech grew more halting by the day. This was because my ears began to hear baffling screeches quite often, between simply ordinary actions such as casually opening windows, pulling a zipper up my back, or peeling onions. Did I not open up something unthinkable as I opened the window? As I was pulling up the zipper, did I not catch in those aluminum teeth and forcibly shut in something never meant to be sealed in? Or perhaps, if what are known as gods, in their innocent fashion, were all diffused unnoticed around us, I, by peeling onions, must have committed the violent deed of peeling the skin off a god's scalp. It assaulted me regardless of time, not with cutely trimmed pity or sentiment such as you might feel for three dead ants, flattened and dried, stuck on the felt sole of a slipper, but accompanied by a remorse like desolate pain which creates unrecoverable differences between me and the world as I take each step. I breathed, trying my best not to make any fissure in the air, then I felt suffocated, so I ran outside gasping for oxygen which would force its way into me.

The shadow of the earth, deep in color, was already upon me. Even though it was a bright and sunny midday my family lost sight of me in our small yard.

ISLAND
Translated by Takako Lento

It so happens that I have made a home in me who is here. Eventually I will live the life of a star. I will live the life of a purse-web spider, an orange hanging on a branch, a turtledove, or a sea horse. Just as it was designed from the beginning.

Often enough I looked out over me who is here, with a far-off gaze as one would look over someone else's island. Scrutinized that way, the island was all the more helplessly unsteady and hollow.

Even so, it seems I've stayed too long. At the end I behaved like its owner, swaggering all around the island. As a matter of fact, I should have settled my affairs each day like a daily hire, and left. To where? To that eternal flow. I had a canoe ready at the inlet in a corner of the island so that I could take it out any time I wanted to. Toward that current.

If I start to say that I've begun to take pity on this island where I had my spirit stay for a while, would that be a lame excuse for this unintended long sojourn? If I decide not to leave before I let this forlorn white island rest under the green shades of areca palms, I don't believe that would be tarrying significantly. All told, from beginning to end, it would be just a modest span of time in which Supervielle's horse could take a swift glance backward.

Mingling body odors, fed up with terrible collusion, I would stay on this island a while. I can wait to live as a purse-web spider, turtle dove, or seahorse, until after that. That great river whispers to me that

I can wait until after that, pushing my canoe past unperturbed waves back to the island as I timidly row out from time to time.

AS I SIT ON THE GRASS
Translated by Takako Lento

As I sit on the grass
listening to the faltering song
of a little boy, so young yet,
having trouble carrying a tune
I feel
I am in my true being
in my only self
a half tone off from the people around me
a half tone off from all in the cosmos
which I believed to be my hundred selves
to be my own thousand selves
... dandelions, fluffy seeds
bursting out, bursting out ...
It would be good to fly away somewhere
or without flying away
it's just as good to sit like this instead
blown in the wind

OVER THE BRIDGE
Translated by Yotsumoto Yasuhiro

It looks
Like there is a nice village
On the other side.
It looks like a kind-hearted person
Is waiting for me.
Cows mooing in peace
And fields of milkvetch in bloom all year round.

Looks like something good is going to happen.
I can't help smiling.
Can't help
Trotting along.

HOW MANY BITTER ...
Translated by Yotsumoto Yasuhiro

How many bushes should I cut
To see the horizon?
How heavy a cart should I pull
To move to daybreak?
How high should I jump
To gain noble wings for my back?
How many bitter tears should I shed
To become one with the roaring waves?
How big should the fire be
To boil my blood thick enough to be served on that plate?
How wide should I rip my throat open
To let my songs reach that ear?

from THE FOREST
Translated by Stuart Cooke

The roots sustain the tree
the tree sustains the blackbird
the blackbird sustains the song
the song sustains life
life sustains the earth
the earth sustains the roots

*

When the blackbird is born
the forest is there already

*

So that he might be of the forest
to each blackbird
the forest gives a name

*

When the blackbird sings
it's not of the forest

*

Not even the blackbird's song
can make
the tree fly

TIME PASSES: THE WINDOW'S LIGHT ON THE FLOOR UNDER THE CHAIR

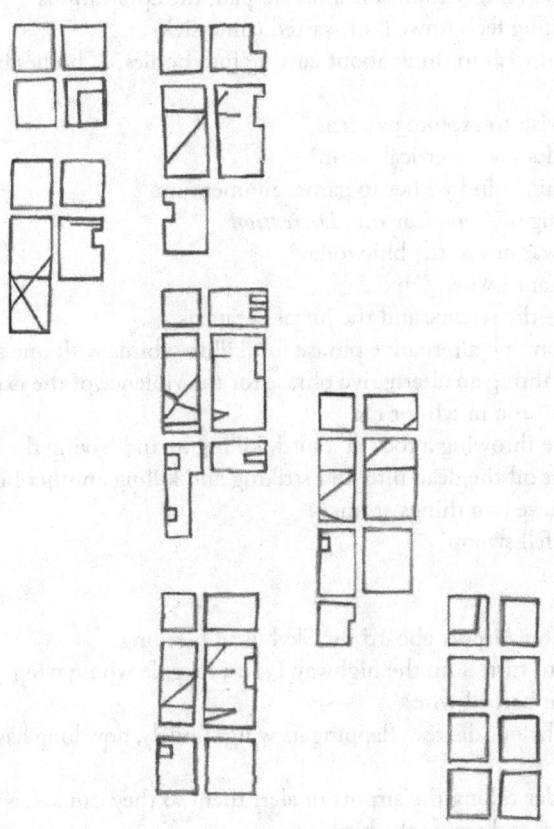

AVALON AIRPORT/HOW TO UNATOMISE THE FRAGMENT

1. Is a day, sending two messages, going for a swim, making a soup & doing the crossword, enough?
2. The human rights watch articulates clearly on tv
3. Debating, not without minimal despair, the applications
4. Something feels unwell, or wasted (time-sick)
5. I do not wish to think about cutting into bodies, of bodies being cut into
6. I still wish to explore patterns
7. What does the metrical mean?
8. The brain/mind wishes to garner momentum
9. Thinking of Anne Carson's *Decreation*
10. What was out of the blue today?
11. Where am I when I'm …
12. There is the science and the jut of parataxis
13. I still have no alternative phrase for 'kill two birds with one stone'
14. I am wanting an alternative phrase for the violence of the expression is just a bit too much for me
15. Imagine throwing a rock at a bird, killing it, and having the rock ricochet off the dead bird and striking and killing another bird
16. To achieve two things at once
17. In one fell swoop
18. Fuck
19. …
20. At Avalon Airport aboard the Skybus to Geelong
21. About to turn onto the highway I see a magpie whose wing is caught between barbed wire
22. It's in obvious distress, flapping its wings futilely, how long has it been there
23. I consider calling the airport to alert them so they can assess the situation and rescue the bird
24. But I do not make the call
25. I am thinking feeling bad is irresponsible if it is not acted on
26. I am irresponsible
27. I am not even close to conceiving of an alternative phrase
28. Though it is daydreamed of
29. Today on the bus, chin on arms leaning on the seat in front of me, I am listening to *Is this desire?* while driving through the Adelaide Hills (I have never been to the Adelaide Hills)
30. Meandering still feels lost on me

31. Happiest when contemplating the crossword grid, the 'performative encounter' which allows for new positions, unexpected collisions, potentialialites
32. The benefit of multidisciplinary (often spoken of) but is it taken on
33. Of metaphor (according to Ricoeur) of placing two different things side by side to create new and meaningful relations
34. I didn't realise people are so scared of metaphor
35. The people who are scared of metaphor are throwing stones and killing their chances
36. Reading about the fragment and blank space
37. Ancient texts are made fragments by history, modern texts by design
38. This is not fragmentary
39. I am more interested in how to be the opposite of atomised
40. How to be the opposite of neo-liberal
41. It's better not to be teleological
42. It's harder
43. How to unatomise the fragment
44. How to not kill birds
45.

THE AUTUMN WINDS ARE COLD

The autumn winds are cold;
snow falls in the mountains
and the Japanese maples are red.
I have lived in this suburb
for over forty years and can't remember
the autumn winds so cold
or the trees being more beautiful.

My children have children of their own,
old friends have moved away;
square-shaped houses
stand like giant cement blocks
where roses once grew.
Sounds of machinery echo from where
a house is being demolished.

My breath condenses
when I breathe out;
and I believe there is nothing
better than to feel the sun
on your face each morning.
Hands in pockets, hunched up, I walk
through layers of red leaves.

Bird songs and twitters
crack the chill air like ice
and autumn winds carry the taste
of snow from the mountains.
Maple leaves make a dry sound
underfoot and crush easily
becoming a reminder of fire and ash.

RAIN AT NIGHT

I thought I heard it faintly
during the night –
sleeping and half asleep –
while it dripped from leaves
on to the front steps
and down the drainpipe –
stopping and starting as if it, also,
wanted to go back to sleep.

What my body needed
was not what the rain wanted
and it continued
with its irregular tap-tapping –
creating voices that came
from a world that was cold and dark
while mine was a world of warm blankets.
I dreamt I was on a journey
travelling in a landscape I didn't recognize.

When I woke up I did
recognize the landscape.
'It's called tomorrow,'
the sound of the rain was saying.
Indoor shadows
had been pushed outside
and belonged to dissolving drops of rain –
while I took a step into the light
and remembered how persistent
those voices had been during the night.

TRAVELLER'S TALE

I heard them making love in the next room
all night on and off at every hour.
I heard moans, whisperings and sighs
and in between silence and its power.

I hardly slept, they kept me half awake.
I saw their young bodies intertwined.
I heard laughter, sniggering and cries,
and passion urgently defined.

Next morning I prepared to leave quite late
and went downstairs to organise the bill.
Such a sense of emptiness about,
the office open, everything still.

I needed coffee and a fresh croissant.
The manager in black at last appeared.
'Those people in the room next door to mine ...'
He looked at me, I smiled; I'd say he leered.

'There was only one man in that room.
Old. We didn't know he was dying.'
I looked at him again, he looked at me.
I could have sworn that he was lying.

(RUNNING: THAT NIGHT 14)
Translated by Leith Morton

Running
Through the sea of fire a road of fire
Stumbling forwards like a pier is
Running
On the road of fire
Like a red nail
I am running
Running
Because the flames on the straight road are Running I am running
Because I can't stop running I am running Because I am
Running I can't stop running
I'm running
Because I can't stand still I'm running Beneath my running feet
Before my running feet
Scorching
Burning
Those running are running
Running running
Overtaking those running
Darting between those running
Those running are running
Running
Those
Not running
Are not
Those not running
Are not running
Those running
Run

Run
Those Running
Are not running
Are not
Those who
Ran
Are not running
Are not

Those who
Are not
Mother!

Is not

Mother is not
Running ran running
Mother is not

Mother!

Running
Me

Mother!
Running
I
Am running
I cannot
Not run
Slippery slippery
Slippery
The thing that
Slipped through slithered down slid away
That was
That was
That hot thing that
Slipped through slipping through
Slithered down slithering down
Slid away sliding away
It was greasy so greasy so so greasy
Was that
My mother's hand in my own?
My hand in my mother's?
Running

Who
Is it?
Who is it in whose hand?

Running
Looking back
Running
Looking back
Running
Tottering
Hopping on a red-hot plate
Hopping looking back at what's behind

Mother!
You
Have collapsed flat on your back
On the road of fire
Raising up
Your face like a summer orange
Your right arm aloft
Like the withered branch of a summer-orange tree
Thrusting out your right hand
Stretching out your right hand
Out towards me

Me
I am hopping on a red-hot plate
A single red nail hopping
Hopping but already
Running
Hopping running
Running hopping

On the road of fire

Mother!
You
flat on your back
Like a summer-orange your face
Burning
Like the withered branch of a summer-orange tree your right hand
Burning
Now
Burning

The road of fire
Running
Can't stop running
Hopping running hopping
Beneath my running feet
Before my running feet
Scorching
Burning
Those running are running
Running hopping
Darting between those running
Overtaking those running
Runners are running

Running
Mother!
Running
Mother!
Road burning
Mother!

---

*The title refers to the night Soh Sakon's mother died in an incendiary bombing raid carried out over Tokyo on 25 May 1945 by 564 B-29 Superfortresses, the largest bombing assault ever carried out over Tokyo in the course of World War II.

HUMMINGBIRDS

We sat and watched
the hummingbirds at sunset

wrens had taken up
the house to nest

life was abundant
I planted herbs for you

rosemary parsley thyme
the flight was somehow

grieved to return was
hard no snow to speak of

only noise and too close
proximity

such noise after
the silence of evergreens

deer foraging
quietly between

and hummingbirds
whizzing like bullets

past our heads
almost countless

to the sugar feeder
those small machines

still mine ten thousand
miles away

APOCALYPTIC SUNSETS AT THE ДАЧА

Бабушка always went to bed early,
the box TV graining our silhouettes
on the sunken couch. I always thought
it could devour us whole, my cousin and me,
dark blue depths the same colour
as the night sky, speckled with white bits of lint.

Our eyes glowed with midnight rapture,
anticipating the mad dash outside
to brush our teeth over the mouldy plastic sink,
the summer day turned frigid and watchful.
Бабушка's cats slinking somewhere in the bush
the only sounds in her yard.

The rest of the world may as well have ceased
to exist. No cars or lights or neighbourly
voices. No barking dogs or crooning birds
or even the swaying of branches. Earlier,
a false alarm in the form of a storm warning;
council had already cut our power nonetheless.

We stayed up waiting out the brownout,
anticipating reruns of dubbed American movies
about mermaids and figure skaters. Back here,
my parents and I are always out too late
in the woods. The ground darkens
before the sky does. Dirt cakes my tattered shoes,

the same ones I wore when I roamed
sprawling meadows behind the дача
while my mother secretly organised
my citizenship. Did she think
I'd have said no? Did she think I wasn't
old enough at seventeen

to make my own decisions and know
what they mean? She may have been right
because I don't feel any more like a person
now than I did then. I don't feel more Russian
than I did on those nights laying half-awake

on Бабушка's blue couch, a breath away
from the forest, a dark cloud of apocalypse.
In the shelter of those woods, I was
my truest self. With my cousin by my side,
laughing unbridled until my ribs ached.
I was a child, then.

from **SILENCE IS OK**

I am in a ground floor turret the shape of a mood
held together by a dream that can't withstand my focus
  a nice idea to let in some temperature
 the sultriest playlist
sonic flex repeating a while
where are my ideals?
  all these stacked books represent such need
  my particular difficulty
 I can't admit
I'm free not thwarted

  use it or lose it
the libido is surfeit self-generating
habits are force-fields
  what I mean feels concussive
invective as in
imagined

    *

  here's what puts me to sleep
wriggling out of a bad feeling
another gaffe
 it's fear leading the posse
while a leaf unfurls

this is not an Ave
 I've wandered down before
 look out for me
biting my thumb
asking the same of you
Seen
 a dewy cosmopolitan mastiff
the fresh sign of my thinking
optimistic
I don't
 believe so

    *

if I may include my analysis of pure pleasure
 the body
jogging itself

 the car braking between two
trunks of certain distance

   *

I won't soften today
sowing lettuces
visualising my intentions
I'll have to drawl
if it's air not jugular
where is my ribbon
  always some new deal
seeding …
no response for ages

 all those boys?
 in the wrong
 missing an enzyme
 between the cut and paste

   *

that last part is an indictment
walking after daylight
 traffic rising
like a natural feat
location sensation emotional
 So
I demand to be remade
much warmer than I feel!

   *

sharpening my insidious streak
I meet the medium of the page
written in the hand
 of someone like who speaks here

I look out the window
  agelessly
at seeds propped up by their network
of aquamarine plastics
what I'm giving off
is a feeling not a lecture

writing after that
the manner in me subsides

    *

I take my books to bed with me
I pause I catch a breath
  if we are all animals
how lovely
we cry and want to participate
raising shells to our ears
  the tide speaks pure verbiage
sentences that twist
  one-too-many times

    *

don't backflip now
I'm aware I'm not everybody's
  sound
a vulnerable Flake
it's a strategy but it's no way
  to live

I'm tired of carrying around
such an old-fashioned symptom

THE WHITE HORSE

Wanting so much to learn the classifier for poems
about classifiers, I sought out the wisest teacher;
she handed me a black ceramic pot the spout of which
now daily flowers into smog. I needed more:
the Second Way, she said, was a devotion
to propaganda, perhaps a shot at life on the petulant seas.
But the white stallion with its cloud-draped hooves
& silk-thread mane never turned up for collection.
Nor did my Vietnamese mother who had forsaken me on this,
the eve of the lunar new year. Only thus did I learn
that I am from Australia, that I am an Australian
– an ungracious people, I have read, whose marketable skills
include pressing the eject button on history,
that constellation of CD players in the sky.
& so I was: a spinning disc who spoke often
but recorded nothing, not even the tiniest byte.
I had a thirst that strong white liquor couldn't quench.
I was always hungry, especially at night.
For hours I would channel surf a TV that had been turned
upside down & emptied of intelligible signs.
Once, I woke up parched in the first gradient of day
when the morning meal is not yet served;
the eggs, alive & cackling. In empty
rooms throughout the hotel, lacy curtains heaved out
– absolute silence – snatching at grey, smoke-laden air.

FOR THE TWILIGHT HOUR WHICH PASSES

Heavy with last leaves, silver birch
chime in late afternoon bluster. Listen,
it's Summer's last trick as it turns its back on us
rides the ocean currents away;
sunlight borne in from the west
freeze-frames its white sails so they hang
like a pendant on the reclining horizon's throat.

There are no heroes left on the beach
just a knotted rope of blue-bottles
which slackens across the sand
barbed tails trailed out in the rising water's edge.

The lick of swell: we hear it from this distant
birch-lined street, even as rush hour traffic
hums along the arterial road like one long
unravelling dream. To pass this time
when nothing more is possible, we trace
internal geographies for ourselves. The wind
blows in from the *paysage*, buffets the study's
wooden blinds, playfully swings
the lounge room's Chinese paper lamp shade
in tethered arcs above our heads.

As dusk finally drops, as a crow drops
swiftly off a building, movement abates, a sentence
cut short. & for the twilight hour which passes,
the vibration of other lives – their viscous
sorrow, their mordant joy – distends into a perfect
stillness, liqueur of aniseed & salt. The high tide
reclaims its lost cargo: blue specks drifting
into blue-black flotsam, greater streams,
abstractions some distance off the coast.

RED CREEK

Leaving the car on the roadside
and vaulting a rusty gate –

it's eighty years or more
since the farmstead was abandoned

to the elements' slow campaign.
Summer smoke-haze –

stubble cropped by sheep,
on the hill-line a drystone wall.

Half a roll of film,
the ruin anchoring the foreground –

low walls, a doorframe silhouetted
against the noonday sky.

Along the slope an old diggings
and a chimney rooted in the paddock

like a carious, yellowing tooth.

CARTE BLANCHE

i.

what to make of this blank space :
this white noise : to score it :
to give it some characters : to put
black marks against it : the way
these lines run on : stack up :
stretch out : ranks of peasants
shaking their rakes & forks :
agitated : jostling : is there
a weak point in the defences :
a vulnerability in the lines : some
place we might break through :
into spaciousness : into nothing :

ii.

whiteness on whiteness : to pluck
a white rabbit from a white hat :
in the middle of a snowstorm : or
a ptarmigan in its winter morph :
the whites of your eyes shining :
the cat who got the cream : your
mouth opening on a porcelain
smile : & death with a moon in
her pocket : song of the pack-ice :
jingle of the permafrost : an army
camouflaged in bedsheets :
gnawing ice : marching out to
battle : under a flag of abject white :

SUB-PRIME ALONG THE MISSISSIPPI

Alone on the road between levee and bayou
we're ushered on a grey breath.
Houses sit quietly, clutching dry land,
facing an eternal slope.

Dogs, quick to bristle in unfenced yards
track our passage with steady gaze;
it's as though, not from around here,
we've walked into the wrong bar.

Perhaps this is a weekday, in winter.

In dreams, some say, the house is the self.
In this American dream the self is boarded up;
the ceiling's caved in. Moss pries every plank
and slat. The light is out.

Sweet haven: to rot in a coocoon.
    Complicity of house and self not well,
and played. The river thunders on, unseen.
    Take the copper wires, and the sink.

THE CATHEDRAL
Translated by Takako Lento

The cathedral's spire
Flared up in crimson
And collapsed

As if …
It was trying to prove
The mutability of this world
Betting on its own existence

But
Nothing has been lost
What is truly durable
Stays outside our world

Indifferent to busily repeated
Additions and subtractions
Day after day
The soul is at peace

In the invisible cathedral
Built outside time

KEEP WRITING
Translated by William I. Elliott & Kazuo Kawamura

A train is running on a single track along the gorge.
Monkeys have already abandoned evolution.
The sounds of the wonderful old bagpipes have receded,
and I have nothing to do but keep writing poems.

A mother is on the sofa giving the breast to her baby,
and on a corner at midday there is suddenly an explosion.
On a new morning noisy opinions are heard
while a boy is sullenly reading a comic strip.

What does it matter?
The official history parades nothing but heroes
and only scratchy old photos remain;
while I have nothing to do but keep writing poems.

We can't find the ending
because we don't know the beginning.
Day after day we continue to doubt believing
and only the sky spreads out widely, like salvation.

Living with garbage that has nowhere to go,
forgetting missing people's names,
pawning what ought to be offered at the altar,
unable to tell a nanometer from a light-year,

being asked the pros and cons without time to breathe,
dodging back and forth between wavering feelings,
seeking a bliss deeper than meaning,
I have nothing to do but keep writing poems.

GOOD-BYE
Translated by William I. Elliott & Kazuo Kawamura

Good-bye, my liver.
Good-bye, also, kidneys and pancreas.
I'm about to die now,
but since there's no one here
I pass all of you my farewell.

You've worked for me for a very long time.
Now, though, you're free.
You can go anywhere you like.
Having bid you all good-bye, I can also be utterly free.
I'm all soul – no make-up.

My heart, I've troubled you, making you pound and throb.
My brain, I've made you think of altogether senseless things.
My eyes, my ears, mouth, and penis, too, I've inflicted pain on you.
All of you – please! Don't hold it against me!
It's because of all of you that I have been myself.

Nevertheless the future without you is bright.
Since I have no more self-regret,
I will willingly forget myself,
dissolve into mud and vanish into the sky.
I'll become friends with wordless things.

ORDINARY PEOPLE
Translated by Takako Lento

Sumiko
walks through town with a liberated rhythm
she stops as she pleases
she examines the goods on the shelves with care, and
does not buy any of them, which pleases her

Atsushi
picks up the wine list
he crosses his legs under the table
he considers himself unremarkable, and
he receives a gift of a fossilized fern

Yukihiko
picks up a puppy
he throws away a collection of literature
he forgets himself admiring an ancient tree, and
listens for noises

Anri
is comparing this and that
looks into the sky at the railroad crossing
she drinks a glass of lukewarm soda water, and
steps on ants

Ordinary people are attentive
to others who are not like them
lest these feel inferior
which, they are also vaguely aware,
is hypocrisy

Kohji
breeds jellyfish in his bedroom
he sends out gift cards as mid-year greetings
he counts his med tablets
he buys a new pillow

Kimiyo
nonchalantly goes on a short trip
is moved by distant vistas
eats a simple lunch
walks into a stream barefoot

Shin'ichiro
goes to the National Museum
brushes past a princess
a train crosses the steel bridge
birds are perched on a dead tree

Harumi
hates competition
she is watching the sunset glow from the rooftop
holding a bagel in her hand
somewhere in the distance a rainbow appears

Kenzo
buys bet slips at the off-track betting window
he trades jokes with
young city councilors
he watches a re-run of a drama

Mr Anonymous
tirelessly sends in submissions
he buys a book of poems for his daughter
he applies eye drops
he avoids health checkups

Minako
is suspicious of beauty
she blanches leafy vegetables
she looks for Aldebaran in the night sky
she focuses her attention on cervical vertebrae

Amane
unabashedly reminisces
he practices the mandolin
he signs a paper form
he secretly prays

Arisu
makes a bamboo dragonfly
she drinks chai on the terrace
she emails her younger brother
she cries once in a while

Fumio
cannot see the end
Hayao
does not see the end, either
no progress is made in decommissioning the nuclear reactor

Kohtaro
commits a harmless crime
ditto with Osamu
his passport expired yesterday
bees gather around acacia flowers

Chin
thinks he will not die
he writes satirical haiku
he washes his briefs
he sighs

The graveyard for generations of a family and
the graveyard for those with no descendants
sit adjacent to the zoo
people are voluble today, too, but
elephants are reticent

Jojo
believes this is the beginning
he walks out favoring his injured leg
to look for pieces of wood
to hang a small shelf on the wall of his shed

I have
a muscle cramp in my leg
I consult a thesaurus
I eat pickles, and
write this

POSTSCRIPT
Translated by Robert Nery

(Italicised expressions are in English in the original)

Adios
        America
                w/all
your star-spangled ideas
You made us idiots
No match for you
                CRAZY MAN
CRAZY   CRAZY
                I get so furious
everytimeIthink
            we were put through school
and come out silly
Because we're out of touch (chua chua)
Because we're out of touch (chua chua)
It's all a matter of pointofview
& ar poinuview's squinty
                CHICKEN-EYED
    Just *think of all the*
finals and seminars for which highbrows
were burned
          jusso we won't be
it's embarrassing after all before our
YANK classmates they're so many
after all   my God   a dimwit
D'ya know I wrote a heaven-knows-how-many-page-paper on
Ver-gi-di-ma-rium by Marston was it or *Hall?*
& for 8125
        I got eyestrain from peering
at the Rules of St. Benedict on *microfilm*
so I could evaluate if *Madame Ovaltine* was a flirt or *saint?*
What kind of sonofabitch iskolarsip [Tagalog accent] apparently was that?
Better to scratch your balls / You might come

I mean it's absoluuuutely ridiculous
              endeavuh so precieuse to stuff
yu'head w/ headnotes footnotes marginalnotes
until your soul's one big fat variorumedition
of pure unmitigated pedantic nonsense

B* E* C* A* U* S* E*

there's nothing nothing
                        you know
                                    about your own
THIRST   SLEEPINESS   FEAR   LUST   FARTS

then you godda nerve to think
you're shuperiah to the [Tagalog accent] *restadapipol*
juz becuz you speak English w/ the twang of angels
from Tallahasee Salinas or Catona
Hey you're really a son of the fleas on the dog of St. Roch!
People who don't know English have intelligence too if you don't mind
Reason has its own structure
derived from inference and a *higher form of algebra*
dealing in estimation and conjecture
I mean to say
              St James
              St Eliot
              St Warren&Wellek
              St Shakespeare&Johnson
              St Donne&Miltonberle
              St Thomasite
              St PeaceCorpse

      When you rise from your various graves
      From a Stateside sophistication save us

CHORUS OF THE STREET
Translated by Robert Nery

You must change your way of life
The shape of a sky the colour of a drain
Make new the wind, the leaning of the moon
Must change Fuck everything has to OK

Shake off the stink of rotten sardine
On the pot-stand pour the lard that has soured
The salt that has scoured the plate cast away
It must change, make new the order of things

Abolish the cardboard wall, make fans
Strip the iron of age-old piss and rust
Torch the fleas on the bamboo bed, the ants
Arise from the mudpond of your debts

The foot needs leather to cover it
A fan in the heat is needed, and flannel to lie on
The brain needs somewhere to shelter
The life needs rice and food to go with it

The fate of the voiceless must be different
On the banks of the canal build anew
Our names must be divested
Of their uniform of grimy rags

My God don't be certain all you kids you old men,
Things will stay the same, Christ, all
Your mother-fucking life, just wait and see
When night comes, when day breaks

A RECORD YEAR FOR RAINFALL

Sometimes we need ambiguity to make things work.
In the early 1700s, an astronomer in Sweden developed
a scale where water boils at a degree of 0 and freezes
at 100. Eventually this representation will be reversed.
That this uncertainty will refer both to a finite point
and the interval between temperatures. In 1985,
the BBC would start using degree Celsius in its forecasts.

I almost caught a bird sleeping on top of the wall.
That was around the same time in the 1980s.
I still feel its heart in my hands.

No thing off in the distance that cannot
flare into presence, someone said once.
We must somersault into it,
that presence. Live in it.

In a recent story, a man converts to the Celsius
and stands in the streets pointing to a confusion,
starts an argument and a conflagration.
The moral: we are all visitors.

Certain words make us fall silent
because they harken to an older conscience,
a raw awe. Like the word *fire*.

Dark harbinger, host of this quiet, I suppose it is right
to mourn with you. We are a magnificence
bound to die out.

All points must be rounded off. Everywhere is water
or what smashes into water. We have to be kind,
become a house made of wood.

ATTACHMENTS

I love how things attach themselves
to other things – the rocks sitting stubbornly
beneath a river, the beards of moss.

I choose a color and it connotes sadness.
But how long must the symbols remain true? Blue
is blue, not lonely. After a time, one gives up

reading the sky for shadows, even rain.
There is no promise, only a possibility.
A moment moves to another, and still it feels

the same. Like old letters in boxes.
Or how the rain, at times, falls invisibly.
Finally, the things we love demand more love,

as if we have always been capable of it. Yet
I can only offer belief, mirages that mean water,
long travels leading somewhere. I am reading

old letters, trying to make something
of what's been said. It might be raining;
some pages are unreadable.

TASMAN SONNET

A, green, the tint of absinthe dripping through
A wad of lawn clippings – E,
Chartreuse, colour that only monks can see –
I, cloudy violet with sparkling points of blue
Or paler, the fresh paint sheen of a car –
When new, easy to buy – old, hard to sell.
O, orange, the sound of a tolling bell
Travelling over town and factory, very far –

U, under clear water, underwear –
Your flight spoiled by lots of crying babies
.ough all of Europe is reflected in your eyes.
You think you hear, as you brush your hair,
The howling of a kennel full of hounds with rabies.
A rainbow as you land; then a career surprise.

CROWDED HOUR

A, Tangerine, lipstick 1962, daring
Hint of flame and wild behaviour,
E, lemon, sour surprise and rave, your
Suspicious self out for a welcome airing
On Fifth Avenue, your midday saviour
A transparent fellow spirit, the caring
Caress of a martini smoothly preparing
Your conscience to accept a second favour –

Bartender's gift; of one half-empty bottle –
I, corn silk hair, love at full throttle,
O, blue shadows, delicate gloom
Pricked with traffic lights in the evening air –
U, olive green of underwater hair –
Scuba, the acronym, in the crowded room.

THE HOTEL

I am at the island airport
waiting for the shuttle bus.
The shuttle bus will take me
to the hotel,
where I will live
that life, usually unspent.

I will meet the man who
has always occupied that life, unspent.
Not even on the fringes of my Tuesdays
to Thursday,
he does not exist when I am outside
of this island.

When the shuttle bus arrives
I take my luggage and load it on myself.
The driver looks offended,
like I have shamed him lifting my own load.

It is a different driver – I have not seen
him before.
I could ask him if he was new, where he was from.
But I am here for only 17 hours,
I must conserve my energy for the man
waiting for me at the hotel.

I drag my luggage across the pavement
and steer straight towards the entrance.
When I get to the glass doors, they do
not open for me.

I step closer. Still,
they remain shut.
I panic for a moment, thinking
it might be someone from my spent life,
interrupting my life here –
stopping me from crossing over.

But then I remember, that with these doors,
if you stand too close – they will not open for you.
I am always arriving at these doors and
forgetting they will only open for you if you
are at a safe, clean distance.
I am not good at keeping distance.

What I need to learn, what I am always learning,
over and over again,
is that some things will only open for you when
you are far away, yet close enough –
the shock of this re-discovery,
always a new phenomenon.

I take a step back, and the doors open for me.
I walk to the elevators,
where I will fly ten storeys high.
I will walk into the hotel room and
meet the man of my unspent life,
then, I will return to my normal storyline,
the one of the wife and bearer.

CRIMINAL INTENT

I was using my finger
to shoot bullets
at the stars
when one of them
fell from the sky

the next day
a black crater
where the dog park had been
and the obliterated remains
of a cat or two

when no one was around
I dropped
the offending weapon
in the deepest part
of the river

I am confident
the fish will destroy any trace
of the evidence
just as soon as they have finished
dining on my eyes

THE DEPARTMENT STORE OF EVERYTHING

while everyone else went home laden
I was left
empty-handed

unable to find
a pair of size nine beds
for my sleepwalking feet

the ensemble mattress kind
with a knick-knack shelf bedhead
and built-in light

like I'd had as a child
when I knew how to sleep
undisturbed

by mistakes I'd made during the day
or the week
or thirty years ago

I'll be back tomorrow
my voucher
is non-transferable

ON NOT GIVING AN ACCOUNT OF ONESELF

I am telling a story without prehistory.
Pocket rockets of pink, the go to temple
of gum blossom. Rays of morning sun
settling on the driver's side. By way of warning,
I would say I am impressionable.
My inability to assume greater agency
offset by being 'on board'
with the attention economy. Pieces of intelligence
fall as spring rain, once more unadvertised.
Breathing in damp grass simply
the work of motor neurones. Be still,
    be mine, my Dixie flatline.
Road trip vs the mechanical commute:
is this shorthand outworn for the human path?
Paddocks disguise a different kind of sprawl, post
the muteness of winter. A Euclidean delisting.
Might I take a wrong turn
at the object of temptation? Mud-spatter
on the high chrome gloss. The tattoo of razor girl
making out with the console cowboy
just visible through the rearview mirror.
If I took a peptide for every disappointment,
would I fail to replicate Love's ideation?
The foreign object unlodged, made mobile
in my basic needs bloodstream. How to drive
beyond an escape clause of origins,
of having started out all wrong, a problem
to be found somewhere, hand in glove,
with my infantile life. Outsider bespoke:
That was then, this is now.

              Listening to bird song. Again.

CONCEPT CREEP

It's not a reflection on you, climbing the stairs to happiness (what flights?),
trying to leaving at the door the low-tops of ambivalent love.
Whose turn is it to shock absorb the ordinary once more?
Emotional labour slides in restaged or rug-stuck rites.
To hum at the grind, clock-work engine in grandstand traffic.
Assumed face of calm as compassion congests in the blood.
Red-corner smiles of encouragement, Marie-Antoinette comfort
for the over-casualised, infantilised offspring
of the stalled revolution. What goes unnoticed spreads to home,
a tirade of to-do chores, outward well-wishing and the warmth
of small invite returns. Evening vigils to dispel
uncertain terrors. Ghost-shopping for milk, discount
packets of human kindness pantried for the winter.
It's not just about taking a leaf out of the book, more out of the gutter.
Roof over our heads, heads-up, everyone's fine.
Maintenance is what holds the body or households together
Sticky-tape rebuilds, take-home projects of heart work.
The hold-all basket of 'working families' still guillotine
feminism's parallel lives and the cause beautiful.

LISTED LAND USES OF MOONEE PONDS CREEK

1. Saltwater marshes, the floodplain fallow. Eels, waterfowl, yam daisy, tuber and gum resin. Red river gums to shade and story.

2. A new entry as Batman's Lagoon. Outspoken against sign-over, Moonee Moonee burns down the gaol (so they name a creek after him). Escapes with Tullamareena, that once 'steady industrious man' turned recalcitrant.

3. Waste waters, an also-ran of the Gold Rush. Repurposed canal for barges to carry coal into Train Town.

4. Tipped in, tipping point. The poor fossick landfill and build Depression shelter. Huts over or under-hanging, scarcely there, insistent. The hard-up urban spread.

5. Post-war mission: a Melbourne-wide slum abolition. Concrete houses with concrete fences, perhaps a concrete dog or two. Prefab experimental design, modernist functionalism. Streetscapes built to the system, a predicate of still life.

6. Harvesting stormwater, the creek is reconstructed as a concrete drain. Moonee and Tullamareena are homaged in a Bon Scott meets Albion music video. The seventies drive past thick with the exhaust fumes of Forbes' 'Tropothesia.'

7. Not the clean exit strategy envisaged: Moran's killer crosses the footbridge to a waiting car.

8. A Melways buffer zone between Citylink and the burbs in boom. Newspaper reads: 'Yarra's most abused tributary.' Cyclists skirt graffiti or spot public art on their daily route to the CBD.

9. Relatively unmodified rows constitute valuable 'historic character' and heritage overlays are briefly imposed. Pre-selection makes for a developer's last promise: prime private dwellings, with 10% additional dwellings for the disadvantaged.

10. Medium to high confidence in estimated value. Easy access to airport and upward mobility. Nearby wetlands and a flourishing café culture. Eradication of Boxthorn, Prickly Pear, and Ash. Decked out capital gains, silver gum *savoir faire*.

FINDING HOME

I hear the call
        from out across the   floodplains
        that separate a   home   unknown
                      from here,
too sacred to answer
with this soft song
        in foreign tongue,
                slimy, slick as it leaves my lips

and only in blood   have I been
        to this place,   unseen,
    so if home is northward,
                then red dust falls
            between walls of golden sedge
    to carry us from   here
                          to there,

        where sheets of paper bark
                peel back to reveal a story
                        bright against the opal
        trunk of tree.

        so I carry saltbush
                between cheek and gum and thumb
        to lick the words
from my mouth
        before calling back
                to Country's song.

IMAGO

I am at a loss of how to say this
        without uttering the same words
                              over and over –
without going on about reverence   for riverbeds
      and the wrens   and oyster shells
           and eternal lomandra blades
                  that grow from between the moss rocks
                        and the poetry
                                that is precipitation
     and the daylight
                and dew,
without stringing the words
          here
               and there,
tiring   the meaning   of their beauty –
but my mother used to pull over on the side of the road
to pick caterpillar weed
             to bring back to us,
                  her children.

I will draw short an image of the lifecycle,
of how we laid chins in palms
             in front of those green branches
that made   a home   of any freshly washed-out jar
to watch bodies silk along the stems
      to those great swollen seed orbs
          that hung weightless upon the branch
                  as if some religious decoration
and of how cocoon-making always occurred
     when no one was around
and we'd return   from beneath the star-blanket
      or the creek   or school
      greeted by those small bright green cocoons
           painted story-like with iridescent gold dots

before going some shade of earth
        and wither to look almost close enough   to death
that I would think *this one mightn't make it*,
        then, despite having planned which flowers I'd place around it
                          as I lay it down to rest,

the cocoon would become transparent
and we would get to know the orange of the wings
    from outside.

       I remember   finding the creature   unfurling
as the new butterfly body clung onto the self
    from which it had emerged,
        and I think about this   constantly,
    about becoming and being a mother,
      familiar,
about returning to   and turning to   nature
    and those cycles within it
      as teacher,
        to lean upon   the trunk
            and sit upon   the dune
        to share the load
     of growth
  and giving.

from SINCE FUKUSHIMA
Translated by Judy Halebsky & Takahashi Ayako

PEBBLES OF POETRY
Part 1: March 16, 2011, 4:23 am – March 17, 2011, 12:24 am

Such a huge catastrophe. I was staying at an evacuation center but I've now pulled myself together and returned home to work. Thank you for worrying about me and encouraging me, everyone.
March 16, 2011. 4:23 a.m.

Today, it is six days since the earthquake. My way of thinking has completely changed.
March 16, 2011. 4:29 a.m.

I finally got to a place where all I could do was cry. My plan now is to write poetry in a wild frenzy.
March 16, 2011. 4:30 a.m.

Radiation is falling. It is a quiet night.
March 16, 2011. 4:30 a.m.

//

This catastrophe is so painful, and for what?
March 16, 2011. 4:31 a.m.

Whatever meaning we can find in all this might come out in the aftermath. If so, what is the meaning of aftermath? Does this mean anything at all?
March 16, 2011. 4:33 a.m.

What does this catastrophe want to teach us? If there's nothing to learn from this, what should I believe in?
March 16, 2011. 4:34 a.m.

Radiation is falling. A quiet quiet night.
March 16, 2011. 4:35 a.m.

//

I was taught, "wash your hands before coming in the house." But there isn't any water for us to use.
MARCH 16, 2011. 4:37 A.M.

Relief supplies haven't arrived in Minamisōma. I've heard that the delivery people don't want to enter the town. Please save Minamisōma.
MARCH 16, 2011. 4:40 A.M.

For you, where do you call home? I'll never abandon this place. It's everything to me.
MARCH 16, 2011. 4:44 A.M.

I'm worried about my family's health. They say that this amount of radiation won't affect us very soon. Is "not very soon" the opposite of "soon"?
MARCH 16, 2011. 4:53 A.M.

//

Well, yes, there's clearly a border between fact and meaning. Some say that they are opposites.
MARCH 16, 2011. 5:32 A.M.

On a hot summer day, I like to go to a beach on the Minami-sanriku coast. On that exact spot, the day before yesterday, a thousand bodies washed ashore.
MARCH 16, 2011. 5:34 A.M.

In a quiet moment, when I try to understand the meaning of this catastrophe, when I try to see it clearly there's nothing, it's meaningless, something close to darkness, that's all.
MARCH 16, 2011. 10:43 P.M.

Just now, while writing, I heard a rumbling underground. Felt the tremors. I held my breath, kneeled down, and scowled at everything swinging. My life or this tragedy. In the radiation, in the rain, no one but me.
MARCH 16, 2011. 10:46 P.M.

//

Do you love someone? If it's possible that everything we have can be lost in an instant, then all we need to do is to find some other way not to be robbed by the world.
MARCH 16, 2011. 10:52 P.M.

The world has repeated both its birth and death, sustained by some celestial spirit which defies all meaning.
MARCH 16, 2011. 10:54 P.M.

My favorite high school gym is being used as a morgue for unidentified bodies. The high school nearby, too.
MARCH 16, 2011. 10:56 P.M.

I asked my mother and father to evacuate but they couldn't stand to leave their home. "You should go," they said to me. I choose them.
MARCH 16, 2011. 11:10 P.M.

//

My wife and son have already evacuated. My son calls me. As a father, do I have to decide?
MARCH 16, 2011. 11:11 P.M.

More and more people are evacuating from this town. I know it's hard to leave. You can do it.
MARCH 16, 2011. 11:39 P.M.

Having evacuated to a safe place, the young man, twenty-something, is looking at the monitor and crying, "Don't give up on our dear Minamisōma," he says. What's the sense of things in your hometown? Our hometown now, overcome with suffering, faces distorted by tears.
MARCH 16, 2011. 11:48 P.M.

Again, big tremors. The aftershocks we were expecting finally came. I was wondering if I should shelter under the stairs or just open the front door. Outside, in the rain, radiation is falling.
MARCH 16, 2011. 11:50 P.M.

//

The gas is on empty. Out of water, out of food, out of my mind. Alone in this apartment.
MARCH 16, 2011. 11:53 P.M.

A long rolling tremor. Let's place our bets, do you win or do I win? This time I lost but next time, I'll come out fighting.
MARCH 16, 2011. 11:54 P.M.

Until now, we carried on the daily lives of generation after generation, we searched for happiness, sincerity, I think.
MARCH 16, 2011. 11:56 P.M.

My elderly neighbor gave me a box full of onions. He grew them himself. Sadly, I'm not much for onions. The box sits in the entryway, I stare at it silently. A few days ago, I was living my ordinary life.
MARCH 16, 2011. 11:59 P.M.

//

12 am. Six days since the disaster. A sick joke! Six days since and for five days, I've wanted this all to be fixed.
MARCH 17, 2011. 12:03 A.M.

In the kitchen. Cleaning up scattered, broken dishes. Aching as I put them one by one into the garbage. Me and the kitchen and the world.
MARCH 17, 2011. 12:05 A.M.

No night no dawn.
MARCH 17, 2011. 12:24 A.M.

LECTURES OF THE ALONE

The skin still unpunctured during
the fire of Gippsland, something
is in this ether, states the school
of commentated epistles.
That cabin, those glistening spiders, quartz tracks
of unknown merchants, a dozen classes
stamp the earth below the unseen Australian Alps,
looking like
lectures of the alone
on feeble legs,
obnubilated with
the dewy absence
of that unseen lark,
that unseen albatross, and
that unseen malleefowl.
She touches the hand I scratch to uncover
the blue provenance, yet in collaboration
we still discover nought but the palm.
She reads it but dozes sibilant moments from
the resolution, 'breath in the air, nightingale-something,'
and she says it's me that laughs asleep.

CHRISTMAS TIME

I was getting flogged
At the age of eight
A strap across the legs
For not standing straight

Where was my mummy?
Where was my mob?
Through teary eyes
I would sob

Footsteps echoing down the hall
The smell of carbolic permeates the air
All the other girls
Would stop and stare

The sound of the bell ringing
Tells us that it's dinner time
Have to go wash our hands and faces
Then stand up in line

And now before we eat
We must say Grace
We must also mind our manners
Before taking our place

The sound of cutlery on chipped enamel plates
The smell of boiled cabbage hangs in the air
I pretend
That I'm not there

We will be singing
Christmas Carols tonight
Don't we look all shiny and pretty?
In our frilly dresses of white

On the back of this big old truck
We would stand and sing
Christmas Carols to the white folks only
The melting candles, little black hands be sting

Then on the ground we would be a scrambling

The old white biddies chucking us lollies
Thought the sight of us children
Quite funny and quite jolly

That night I try
Try to sleep in my bed
Thoughts of mummy
Go through my head

Through the window
I see the moon
Mummy will come get me
She will be here soon

Christmas morning, with no wrapping
And with no name
Each and every one of our gifts
Were perfectly the same

I had never had such a gift
The smell of something new
Over time, the longer I was there
Thoughts of mummy were becoming just a few

My only comfort was my precious doll
Which was exactly the same as all the others
All here like me
All here without our Mothers

FREE

The sea breeze
Is free

The feeling of sand under my bare feet
Is free

The sound of the waves as they crash to shore
Is free

The air that I breathe
Is free

The warmth of the sun
Is free

The sound of the birds chirping
Is free

The feeling of cool grass under my bare feet
Is free

The sight of the blue sky
Is free

The sight of the white clouds
Is free

The aroma of a freshly baked damper
Is free

A recollection of a nice dream when I awake
Is free

FAMILY TALE
for Evelyn

In time's blackness, before you or I were born,
your grandfather pulling your grandmother
back from a tropical cyclone, that sucked for hours at
the shattered louvre window
of a little green tiled fifth floor bathroom.
Wind squealing like a stuck god
he tried to make heavy her body with his own scrawny frame.
Outside, their rusty red car leaping up in the wind's hands.

In his white, high-ceilinged living room, my father's hands
tremble over red wine, potatoes and roast lamb as he tells this story
half to me, half to my mother's ghost.
Is she listening?
She never spoke of it.
My father and I gather up the scraps of our feast
and disappear into our silences,
into the night where truth swims against truth.

My parents hold each other long and hard
through warring particles of air.
Something creates, and recreates them.
The bare, skinny, shiny thing of mere life.

SIE T-INS 88

1885 his bowling was the match the original paintings in the

flowerless flowers
the towers call beehives calls
8 mins ago the score sounded

called wasps / bees from the kitchen ah
fetched a t-spoon ah was meant to fetch sugar (already had a t-spoon)

returning to the (bee) ah placed
the sugar at m feet and hunted around for a t-spoon ah already had

bradmans private obsessions like putting on (white) sneakers before tennis
or blue bags (high) in the laundry

counting overs w moonsnail shells
w dukes w kings ceausescu w mao
long live beeradman (bot) the breads outside the capital

breads the city breads bees works the city
city works to produce bread / bees – as is the case with all cities ultimately producing bradman

s high on something or something folds n the light changes (trees)
whatre all these trees everywhere doing here

(people) work
choc ices

8
8
people (trees)re a habit cultivate em warsawllve groves of orange trees bucharest trees
above ground trees below ground shanghai underground mumbai flyovers trees
   (bradman) in the root system n pylonsre leaves photographs of beeradman
   (trees) above ground flashlight feeds
(trees) below ground in suriname people fold n the light changes (whatre all
   these people everywhere doing here?) in brogo

trees (watertanks)re trees trees watertanks those useless watertanks,
take the log way.

THE TWELVE

CHOREOGRAPHY: GEORGE BALANCHINE, YOUNG BALLET, 1923
Accompaniment: Chanting of Aleksandr Blok's *The Twelve* and other poems by chorus of fifty voices

Today I am a genius.
Aleksandr Blok

two days: upheaval and topsy-turvy all around those dark streets the blizzard blinds all such terrible noise *crack-crack-crack* fragments flying as Red Guards patrol the city raid the school with their bayonets close it down, up rise in a blazing Bolshevik dawn: violence, hunger, disease *a joyous, if disorderly carnival*. Georges, fourteen, sews saddles, runs messages, plays piano in a movie theatre. Long days for scraps of food to sate the gnawing worm; the children check daily for signs of reopening. Luna- charsky, new minister of fine arts and per- suasive in his gest- ures that opera and ballet could be propaganda machines: *Rat-a-tat-tat!* Suddenly every- thing is free! But there isn't anything to take. Hunger hollows Gnawing ground the flat one no fuel to slip - hunting for wood; the theatre! Georges & friends present another *Evenings*; he assembles folk dances with difficult rhythm, performed fluid in the round against the chant- ing of the people, vulgar lines, over- lapping at the heels of critics and con- servatives a kind of heresy aimed square at the wind- ow, to the west.

ELEGY

Choreography: George Balanchine, Young Ballet, 1923/24
Music: Sergei Rachmaninoff (*Élégie* for piano)

Goodbye St. Petersburg, goodbye Petrograd,
goodbye hungry days and freezing nights.
Farewell mother, father, sister, brother –
it will never be the same; we sail for Stettin
as Soviet Dancers, our steamship full
of bread; we gorge and fill our pockets.
Farewell youth, we won't return. Berlin
burns bright in the indigo evening; clean
comfort and whipped cream, traffic and so
many trees. We dance and eat in Rhineland
resorts, leave a mild mark, keep moving.
Choura is a barrel, a piano. Kola likes to nap
and is unimpressed by river-side castles.
Dmitriev can do only so much with those
sawn-off fingers – he overestimates his value;
we will run out of money, Tamara will sell
her hair. London, Paris; we nibble cheese, play
dominoes for distraction. Then out of no-
where: *téléphone pour Monsieur George*;
C'est en bas.

BROADWAY

'It should be Balanchine, of course.' And so they hired him.
ALEXANDRA DANILOVA

Successes and flops. On Broadway, George learns the basic challenge is to keep people awake. He embraces the concentrated genius of Fred Astaire, fiddles with the pleasures of a hoedown. Dramatic invention in footwork starts the motors on a shoulder-based airplane and he says *Tha-at's right. Bam!* He earns huge sums and spends them all on fine champagne, grand pianos, and poker nights with the theatre crowd. Nothing but climaxes. At rehearsal, it's a different story: that travelling mind swivels satire through the Big Easy, taps out an upstate New York Comedy of Errors. Later, Griegian landscapes chart a solo fantasy of compositional brilliance. Remember Peter's surprisingly long dream sequence? It sparked a vogue, those irresistible clichés of excitement and terror. Always, the dream is to get the girl. Or to be wealthy and successful. Or to develop a national music? Or … something about marital discord. I do know that George, like Little Joe, is trapped at the crossroads of Heaven and Hell and needs to rise from a slumberous sentiment, to stop being a fool in love, serenading her window, unshaven, and instead to pool his resources: twenty tooth-brushes threaded on a string and a foolproof affirmation to Zorina: *You see, will be okay. How can you fail?*

Ziegfeld Follies of 1936
On Your Toes (1936)
Babes in Arms (1937)
I Married an Angel (1938)
The Boys from Syracuse (1938)
Great Lady (1938)
Keep Off the Grass (1940)
Louisiana Purchase (1940)
Cabin in the Sky (1940)
The Lady Comes Across (1942)
Rosalinda (1942)
The Merry Widow (1943)
What's Up? (1943)
Dream with Music (1944)
Song of Norway (1944)
Mr. Strauss Goes to Boston (1945)
The Chocolate Soldier (1947)
Where's Charley? (1948)
Courtin' Time (1951)
House of Flowers (1954)

And later:

> 'Hello, I'm an angel.'
> 'Hello, I'm a potato.'
> 'Hello, Salvador? I've had another nightmare.'

HOLLYWOOD

Choreographs dances for: The Goldwyn Follies (1938)—On Your Toes (1939)—I Was an Adventuress (1940)—Star Spangled Rhythm (1942)—Follow the Boys (1944)

He took the train with Kolya to blue skies and balmy air, settled in a house on North Fairfax. Fine weather for fresh produce and tooling around. Good for the lungs. George U-turns on wonderful legs, Percheron ankles. He is slicing lemons for his tea. COME EARLY, he writes to Brigitta. WE'LL HAVE FUN. It mostly involves the hip, and liberal spoonfuls of caviar with black bread and sweet butter. Another directive: toss the vodka in one go. She has high cheekbones and a generous mouth and he cannot control his proposals. *JEG ELSKER DIG.* George loves Zorina loves Orson Welles but somewhere along the line she says *okay*. He could fantasise anything. Corned beef and cabbage. An upturned wrist. A Swiss watch. He is mystical Prince Myshkin with a montage of dance shots. Goldwyn, his angry arm bouncing in a sling, is not pleased with all the moving around; his jutting jaw shapes *dancing wonderful, but too much ballet*. Back and forth. There are no miners in Harrisburg. George doesn't mind peeling onions while she dances on the lily pond. In the end, a glycerine teardrop rolls down her cheek. The sun and the moon caress the floor. He solves perspective. Laundry disappears. He loves ironing. He loves her grey eyes in the compact, singing *Ochi chornye, Vera Barnova. Vera Barnova je t'adore*. Love is blinded by klieg lights and the occasional shower of untoasted cornflakes. Love is poured on through Cartier trinkets and magical raincoats and a custom-built house on Long Island painted pink. Wingolf feels the wind through his fur. Was that tempo right? I tried to restrain myself. The conductor has no real control, of course. Without need for another cigarette case, car or country house, he commissions a score from Hindemith. Zorina eats coffee rings in secret, with more raisins than there are in the flag. When a fire breaks out, his heart. George is lying on a steamer, returning from Cuba, and talking about potatoes. The psychiatrist says nothing, just clutches his own belly as he listens.

from JANUARY

You go to bed wondering what will be happening
in the morning, and in the morning you wake up
and over there in another country crowds
have stormed the national seat of government –
predictable, predicted, business of politics
interrupted, lawmakers in gas masks, who knew
they had gas masks under their seats? Some
people think of everything. Is this
a coup, or an outrageous intrusion on what
passes for normal, or a few idiots getting
out of hand for an hour or two – didn't
they have barbed wire round the White House,
where's barbed wire when you need it? I have
myself been involved in the cutting of barbed wire
but that was us not them. How last night
there was a man dressed as a swamp creature
and a placard saying drain the swamp, clever,
and someone with a staffy on a lead. There were
women in red coats and boots in the cold
weather, bit of a party, you could have walked
safely through that crowd. What I am failing
to say. How your body changes in an angry crowd,
your heart rate, your voice, your actions
no longer entirely your own, channelling
the energy of thousands. Us not them.
In these times better to be working at putting
people back together, assessing injuries
in a wounded human, blood pressure, heart rate,
level and location of pain. Identifying
and preventing bleeding by whatever means.
We've been watching reality TV. How a team
of people work together in Emergency: calm,
skilful, each one with a task, using their words.

*

Who wants a saviour? What is needed is
the one who refuses any system, the one
who'll pick up any useful system, examine
it, use it for a while in a new way then walk
off leaving something unexpected behind –
a new product of that system made extremely well
and abandoned: placed alongside others made in other
ways, as the products of other systems. Orphan
products, no loyalty. The frameworks are there
to be used for what they can do. Don't come here
for lifelong commitment to anything except
the moment of perception which destabilises
everything else. And bring that into
everyday life: to each human being
that crosses your path, say. Otherwise known
as charm: intense attention, dangling
a little joke in mid-air, unheralded and no
label, no punch line – to see who gets it
and one joke leads to another, or allowing
surprising behaviour to occupy your mind
apropos of nothing. It is as though you left
behind small explosions on very long fuses –
to have been seen clearly and with the same
curiosity you might bring to a work
of literature, say, a poem that will always
escape analysis, resist all intellectual
attempts at definition, continue to be
serenely itself while generations of scholars
apply their best powers of historical analysis,
their explorations of its ambiguities, the other poems
on which it draws, the social conditions that
allowed it to be written. You chose to remain
astonished by the original thing, black type
on a yellowed page slightly tattered at the edges.

THE MANGO TREE IN KHAI VILLAGE

If this branch should break my brother and I will be washed, and as there is only cold water to be washed with neither of us are leaving. We don't want to go to prayers at the local mosque but it is getting dark, and my father is now calling us down. He tells us that the whole village is talking about his wretched children. He doesn't mean it because he is laughing – our insolence reminds him of his childhood when he would skip Friday's prayers and sit instead on the walls of an old forte and eat over-ripened mangoes. Many people stop by on their way to the mosque, they try to persuade us down, some joke with my father and tell him two little jinns are sitting in the tree and must be placated because they have hidden the two children. The other kids ask their parents if they can join us in the tree but no one in the village is as agile as us. We squeal in delight because this afternoon we have become famous for our disobedience. We are little children and understand that disobedience and the tree hold more delights than any eternity in paradise can bring.

A LITTLE HISTORY OF THE WORLD

Beside the bed is a fluoro lamp. Outside, the street is filled with army tanks and police cars and people protesting. Under the lamp a woman examines the length of her nails and, satisfied that they are short enough, leans across the bed to pick up some European fashion magazines. Several other women are on their way to give birth in this room: they groan a little and pace up and down the ward. Sometime after seven there is no more running water. It is high summer and there has been no rain for many months. But still the women give birth and babies are born wet and pink. At midnight the tanks are still roaming but the protesters on the street have dispersed. One woman, after a labour of only eight hours, gives birth to her first child. There is still no running water and she longs to wash herself but is told she cannot leave because of the curfew outside. She insists and leaves with her newborn daughter.

THE EMPTY ROOM

the moment you decide you want
the room loses its innocence

the moment you decide you want
or the want decides on you
the moment you want
on the white walls
a future shapes
like shadow puppets
fingers of hope and fear

the moment you want
the easy awareness
of the empty room
is gone.

CHARTER SONNET
Translated by Ao Wang and Eleanor Goodman

to be read with electric guitar and mini Marshall amp; also known as 'Charter 09'

I demand the abolition of the subway's automatic ticket checking system, continuing manual ticket checking until the world ends;
I demand that the whole of mankind have the right to vote for the president of the United States;
I demand an increase in birth control, the encouragement of same-sex marriage, and the imposition of fines on heterosexual marriage;
I demand the revision of constitutional law, deleting all semicolons and series commas;
I demand a ban on mahjong and KTV, the detainment of those who walk their dogs at 5 a.m., and the holding of regular poetry readings in police stations;
I demand the abolition of art and of changing one's life;
I demand that salt be rubbed in wounds, that wine be poisoned, that a cold ass be pasted on every hot face;
I demand the erection of two amps the size of buildings and the holding of unattended noise concerts in scenic locales;
I demand that you and I be together, never to be separated;
I demand memories, black flowers, stars that shine above bicycles and turn into kids' faces;
I demand the release of imprisoned words like 'your mother's cunt' and 'Jiang Zemin';
I demand demands, forbidden forbiddenments, annulled annulments, sneering sneers, and the tying up of the guy who's always pouring out his heart;
I demand loud singing at the gates of hell and sleeping on the bus;
I demand that we maintain quiet ...

THE LAST STARLIT SKY AT FIFTY-FIVE
Translated by Naikan Tao & Tony Prince

For Linlin

A pitch-black seagull entrusts the helm to those little hands
Steadily   the night sky hangs on a mast in the park
Another year has been erased   stars twinkle between the wings
He's not here yet   only the smell of green grass peers into the distance

When waiting for another birth   he heard you ask
'Who is it?'   The sea roses stretch up their tender fingers
And the sea too is like a daughter that rhymes with his blood
How much time and space there is in this question   and how difficult it is
   to answer

Love is also an echo   crystal   spilt from the corolla of night
The tranquillity of this place lets the light held in a deep embrace illuminate it
Clear rippling water (linlin) is also his name   picked up by the seagull's beak

At the zero instant   the daughter's phosphorescent feathers
Lead him to a birth   using all of the world's beauty
He feels within his body a tiny heart beating

STARBOARD OF MY WIFE
Translated by Takako Lento

In my dream at daybreak
My wife is a boat
Lying on tidal flats

Her tilted and immobile shadow
Falls on wet sand
Stroking the dry wooden skin of her starboard
I prowl around like a dog

I sneak out of the dream and go downstairs
Taking a pee, I look up at the bathroom window
Snow is falling steadily, and flakes
Get caught in a spider's web, shivering

In the kitchen I see a child I've never seen before
The child says, in a detached voice
'I am not scared of dying. Because everyone comes and goes
When the tide ebbs.'

Then he walks into the bright light beyond the glass door,
Leaving wet footprints on the floor

ON THE LAKE
Translated by Takako Lento

On the edge of the water
I walk with my wife
The lake is large, so large as to look like the sea
The other shore is dimly blurred

Our two kids are swimming about
Like dogs
Then they run toward us kicking up sands
The rest is silent

Once in a while a boat goes out to the open water
Someone sitting in it keeps his eyes on us
The oarsman will not look at us

She and I got here from far away
But this is the dead end of our journey
All we have to do is to walk on along the water's edge

I wonder if it clears up so
We can see the other shore
Standing in the water up to her hips
She, smiling, beckons me

In the numbing cold we taste
The faint warmth of our mouths
Countless trivial taboos and
Only one fathomless forgiveness

Limpid droplets slide down each single strand of hair

From the edge of the cloud
The sun comes in and goes out

from LOVE BREATHES HARD

After short struggles against ergonomics
I cook breakfast
And we gain one more day because of storytelling

//

All we had to offer then was our obedience
And they accepted it
Although – in truth – it was never enough
To build a comfortable story around childhood
Or about the nothingness of our modified resumes
Our cities were dusty
Our cities were massacre ready:
They taught the shapes of our bodies to all kind of sociologists
And transformed our obedience into mild ridiculousness
Then secured our existence from staff changes in the middle of the shift
We drank alcohol safely
It was worth the blood …

//

These cracks
Filled with carbohydrates
In the dust of the bourgeoisie
And its imposed death
We are created equals
Within an illigitimate love
And the different shapes of fear

//

We have to accept the naiveté of the world
As money moves us from one parking lot to the next
While chanthing useless words to mark our involvement
In these deaths – now I look at a long street daily
And it doesn't help to think of the division of labor
As the starting point of this elaborate mess

It is admirable to do things other than touching one another
I'm talking here about language – its fumes, and miniature arguments
This is a salute to desire as the mad ones linger behind
We ride the cart – socialist and business strategists
To go there – a clean suburb of Facebook posts

//

It is an ending world, so no one writes us
In the middle of it I mentioned you
And now I am Northbound –
So I cry when seeing things melting –
In this great melting pot

//

Feeding our devices electricity
They produce imaginary lovers
Tonight I will hitchhike
Through many doorknobs
Maybe all of this hinges on Aristotle
We still have to find an exit strategy
Through these black and white squares

//

Poets should save us from happiness
Out in the lab they are studying natives
I vowed to stay cryptic
As I am keeping you posted
About the joys of life
And as I touch you
As if we exist
I will keep looking in design books
For shapes that help the world
Drag its infinity behind

Death happens to others
Meanwhile we fly everywhere
To praise its effect
Like a nomad
I am sure
Cairo is an abstraction
Despite its existence
To amuse us about tears

//

The gestures of the world
Are enough
Everything here is exact
As if God never left
And as if there is time

//

A paper cut
While exploring humanity
The world is salt
But poetry helps
As the city disavows me
With fragility
And precision

HISTORY OF DAFFODILS, A BOOK SERIES
Translated by Ming Di

The aftershocks continue in Fukushima. Half the earth
is gradually pulled into the whirlpool of truth,
More unrest is heard, political or not, far and near,
the fate of the foam clinging to its lip.
But these yellow daffodils remain absolutely still.
Or they move like the spines of dinosaurs, dynamically static.
They choose to bloom in April, like us
when we sometimes try to race against time.
(Very often you like to race against me, no need to shy away.)
They look like green onions but are not for eating –
they are prepared to be looked at, for us to see
the different us. Sometimes I go much further
than loneliness, I see you spitting into a void,
making me aware of what these daffodils have done
to this history of ours. Their history is not a history
of planting or distributor distributed, but a series of records
of what's blossomed on you as we saw at a certain time.
They've brought us from behind the history to the front of time.
I will not apologize for not being enthusiastic enough.
I will only apologize for not being subtle enough.
Let's make it here in Kanazawa then. Here
a remoteness allows me to walk into their history.
Let it be, this deep way.
Let it be, the way we look at their movement.
They see us from where we have never been,
the same way that we, in their absence, see their spirit
tranquil in the enormous shadows of reality.

IN THE OLD DAYS
Translated by Naikan Tao & Tony Prince

In the old days I could write you
A letter only this way   and I didn't know
Where we were likely to meet
Face to face again

Nowadays   I fill your inbox
With a galaxy   of keyed-in Chinese characters
They stand up   and run off in search of you
They may end up somewhere in the sky
But I don't care about that at all

In the old days   the blue mountains led a dignified existence
Even when the green rivers fell drunk at their feet
We bowed once to each other with cupped hands
And knew we would certainly meet again one day

Now   you fly to and fro in the skies
Where stars rush about everywhere
To run into you is to run into a sore spot
Like innumerable patches they try to block out
A blue screen   but they are by no means hysterical

In the old days   how many poems people had to write
Before they could become Daoist adepts from Mt. Lao passing through walls
Through the air   and even through a cup of bamboo-leaf wine
To seize hold of you   although more often than not
They would be sprawled on the ground   with battered and bleeding heads
Now   you're dialling a mobile phone number
It transmits thousands of odours
And is filled with the scent of someone's body
When one part trembles the whole world trembles

In the old days   we really didn't do things this way
We only rode our horses side by side for dozens of miles
When my earrings jingled   you smiled at me
And when I lowered my head   we rode on for dozens of miles further

海の巻
海之卷
바다
THE ROLE OF 'SEA'

from **TRILINGUAL RENSHI**

Yotsumoto Yasuhiro
Ming Di
Kim Hyesoon
Tanikawa Shuntarō

Translated by the authors and
Don Mee Choi

1.   (康/Yasuhiro)

サンマルコ広場の波止場でスーツケースを引き摺る
三人の娘たち　黒い髪　黒い眼
どこから来たのかな？　黙っていたなら
三羽の鴎みたいに区別がつかない
ねえ、声を聴かせて

三个女孩提着行李箱来到圣马尔谷广场
码头上，三个女孩黑发，黑眼睛
不知来自哪里
她们沉默，像三只海鸥，分不清谁是谁
嘿，让我们听一听你们的声音

검은 머리 검은 눈 세 소녀가
산 마르코 광장의 부두에서 가방을 끌고 가고 있다
이 소녀들은 어디에서 왔을까
서로를 분간하기 힘든 갈매기들처럼 아무 말도 없이
헤이, 너희들 목소리를 들려줘봐

Three girls with black hair and black eyes
carrying suitcases on the pier of Piazza San Marco.
I wonder where they come from? Silent, they are
like three seagulls, hard to tell one from the others.
Hey, let us hear your voices!

2.   (迪/Mindy)

爱丽尔哼起一支曲，海风把声音传送
至咖啡馆，一位白发男子抬头
看见三姐妹，白杨树影在他眼中晃动

아리엘은 작게 노래 흥얼거리고 바다 바람은 노래의 선율을 나른다
카페에선 백발 노인이 그 세 자매를 바라보고 있는데
포플라나무 그림자가 그의 눈에 어린다

エリアルが口ずさんだ鼻歌を、海風がカフェへと
運んでゆく、すると白髪のおじいさんがふと顔をあげて
三人の姉妹を見つめる、その瞳に白樺の木の影が映っている

Ariel hums a little song, the sea wind carries her tune
to a cafe, where a white-haired man looks up
and sees the three sisters, poplar shadows in his eyes

3.   (惠/Hyesoon)

갈매기도 잠든 깜깜한 밤
아이들이 슈트케이스를 끌고 떠나고 있다
모두 잠들었는데 아이들만 깨어 있다
서쪽 부두에서 아무도 몰래 배가 출항하고 있다
일 년 째 같은 아이들, 같은 배, 같은 구름, 같은 하늘이 떠나고 있다.

鴎も眠る、丑三つ時
子供たちは立ち去ってゆく、スーツケースをがらがら引いて
誰もかもが眠っている　子供たちのほかは
西向きの岸壁から、人知れずフェリーが出てゆく
この一年というもの、同じ子らの出発、同じフェリー、同じ雲、同じ空。

漆黑的夜晚，海鸥在睡眠
孩子们在离开，拖着行李箱
所有人都睡着了，除了孩子们
西边码头，轮渡悄悄离开。一年了
同一只船，孩子们离开，如同样的云，离开同样的天。

A pitch-dark night, even the seagulls are asleep
The children are leaving, dragging along their suitcases
Everyone's asleep except for the children
From the western pier, a ferry departs secretly
For a year, same departing children, same ferry, same clouds, same sky.

4.   (俊/Shuntarō)

前世で乗っていたノアの方舟
今は海底で朽ち果てている
結局地球の外には出られなかったのだ

우리가 전생에 승선했던 노아의 방주는
이제 심해의 바닥에서 썩고 있다
결국, 지구 밖으로는 나갈 수 없다

前世乘过的诺亚方舟
此刻腐烂在海底
毕竟，它走不出地球

The Noah's Ark we boarded in our previous lives
now lies rotten on the ocean floor.
After all, it couldn't get out of the earth ...

5.   (康/Yasuhiro)

詩を書くたびに僕は月へ昇り
静かの底に座ってわが故郷を見下ろす
その冷たい青に秘められた血の赤に目を凝らして
海が僕らを互いから分け隔て
海が僕らを互いに結び付けている

每次写诗我都会爬到月亮上
坐在静谧深处，俯瞰我的家乡
试图看清那隐藏在冷蓝中，血一样的红色
同一个海连接我们
同一个海分离我们

나는 시를 쓸 때마다 달에 올라가
고요의 바닥에 앉아 우리 집을 내려다보면서
차가운 파랑에서 피의 붉음을 보려고 애쓰고 있다
바다는 우리를 서로 서로 나누어 놓지만
그 바다는 또 우리 서로 서로를 이어준다

Each time I write a poem I climb up to the moon, and sit
at the bottom of Tranquility, looking down on my home,
trying to see the red of blood hidden in that cold blue.
It's the sea that separates us from each other,
the same sea that connects us to each other.

6.   (迪/Mindy)

今晚，天空是黯淡的船舱——
我们醒着，眼睛是一只只新月
驶向彼此共和的太阳

오늘밤 하늘은 깜깜한 선실이다——
우리는 깨어 있고, 우리의 눈동자 각각은 새로 뜨는 달이다
태양 공화국으로 노 저어가는

今宵、空は昏い船室——
私たちは目覚めている、それぞれに新月の眼を見開いて
太陽を共に和するために船出してゆく

Tonight the sky is a dark cabin –
we're awake, our eyes each a new moon
sailing to a Sun Republic

7.   (惠/Hyesoon)

열리지 않는 문을 긁어대던 손톱들처럼 벚꽃잎이 지고 있다
먼 산 위의 태양이 흠뻑 젖어 무거워지고 있다
바다로 만든 사람이 창문 밖에 서 있다
새벽 안개처럼 얇아 안을 수 없는 사람이다

電線に止まった小鳥たちの翼が濡れている
桜の花の散りゆくさまは開かずの扉を引っかく指爪のようだ
遠い山並みの上に、びしょびしょの太陽がのしかかる
窓の外には海で出来た誰かが佇んでいるけれど
その人を抱きしめることはできない、朝靄みたいにすかすかなので

鸟栖息在电线上，羽翼潮湿
樱花落下，像指甲抓打那打不开的门
远处山上，湿透的太阳沉重
一个水做的人站在窗外
无法支撑，枯瘦如早晨的雾

Perched on a power line, the birds' wings are wet
Cherry blossoms fall like fingernails scratching a door that won't open
Above the faraway mountain, the drenched sun becomes heavy
Someone made of ocean stands outside the window
That someone can't be held, so thin like the morning fog

8.   (俊/Shuntarō)

プランクトンはどんなソフトでデザインされたのだろう
顕微鏡から目を離していっとき放心している少年は
神という言葉を使わずに世界を夢想したいのだ

什么样的软件设计出这些浮游生物？
小男孩纳闷了片刻，目光离开显微镜
他想不用"上帝"这个词来幻想世界

무슨 소프트웨어 앱이 플랑크톤을 디자인했을까
현미경에서 눈을 뗀 소년이 잠시 마음을 내려놓는다
소년은 '신'이란 단어를 쓰지 않고도 세상을 꿈 꾸고 싶다

What kind of software application designed plankton?
The boy lets his mind wander for a moment, his eyes away from the microscope.
He wants to dream about the world without using the word 'God'.

9.   (迪/Mindy)

文字穿行——如影子。苹果高歌——
iPhone,iPad,iPod,iTunes——掀动海底。
飓风，海啸。然后是寂静，寂静。爱丽儿姐妹们
将语言藏于金色的珊瑚中。深水之上，
文字再次启程，如鱼群，穿行于有咸味的海浪与海草。

문자는 여행한다——그림자처럼, 애플은 노래한다——
iPhone,iPad,iPod,iTunes——바다를 휘저으며.
허리케인과 쓰나미, 그 다음 모두 정적, 정적. 아리엘의 자매들은
금빛 산호 속에서 그들의 말을 지켜냈다. 심해를 넘어,
문자들은 다시 여행한다, 물고기처럼, 소금바다와 해초를 넘어.

文字は旅する——影のように。林檎は歌う——
iPhone,iPad,iPod,iTunes——海原を振るわせながら。
台風そして津波。それからみんなしーんと静まりかえる。エリアル姉妹が
自分たちのお喋りを金の珊瑚に仕舞いこむ。深い水のなかでは、
ふたたび文字が旅に出る、魚のように、しょっぱい波と海藻を潜り抜けて。

Words travel – as shadows. Apples sing –
iPhone, iPad, iPod, iTunes – stir the oceans.
Hurricanes and tsunamis. Then all is quiet, quiet. Ariel sisters
guard their speeches in golden corals. Above the deep water,
words travel again, as fishes, over the salty waves and seaweed.

10.   (康/Yasuhiro)

窓から見下ろす北斎の駿河湾
高度3万フィートで頬張る海苔巻き
あの人の頬伝う涙の味を思い出している心の雲……

眺望窗外，下面是北斋画过的骏河湾
三万米高处，满嘴海苔寿司
她心中的云铭记着面颊上滚落的泪水味道……

창문으로 호쿠사이의 스루가만을 내려다본다
3만 피트 높이에서 입안 가득 노리마끼를 입에 물고
그녀의 뺨위로 굴러떨어지던 눈물의 맛을 마음에 피는 구름으로 떠올리면서

Hokusai's Suruga Bay gazed upon through the window.
Mouthful of Norimaki at an altitude of 30,000 feet.
Clouds in the heart remember the taste of the tears rolling down on her cheeks …

11.   (俊/Shuntarō)

巨大な氷惑星と呼ばれている海王星の
表面温度は摂氏マイナス２１８度
中心温度は５０００度
体温３６度５分の私は地球上の室温２１度の部屋で
４月７日１２時１６分現在 生存中で〜す

거대한 얼음 행성으로 분류되는 해왕성
구름의 표면 온도는 섭씨 영하 218도
중심온도 5천도
지구 행성의 상온 21도에 방에 머무는 나의 체온은 36.5도,
4월 7일 12시 16분 지나 나는 아직 살아 있다(^^) !

海王星被称为"巨冰"行星
在云端，表面温度摄氏零下218
中心温度5000
而在地球上21度常温的房间里，我体温36.5
4月7日12点16分，还活着~

The temperature of Neptune, categorized as 'ice giant', is
minus 218 degrees Celsius at its cloud tops, and
5,000 degrees at its center. I, with a body temperature of 36.5 degrees,
in a 21-degree room on planet Earth,
as of 16 minutes past 12 o'clock on the 7th of April, am still alive (^^)!

12.   (惠/Hyesoon)

나는 책상 위에 해왕성에서 온 바다를 쏟는다
한 편의 시가 끝나자 우주 정거장의 불은 꺼졌다
나는 의자에 앉아 그 깜깜한 바닷물 속에 두 손을 담근다

海王星から海を掬って机の上に注ぐ
私たちの詩の最初の一巻が終わったら、宇宙の駅の灯りが消えた
私は椅子に座り両手を真っ黒な海原に浸す

我把海王星的海，泼在书桌上
我们的第一卷诗结束，灯光熄落在宇宙站台
我坐在椅子上，双手蘸进漆黑的海洋

I pour Neptune's sea on top of my desk
When our first round of poems is finished, the lights go out at the cosmos station
I sit in my chair and dip my hands into the pitch-black ocean

ACKNOWLEDGEMENTS

We respectfully acknowledge the Bidjigal, Birrabirragal, Gadigal and Wangal people as the First Peoples and Traditional Custodians of the unceded lands and waterways on which Vagabond Press is located and where we work and live. We pay our respects to Indigenous Elders past and present and recognise their continuous connection to Country.

Vagabond Press started thanks to Professor Elizabeth Webby (1942-2023). Without Elizabeth's encouragement, wry humour and confidence over decades, neither the press nor this anthology would exist today. This anthology was made in tribute to her constant and decades-long generosity, friendship, and kindness.

Thanks to Elizabeth Allen, Kay Orchison, Jane Gibian, Chris Edwards, and Mel Swann for work, time and friendship shared. Thank you to every writer, translator and artist who has trusted us with their work. Especial thanks to: Mabel Lee, Dot Porter, Jann Harry, Martin Harrison, Noel Rowe, Vivian Smith, Lucy Holt, Bella Li, John Kinsella, Peter Boyle, Pam Brown, David Malouf, Natalie Harkin, Emilie Collyer, Yasuhiro Yotsumoto, Uncle Ken Canning, Shuntarō Tanikawa, Bill Elliott, Tomaž Šalamun, Jeffrey Angles, Takako Lento, Ali Cobby Eckermann, Kate Lilley, Ann Vickery, Felicity Plunkett, Judy Beveridge, Philip Mead, Don Mee Choi, Jake Levine, Kevin Hart, Jessica Wilkinson, and Louise Carter; to literary executors Andrea Goldsmith, William and Sarah Gregerson, Paul Carter, Jess Brooks, Reina Loyola and Lyn Tranter; and also, Helen Brennan, Sarah Tran, Ivor Indyk, Bernadette Brennan and Justin Gleeson. Thanks to the many guest editors who brought in new voices through the Rare Objects, the deciBels, the Asia Pacific and Americas series: Pam Brown, Elizabeth Allen, Chris Edwards, Mookie Katigbak-Lacuesta, Carlomar Arcangel Daoana, Michelle Cahill, Dimitra Harvey, Leith Morton, Robert Nery, Ouyang Yu, Nguyên Tiên Hoàng, Violet Cho, David Gilbert, Mabel Lee, Nguyên Hưng Quốc, Nhã Thuyên, Dinah Roma, Jeffrey Angles, Jake Levine, Peter Boyle, Mario Licón Cabrera; our printers Chaiporn Intuvisankul, Teerasin Khampan, Kunakorn Intuvisankul, and Greg Barnes; our bookshop partners, especially David Gaunt and Robert Mackell at Gleebooks for stocking us when we started publishing zines, and more recently Mark Rubbo and Readings, Robert Albazi at Paperback Books, and Kym Bagley; Mothership Studios in Sydney and the Alderman in Melbourne. Thanks to the Helen Anne Bell Poetry Bequest, Create NSW, and universities, groups and individuals who have supported specific titles. Thanks to everyone who has contributed to our GoFundMe and annual 'Just One Book' campaigns, and to the generous souls who have kicked in as patrons via the Buy Me A Coffee platform: Adam Aitken, Elizabeth Allen, Pam Brown, Dan Disney, Johanna Featherstone, Adam Gall, Jo Gardiner, Flynn Howard, Kate Lilley, Rosie Maia, Elaine Minor, Pij Olijynk, Thom Sullivan, The Other Beauty, Susan Thomas, Rory Waldron-Glyde, Michael Witts. The ongoing and occassional patronage makes a huge difference to the viability of the press.

In recent years, we would not have survived without the support of Creative Australia and its predecessor the Australia Council for the Arts. From recovering after the February 2019 flood in Marrickville then through Covid and now to this anthology,

Creative Australia's support has been and remains essential to our existence. Creative Australia has helped us give new writers their first opportunity, give established writers space to explore their imaginative reach, and the press the chance to keep doing what we love doing: making books and creating space for new writing and writers to emerge. We're grateful to the assessors who have viewed our projects positively, including this anthology, and the tireless and responsive staff at Creative Australia who make funding and so our books possible. Thanks to the team at Auspicious Arts, especially Christiane Carr and Pip O'Brien, for managing the grants, and to the very many generous writers who have written letters of support for applications over the years, including the grant that made this anthology possible. Finally thank you to every single reader who has bought one of our books and kept us publishing.

Please note, we have aimed to keep the transcription and order of names according to contributors' wishes. In some instances, there are variations across the text in line with this. Differences in spelling (including between American English, Commonwealth English and other variants), use of capitals, use of single or double quotation marks, spaced en-dashes and unspaced em-dashes among other variations at times also vary across the text.

All of the poems in this anthology were published in Vagabond Press collections previously. Some of the poems were previously published or subsequently republished in collections by other publishers: Anselm Berrigan, *Pregrets* (2014) and in *Pregrets* (Black Square Editions, 2021); Judith Beveridge, *Peregrine* (2001) and in *Sun Music: New and Selected Poems* (Giramondo, 2018); Javant Biarujia, *Anagoge of Fire* (2004) and in *Pointcounterpoint: New and selected poems* (Salt Publishing, 2007); Judith Bishop, *Aftermarks* (2012) and in *Interval* by Judith Bishop © 2018 University of Queensland Press; Bonny Cassidy, *Said to be Standing* (2010); Justin Clemens, *Me'n'Me Trumpet* (2011) and in *A Foul Wind* (Hunter, 2022); Ali Cobby Eckermann 'First Time' and 'Intervention Pay Back' first published in *little bit long time* (Picaro Press, 2009; Ginniderra Press, 2017) and in *Love Dreaming & other poems* (2012); Rodrigo Dela Peña, Jr., *Hymnal* (2017) and in *Aria and Trumpet Flourish* (Math Paper Press, 2018); Kate Fagan, *return to a new physics* (2000) and in *The Long Moment* (Salt Publishing, 2002); Michael Farrell, *Living at the Z* (2000) amd in *ode ode* (Salt, 2002); Liam Ferney, *Career* (2011) and in *Boom* (Grand Parade Poets, 2013); Jane Gibian, *tidemark* (2013) and *long shadows* (2005) and in *Ardent* (Giramondo, 2007) and *Beneath the Tree Line* (2021); Keri Glastonbury, *super-regional* (2001) and in *grit salute* (Papertiger, 2012); Martin Harrison, *Music: Prose and Poems* (2015) and in *Wild Bees: New and Selected Poems* (UWAP, 2008); J.S.Harry, *Sun Shadow, Moon Shadow* (2000) and *Public Private* (2013) and in *J.S. Harry: New and Selected Poems*, edited by Nicolette Stasko (Giramondo, 2021); Kevin Hart, *Nineteen Songs* (1999) and *Wild Track: New and Selected Poems*, Kevn Hart © 2015 by the University of Notre Dame. Reprinted by permission of Notre Dame Press; Jill Jones in *Fold Unfold* (2005) and 'Erosions' in *The Beautiful Anxiety* (Puncher and Wattmann, 2014); S.K.Kelen, *Don Juan Variations* (2012) and in *A Happening in Hades* (Puncher & Wattmann, 2020); Jennifer Maiden, *The Violence of Waiting* (2013) and *Drones and Phantoms* (Giramondo, 2014) and *Selected Poems:1967-2018* by Jennifer Maiden (Quemar Press, 2018); David Malouf, *Sky News* (2013) and in *Earth Hour* by David Malouf © 2014 University of Queensland Press; Greg McLaren, *Everything Falls In* (2002) and in *The Kurri Kurri Book of the Dead* (Puncher & Wattmann, 2007); Peter Minter, *morning, hyphen* (2000) and in *morning, hyphen* (Equipage, 2003); Dorothy Porter, *Comets* (2001) and *Poems January-August 2004* (2004) and in *The Bee Hut* (Black Inc., 2009) and also in *The Best 100 Poems of Dorothy Porter* (Black Inc., 2013). Courtesy and copyright of the Estate of Dorothy Porter; Jaya Savige, *Maze Bright* (2014) and in *Change Machine* by Jaya Savige © 2020 University of Queensland Press; Vivian Smith, *Late News* (2000) and in *Traveller's Tale and other poems* (Picaro Press, June 2011); Nicolette Stasko, *Under Rats* (2012) and in *Glass Cathedrals: New and Selected Poems* (Salt Publishing, 2006); Ed Wright, *The Empty Room* (2002) and in *When Sky Becomes the Space Inside Your Head* (Puncher & Wattmann, 2012).

CONTRIBUTORS

Adam Aitken was born in London and lives in Sydney. He spent his early childhood in Thailand and Malaysia. *Archipelago* (2018) was shortlisted for the Kenneth Slessor Prize for Poetry and the Prime Minister's Literary Awards. He received the Patrick White Award in 2021. He teaches Creative Writing. His latest book is *Revenants* (2022).

Ali Alizadeh is a senior lecturer in literary studies at Monash University and a creative writer. His books include *Towards the End* (2020), *The Last Days of Jeanne d'Arc* (2017), *Transactions* (2013), *Ashes in the Air* (2011), *Iran, My Grandfather* (2010), and a philosophical study, titled *Marx and Art* (2019).

Elizabeth Allen writes in Sydney. The author of two full-length collections of poetry, *Body Language* (2012) and *Present* (2017), Elizabeth won the Dame Leonie Kramer Prize in 2001 and the Anne Elder Award in 2012.

Rio Alma is the nom de plume of Virgilio Almario. A university academic and public servant, born in 1944 to a rural family, Almario is a prolific author and his indispensable work looms large in Tagalog poetry produced since the sixties. His collection of criticism *Ang Makata sa Panahon ng Makina* (The Poet in the Age of Machines) is one of the founding works of modernist criticism in Tagalog.

Jeffrey Angles is a poet, translator, and professor of Japanese literature at Western Michigan University. His collection of original Japanese-language poetry won the Yomiuri Prize for Literature, a rare honor accorded only a few non-native speakers since the award began in 1949. He has translated dozens of translations of Japan's most important modern authors and poets into English. Among his recent translations is Orikuchi Shinobu's modernist classic, *The Book of the Dead* (2017) (which won two awards for translation, the Miyoshi Prize and the MLA's Scaglione Prize) and the feminist writer Itō Hiromi's long novel *The Thorn-Puller* (2022).

Takako Arai (1966 —) was born into a silk-weaving family in Kiryū city, Gunma Prefecture, on the outskirts of Tokyo. She began publishing poems in the early 1990s, and since 1998 has run a poetry magazine, *Mi'Te*, which features poems, translations and poetry criticism. Her second poetry collection, *Tamashii Dansu* (*Soul Dance*) published in 2007, received the Oguma Hideo Poetry Prize. Her collection, *Betto to Shokki* (*Beds and Looms*), published in 2013, explores the lives of female textile workers, applying a unique language inspired by the local dialect of Kiryū.

Avianti Armand is a writer, architect, and curator. She writes short stories, architectural criticism, literary essays, and poetry. Her poetry collection *Women Whose Names Were Erased* was published by Vagabond in 2018. In recent years, she has been writing illustrated children's stories on the theme of empathy.

Louis Armand's poetry collections include *Infantilisms* (2023), *Monument* (with John Kinsella, 2020), *East Broadway Rundown* (2015), *Indirect Objects* (2014), *Letters from Ausland* (2011) and *Strange Attractors* (2003). He is the author of the libretto *A House for Hanne Darboven* (2021) and novels including *The Garden* (2020), *The Combinations* (2016), *Abacus* (2015) and *Clair Obscur* (2011). His critical works include *Videology* (2015), *The Organ-Grinder's Monkey: Culture after the Avantgarde* (2013) and *Incendiary Devices* (1993). He is formerly an editor of the international arts journal VLAK & co-directs the Prague Microfestival.

Tamryn Bennett is a poet, artist and Artistic Director of Red Room Poetry. Her books include *phosphene* (2016) and *icaros* (2023). She is the editor of *Líneas en tierra / Lines in land* a bilingual collection of Mexican poetry. She has been poet-in-residence at Royal Botanic Gardens, Kew (UK), El Centro de Cultura (MX), Bundanon Trust and Wollongong Art Gallery (AU) with poetic works and exhibitions held in Australia and overseas.

Lawrence Bernabe lives in Quezon City and has published his poems in several independent presses and university journals, including High Chair Philippines and The Kritika Kultura Anthology of New Philippine Writing in English. *Transitoria* (2017) was his first collection.

Anselm Berrigan is a poet, teacher, and editor living in New York City, where he grew up. His newest book of poems is *Don't Forget to Love Me* (Wave Books).

Judith Beveridge is the author of seven previous collections of poetry, most recently *Sun Music: New and Selected Poems*, which won the 2019 Prime Minister's Prize for Poetry. She taught poetry at the University of Sydney from 2003-2018 and was poetry editor of *Meanjin* 2005-2016. She is a recipient of the Philip Hodgins Memorial Medal and the Christopher Brennan Award for lifetime achievement. Her latest collection is *Tintinnabulum* (2024).

Javant Biarujia is the author of eight books of poetry, including *Calques* and *Low/Life*, the latter written while on Asialink's writer-in-residence in Indonesia in 1998. In 2007, he published pointcounterpoint: *New and selected poems 1983-2008*. *Spelter to Pewter* (2016) is his latest book.

Angelita Biscotti has written for *Sydney Review of Books*, *Jacobin*, *Overland*, *Australian Poetry Journal*, *Cordite*, *Liminal*, and more. Angelita is currently working on a practice-based PhD in Creative Arts and English. Angelita lives on unceded Wurundjeri and Boon Wurrung Country.

Judith Bishop's latest poetry collection is *Circadia* (2024). Her poems feature on Jane Stanley's Cerulean Orbits album (Delphian Records 2024) and the Glasgow School of Art Choir's Composeher album (2024).

Pooja Mittal Biswas, born in Nigeria to Indian parents, grew up around the world before settling in Australia. She is the author of ten books of fiction, poetry and non-fiction, and has been anthologised in both *The Best Australian Poems* and *The Best Australian Poetry*, and widely published in literary journals such as *Meanjin*, *Overland*, *Cordite*, *TEXT*, *Hecate* and *Jacket*.

Mario Bojórquez is a poet, essayist, and translator. His first books have been collected in the anthologies *El ray y la memoria* (2012), *Aquí todo es memoria* (2016), *Memoria de lo vivido* (2020), and *El fuego es mi nombre exacto* (2021). He has received numerous awards, including the Aguascalientes National Poetry Prize (2007), the Klísthenes Medal of the Demos Aigaleo of Athens, Greece (2017), the Prize Cardenal for Poetic Merit (2019), and the Sinaloa National Letters Award for Literary Career (2023).

Ken Bolton (1949) is a Sydney poet, living, since 1982, in Adelaide, where he has been associated with the Experimental Art Foundation. He lives with author Cath Kenneally. His books include *Fantastic Day* (2023), *Lonnie's Lament* (2017) and *Starting At Basheer's* (2018). His *Selected Poems* was published by Shearsman Books in the UK. He edited *Homage to John Forbes* and wrote the artist monograph *Michele Nikou*.

Peter Boyle is a poet and translator of poetry living and working on Dharug land. He has ten books of poetry published and eight books as a translator of poetry from Spanish and French. His collections include *Companions, Ancestors, Inscriptions* (2024), *Ideas of Travel* (2022), *Notes Towards the Dreambook of Endings* (2021), *Enfolded in the Wings of a Great Darkness* (2019), *Ghostspeaking* (2016), *Apocrypha* (2009), *The Blue Cloud of Crying* (1997) and *Coming Home from the World* (1993). He has won New South Wales Premier's Award for Poetry three times, and the Judith Wright Calanthe Prize for Poetry, among other awards.

Michael Brennan set-up Vagabond Press in 1999. He taught at universities in Sydney, Nagoya and Tokyo over twenty years. In 2018, he resigned from a tenured gig in Tokyo to work full-time as a publisher.

Jen Jewel Brown is a Melbourne cross-genre author, journalist and editor. Before instigating, collecting and editing Lisa Bellear's *Aboriginal Country*, she co-edited Shelton Lea's final collection *Nebuchadnezzar* (2005) with Gig Ryan. Jen won the 2006 Greater Dandenong Writing Awards Open Poetry Prize and the 2010 June Shenfield Poetry Award.

Pam Brown has been active in the Australian poetry scene in diverse modes for five decades. Vagabond Press published her collections *Missing up* (2015) and *Click here for what we do* (2018), both of which received significant awards. Her most recent book is *Stasis Shuffle* (Hunter Publishers, 2021). Pam lives on Gadigal land.

Melinda Bufton is the author of *Girlery* (2014) and *Superette (2018)*. Her poetry has appeared in numerous publications, including anthologies *Contemporary Australian Poetry* (2016) and *Contemporary Australian Feminist Poetry* (2016). In 2019, she was the winner of the Charles Rischbieth Jury Poetry Prize as well as the Helen Anne Bell Poetry Bequest Award, the latter resulting in the publication of her third collection, *Moxie* (2020).

Alí Calderón is a poet, professor and literary critic. Calderón has received the National Poetry Prize Ramón López Velarde and the Latin American Poetry Prize Benemérito de América. In 2015, his books include *Las Correspondencias* (2015), *Del poema al transtexto: Essays on How to Read Mexican Poetry* (2015), *Reinventando el Lirismo* (2015), and *El sin ventura Juan de Yuste* (2023). Calderón is the director of the Círculo de Poesía Editores and co-director of Valparaíso México Press. He is a member of the Sistema Nacional de Investigadores.

Ken Canning/ Burraga Gutya is from the Kunja Clan of the Bidjara Peoples of South West Queensland. His language name is Burraga Gutya. Poet and playwright, he started writing over 40 years ago from a prison cell in the old Boggo Road Jail in Brisbane, learning how to read and write from a fellow inmate. He worked for many years in Aboriginal Education, and was a founder and former Academic and Cultural advisor at the Jumbunna Indigenous House of Learning.

Broede Carmody is a poet from Dhudhuroa country in north-east Victoria. He has published *Flat Exit* (2017) and *Shouldering Pine* (2022). His poetry has also appeared in journals such as Meanjin, Cordite and Voiceworks. He is currently a journalist for The Age and The Sydney Morning Herald. He is currently based in Melbourne.

a. j. carruthers is a poet, author of *AXIS Z Book 3* (Cordite, 2023), *AXIS Book 2* (2019), *AXIS Book 1: 'Areal,'* (2014), and books of criticism; *Literary History and Avant-Gardes in the Antipodes: Languages of Invention* (2024), and *Notational Experiments in North American Long Poems: Stave Sightings* (2017).

Bonny Cassidy is the author of *Certain Fathoms* (2012), *Final Theory* (2014) and *Chatelaine* (2007) (shortlisted for the Prime Minister's Award for Poetry and the Judith Wright Calanthe Award) – and co-editor of the anthology *Contemporary Australian Feminist Poetry* (2016). She teaches Creative Writing at RMIT University and lives in the bush on Dja Dja Wurrung Country, Central Victoria. Her latest book is *Monument* (2024).

Jacqueline Cavallaro studied at COFA UNSW where she received the Basil and Muriel Hooper Scholarship from AGNSW. Her works are held in private and public collections and have been exhibited with Sheahan Galleries, Flinders Lane Gallery Melbourne, NG Art Sydney, JanKossen Contemporary New York, Wollongong Art Gallery as well as numerous prizes.

Don Mee Choi is the author of the KOR-US trilogy published by Wave Books: *Mirror Nation* (2024), the National Book Award winning collection *DMZ Colony* (2020), and *Hardly War* (2016).

Hedgie Choi received her MFA in poetry from The Michener Center at UT Austin and her MFA in fiction from The Writing Seminars at Johns Hopkins. She co-translated *Hysteria* by Kim Yideum, which won the 2020 Lucien Stryk Asian Translation Prize and the 2020 National Translation Award. Her translation of *Pillar of Books* by Moon Bo Young was published by Black Ocean in 2021. Her poetry collection, *Salvage*, is forthcoming with University of Wisconsin Press in 2025.

Stephanie Christie (also published as Will Christie) creates poetry in the form of page poems, text art, installations, theatre, video and sound. They're curious about what words do to us.

Justin Clemens has published many books of poetry and criticism. His most recent poetry collection is *A Foul Wind* (2022).

Ali Cobby Eckermann is a Yankunytjatjara poet and artist from South Australia whose work has been published and celebrated around the world. Her poetry collections include *little bit long time* (2009) and the award-winning collection *Inside My Mother* (2015). Her verse novels are *His Father's Eyes* (2011), *Ruby Moonlight* (2012), which won the inaugural black&write! Indigenous fellowship, the Kenneth Slessor Prize, a Deadly Award and was named the NSW Premier's Literary Awards Book of the Year, and *She is the earth* (2023), which won NSW Premier's Literary Awards Indigenous Writers Award and Book of the Year. In 2013 Ali toured Ireland as Australia's Poetry Ambassador, and in 2017 she received the Windham-Campbell Prize from Yale University.

Emilie Collyer lives in Naarm/Melbourne's west, on Wurundjeri land, where she writes poetry, plays and prose. Her debut full-length poetry collection *Do you have anything less domestic?* (2022) won the inaugural Five Islands First Book Prize and she was runner-up in the Gwen Harwood Poetry Prize 2024. She was the 2020 recipient of a Varuna Publishing Fellowship with Giramondo Publishing and recent accolades include shortlisting for Melbourne Poets Union International Poetry Competition 2019 & 2020 and runner-up Ada Cambridge Poetry Prize 2019.

Stuart Cooke is a poet, critic and translator. His books include George Dyungayan's *Bulu Line: a West Kimberley song cycle* (2014), *Speaking the Earth's Languages: a theory for Australian-Chilean postcolonial poetics* (2013), and the poetry collections *Opera* (2016) and *Edge Music* (2011). He lectures in creative writing and literary studies at Griffith University.

MTC Cronin has published over twenty books (poetry, prose poems and essays) and half a dozen of these volumes have also appeared in translation (Italian, French, Spanish and Macedonian). Her most recent book is *Who Was by Alex Quel* (2022), a collaboration with Peter Boyle.

Brett Cross has been a small press publisher in New Zealand for close to twenty years, operating the avant-garde lit. publisher Titus Books as well as the nonfiction Pacific publisher Atuanui Press. *Islands* (2024) is his debut collection of poetry.

Mikael de Lara Co has won awards in the Philippines for his poetry and literary translations. He works in strategic political communications and advertising, and is based in Cagayan de Oro City.

Noelle Leslie dela Cruz is Full Professor of Philosophy at De La Salle University in Manila. She is author of the poetry chapbook *Sisyphus on the Penrose Stairs: Meta-Reveries* (2017), lead author of *Philosophy of the Human Person: Giving Meaning to Life* (OUP), and co-editor of the anthology *Feminista: Gender, Race, and Class in the Philippines* (2011).

Rodrigo Dela Peña, Jr. is the author of *Tangere* (University of the Philippines Press, 2021) and *Aria and Trumpet Flourish* (Math Paper Press, 2018). He also edited *A/PART: An Anthology of Queer Southeast Asian Poetry in the Pandemic*.

Dan Disney's previous full-length collections are *and then when the* (2011), *Mannequin's Guide to Utopias* (2013), and *Either, Orpheus* (2016). Alongside an experimental verse novella, *Report from a border* (2016, co-devised with John Warwicker), he is the editor of *Beyond Babel* (2014), and co-edited *Writing to the Wire* (2016, with Kit Kelen) and *New Directions in Contemporary Australian Poetry* (2021, with Matthew Hall). He teaches with the English Literature Program at Sogang University, in Seoul. His most recent book, *accelerations & inertias* (2021), was shortlisted for the Judith Wright Calanthe Award and received the Kenneth Slessor Prize.

Đỗ Lê Anhdao is a bilingual and bicultural writer, performer, and activist. With the group Mai Piece, she co-founded One Mic in January 2004, the first open mic to bring multi-generation writers and musicians to Little Saigon – hailed as the 'Harlem in Bolsa' by *OC Weekly*. Đỗ's writings can be found in *Nha Magazine* and various Vietnamese literary journals such as T*ap Chi Tho, Hop Luu*, and *Van Hoc*. Đỗ graduated from UCLA and now lives in Las Vegas. Her present advocacy includes working as a sexual violence prevention educator for the Nevada Coalition Against Sexual Violence and serving as Literary Committee Chairperson for the Vietnamese American Arts & Letters Association.

Chris Edwards is a Sydney-based poet whose publications include *People of Earth* (2011) and *After Naptime* (2014).

William I. Elliott has lived for forty years in Yokohama, teaching literature at Kanto Gakuin University. His books include criticism and thirty translations of Japanese poetry, ancient and modern. With colleague Kawamura Kazuo he has translated fifty-four collections of Japan's best-known living poet, Tanikawa Shuntarō. Elliott has published seven collections of his own poems, including *An Evening's Entertainment* (2009). He founded the Kanto Poetry Center and the bilingual journal *Poetry Kanto*.

Joel Ephraims won the 2011 *Overland* Judith Wright Prize for new and emerging poets and the 2016 *Overland* NUW Fair Australia prize for poetry. His works include *Through the Forest* (2013), Biota (2022), and *Flying Car Kaleidoscope* (2024).

Kate Fagan is a writer, musician and scholar whose third volume, *First Light*, was shortlisted for the NSW Premier's Literary Awards and the Age Book of the Year Award. She directs The Writing Zone, a mentoring program for emerging writers and arts workers from Western Sydney, a former Editor of *How2* magazine (US), and Director of the WSU Writing and Society Research Centre and Chair of the Sydney Review of Books Advisory Board. Her most recent book is *Song in the Grass* (2024).

Michael Farrell (born Bombala NSW, lives Melbourne) has published nine books of poetry, and edited two; most recently *Googlecholia* (Giramondo 2022).

Johanna Featherstone established The Red Room Company in 2003 and created a series of literary TV shows, The Wordshed, in partnership with The University of Western Sydney. She is an honorary associate of The University of Sydney's School of Letters, Arts and Media and a co-director of Oranges & Sardines, her family foundation. Her chapbook *Felt* was released in 2010.

Liam Ferney's most recent collection *Hot Take* (2018) was shortlisted for the Judith Wright Calanthe Award. His previous volumes include *Content* (2016) and *Boom* (2013).

Luke Fischer is a prize-winning poet and philosopher. He has authored and co-edited seven books, including three poetry collections *Paths of Flight* (2013), *A Personal History of Vision* (2017), and *A Gamble for my Daughter* (2022, as well as the critical study *The Poet as Phenomenologist: Rilke and the New Poems* (2015).

Toby Fitch is a poet, critic, teacher and editor. He is the current poetry editor of *Overland* and a lecturer in creative writing at the University of Sydney. He is the author of *Rawshock* (2012), which won the 2012 Grace Leven Prize for Poetry; *Jerilderies* (2014); *The Bloomin' Notions of Other & Beau* (2016); *ILL LIT POP* (2018); *Where Only the Sky had Hung Before* (2019); *Object Permanence: Selected Calligrammes* (2019); *Sydney Spleen* (2021).

Lionel Fogarty was born on Wakka Wakka land, at Cherbourg Aboriginal Reserve in south-east Queensland in 1957. Throughout the 1970s he worked as an activist for Aboriginal Land Rights, and in the 1990s, after the death of his brother Daniel Yock, protesting against Aboriginal Deaths in Custody. His poetry collections date from the early 1980s; his most recent collections are *Connection Requital* (2010), *Mogwie-Idan: Stories of the Land* (2012), *Eelahroo (Long Ago) Nyah (Looking) Mobo-Mobo (Future)* (2014), *Lionel Fogarty: Selected Poems 1980-2017* (2017), *Harvest Lingo* (2022). He has won the Judith Wright Calanthe Award for Poetry and the Kate Challis RAKA Award.

Katherine Gallagher is a widely-acclaimed poet with eight books published as well as four chapbooks. Gallagher's own poetry has been translated into French, German, Hebrew, Italian, Romanian, and Serbo-Croat.

Jo Gardiner worked as a teacher and a psychologist. Most recently she was a finalist in the 2022 Montreal International Poetry Prize. Her novel, *The Concerto Inn*, was published in 2006. *The Impossible Shore* (2024) was her first poetry collection.

Angela Gardner has six poetry collections including *Some Sketchy Notes on Matter* (2020) shortlisted for the Dorothy Hewett Award and the Thomas Shapcott Prize winning *Parts of Speech* (2007). Her verse novel *The Sorry Tale of the Mignonette* (2022), was shortlisted for Wales Book of the Year 2022.

Jane Gibian is the author of five poetry collections, *tidemark* (2013), *Ardent* (2007), *long shadows* (2005) and *The Body's Navigation* (1998) and *Beneath the Tree Line* (2021). Her poetry has been widely anthologised in publications such as *Contemporary Australian Poetry* and *Contemporary Australian Feminist Poetry*. She works as a librarian and also writes about libraries, history and the environment.

Keri Glastonbury is an Associate Professor in English and Writing at The University of Newcastle. Her poetry collection *Newcastle Sonnets* (2018) was shortlisted for the 2019 Prime Minister's Literary Award for Poetry.

Eleanor Goodman is the author of the poetry collection *Nine Dragon Island*, and the translator of five books from Chinese, most recently *In the Roar of the Machine: Selected Poems by Zheng Xiaoqiong*.

Johannes Göransson was born and raised in Sweden. He is the author of six books of poetry, most recently *The Sugar Book* (Tarpaulin Sky Press, 2015), and the translator of six books, including work by Aase Berg, Johan Jönson and Henry Parland. He is the co-editor of Action Books and teaches at the University of Notre Dame.

Jaimie Gusman lives and works as a potter in Ka'a'awa, Hawai'i. Her first book, *Anyjar*, was published in September 2017. She is a recipient of the Ian MacMillan Prize (2012) and the Rita Dove Poetry Award (2015). She also has three chapbooks: *Gertrude's Attic* (2012), *The Anyjar* (2011), and *One Petal Row* (2011).

Ha Jaeyoun was born in 1975. In 2002 she won the best new poet's award. She writes poetry and researches and teaches contemporary Korean literature. Her three books of poems, *Radio Days* (2006), *Like All the Beaches in The World* (2012), *Universal Hello* (2019), and the academic books *Adventures of Modern Poetry and Moving Chosun Language* (2012), *The Imagination of Literature and the Action of Poetry* (2022) and *Infinite Love of Paradox* (2022), and the essay collection *To the Darkened Lights by the Coming of Me* (2023).

Contributors

Judy Halebsky is a poet and translator. She is the author of *Spring and a Thousand Years* (Unabridged) (2020), *Tree Line* (2014) and *Sky=Empty*, winner of the New Issue Prize (2010). She has also published articles on cultural translation and noh theatre. She is a professor of Literature and Language and director of the MFA in Creative Writing program at Dominican University of California.

Eliza Vitri Handayani is an author and literary translator. Her novel *From Now On Everything Will Be Different* came out in 2015 by Vagabond Press. Her translation of short stories, essays, and poems have appeared in numerous literary periodicals all over the world. She also directed the art projects House of the Unsilenced, Fashion ForWords, and Ceritrans.

Natalie Harkin is a Narungga woman and activist-poet from South Australia. She is a Associate Professor at Flinders University with an interest in decolonising state archives, currently engaging archival-poetic methods to research and document Aboriginal women's domestic service and labour histories in SA. Her words have been installed and projected in exhibitions comprising text-object-video projection, including creative-arts research collaboration with the Unbound Collective. She has published widely, including her poetry manuscripts include *Dirty Words* (2015) and *Archival-Poetics* (2019).

Martin Harrison (1949-2014) was an Australian poet. He published poems and limited edition books in London and New Zealand followed by *The Distribution of Voice* (1993), The Kangaroo Farm (1997), which was shortlisted for the Victorian Premiers Award, Summer (2001), which won the Wesley Michel Wright Award, and Wild Bees: New and Selected Poems (2008) was shortlisted for both the South Australian Premiers Awards and the ACT Poetry Prize, and the internationally acclaimed volume of essays *Who Wants to Create Australia?* (2004), which was a *Times Literary Supplement* book of the year selection for 2004.

J.S. Harry (1939-2015) published eight books of poetry in her lifetime, including *The Deer Under The Skin* (1971), *Hold, for a little while, and turn gently* (1979), *A Dandelion for Van Gogh* (1985), which was shortlisted for the National Book Council and the Adelaide Festival Poetry Awards, *The Life on Water and the Life Beneath* (1995), *Selected Poems* (1995), winner of the NSW Premier's Award for Poetry, *Sun Shadow, Moon Shadow* (2000) and *Public Private* (2013). Her collection of Peter Henry Lepus poems, *Not Finding Wittgenstein* (2007) won the Age Poetry Book of the Year Award, and Giramondo published *J.S. Harry: New and Selected Poems* (2021).

Kevin Hart is internationally recognised as a poet, critic, philosopher and theologian. Born in England, he grew up in Brisbane, and taught Philosophy and English at the University of Melbourne. He has recently taken up a position at the University of Virginia. His collections of poetry include *The Departure* (1978), *New and Selected Poems* (1995), *Flame Tree* (2002), *Young Rain* (2009), *Morning Knowledge* (2011), and received many awards including the Christopher Brennan Award and the Grace Leven Prize for Poetry twice.

Dimitra Harvey was born in Sydney to a Greek mother and grew up on Wangal country. Her poetry chapbook, *A Fistful of Hail*, was published in 2018 and has appeared in *Meanjin, Southerly, Cordite, SBS Voices, and Mascara Literary Review*, as well as anthologies such as *The Best Australian Poems*.

Ashley Haywood is writer, artist and poet whose work often dwells in the art-science nexus. She is the inaugural UQ Fryer Library Creative Writing Fellow (2017-2018), thrice shortlisted for the Thomas Shapcott Poetry Prize (2020 Runner-up, 2021, 2022), and winner of the QRAA Ekphrasis Challenge (2020) in her category. She holds a PhD on signs, minds and creativity, or how to write like painting, and has a background in biological science.

Fiona Hile's first full-length collection, *Novelties* (2013), was awarded the Kenneth Slessor Prize for Poetry. Her most recent book, *Subtraction* (2017) won the Helen Anne Bell Poetry Award.

Hirata Toshiko is one of Japan's best-known contemporary poets, as well as a renowned playwright and author of seventeen novels. She is associated with the 'women's boom' in contemporary Japanese literature. Her collection, *Shinanoka* (2004) which will be called, in English, *Is It Poetry?* earned Hirata the Hagiwara Sakutarō Prize for poetry.

Contributors | 429

LK Holt has published six full-length collections of poems. Her book *Birth Plan* was shortlisted for the 2020 Prime Minister's Award for Poetry and the 2020 Victorian Premier's Award for Poetry. Her most *Three Books* (2024) won the Judith Wright Calanthe Award. She is the recipient of the NSW Premier's Award for Poetry and the Grace Leven Prize for an Australian poetry collection, and has been longlisted for the Australian Literature Society's Gold Medal. She lives in Narrm/Melbourne.

Hong Ying, the author of the novel *Summer of Betrayal* and the memoir *Daughter of the River*, was born into a sailor's family in 1962 in the city of Chongqing, China. In 1989 she entered the Lu Xun Writers' Academy in Beijing. She left China to study in London in 1991. She is also the author of seven collections of stories and novellas, four poetry collections, including her first collection in English translation *I Too Am Salammbo* (2015, translated by Mabel Lee) and two other novels.

Hwang Yuwon was born in Ulsan in 1982. He received a B.A in Religious Studies and Philosophy from Sogang University and is currently getting his Ph.D in Indian Philosophy at Dongguk University. His book of poetry *Everything in the World, Maximized* won the Kim Soo-young prize.

Holly Isemonger is a poet from Gerringong, NSW. She was the joint winner of the Judith Wright Poetry Prize. Her work has appeared in journals such as *Cordite, Overland and Westerly* and her debut collection *Greatest Hit* was released in 2023.

Ishigaki Rin was born in Akasaka in downtown Tokyo in 1920. From 1934 to 1975 she worked as a bank clerk and thus first became known as the 'bank clerk poet'. She was also an active trade unionist, holding a number of positions in the bank employees' union. Her four major poetry collections were published between 1959 and 1984 and were awarded a number of literary prizes including the Mr H. Prize and the Tamura Toshiko Prize.

Itō Hiromi is one of the most important poets of contemporary Japan. She is often credited with revolutionizing postwar Japanese poetry with her work focusing on sexuality, childbirth, and women's bodies. She later moved to the U.S., and has since focused on migration and the psychological effects of linguistic and cultural alienation. She is the multi-award-winning author of over ten collections of poetry, numerous essay collections and translations and several novellas and novels. She is the author of *Killing Kanoko* and *Wild Grass on the Riverbank* (translated by Jeffrey Angles).

Joy Anne Icayan's work has appeared in various publications including *Broadsided Press, Likhaan Journal*, and the *Philippines Free Press*. She works in the field of human rights, currently focusing on issues of civic space.

Eleanor Jackson is a Filipino Australian poet, performer, arts producer and sometimes community radio broadcaster. She is the author of *Gravidity and Parity*, winner of Small Press Network's Book of the Year (2022), and *A Leaving* (2018). Her live album, *One Night Wonders*, is produced by Going Down Swinging. She is the producer of the Melbourne Poetry Map and a former Editor in Chief and current Chair of *Peril Magazine*, Board Member of Queensland Poetry Festival and Vice-Chair of the Stella Prize.

Anna Jacobson is an award-winning writer and artist. Her books include *How to Knit a Human* (2024), *Anxious in a Sweet Store* (2023), *Amnesia Findings* (2019), and a chapbook *The Last Postman* (2018).

Jill Jones' latest book is *Acrobat Music: New and Selected Poems* (2022), which was longlisted for the 2024 ALS Gold Medal. Other recent books include *Wild Curious Air* (2020), winner of the 2021 Wesley Michel Wright Prize, and *A History Of What I'll Become* (2020), shortlisted for the 2021 Kenneth Slessor Award and the 2022 John Bray Award. In 2015 she won the Victorian Premier's Prize for Poetry for *The Beautiful Anxiety* (2014). She was, from 2008-2022, Senior Lecturer in English and Creative Writing, University of Adelaide.

Mookie Katigbak-Lacuesta is an award-winning writer from the Philippines. She has published five collections of poetry, as well as a novel, *Assembling Alice*, which was published by Penguin SEA in 2021. In 2023, her poetry collection, *College Boy*, won a National Book Award. She has also been the Filipino delegate to international literary festivals in Dubai, Rotterdam, Medellín, San Francisco, Macau, Kuala Lumpur and South Korea. In 2015, she completed a writing residency for the International Writing Program at the University of Iowa.

Kazuo Kawamura (1933-2015) lived virtually life-long in celebration of the poetry of Percy Bysshe Shelley. He gave critical attention to such other poets as Wordsworth, Yeats, Larkin, and Shuntarō Tanikawa. From 1947-2015 every day, literally, found him engaged in the translation of Tanikawa's poems. He spent the final seventeen years of his life as Professor Emeritus of English Literature at Kanto Gakuin University in Yokohama, Japan.

Christopher (Kit) Kelen is a poet, painter and recovering academic, resident in the Myall Lakes of NSW. Published widely since the seventies, he has a dozen full length collections in English as well as translated books of poetry in Chinese, Portuguese, French, Italian, Spanish, Indonesian, Swedish and Filipino. Emeritus Professor at the University of Macau.

S. K. Kelen has been writing poems since longer than he cares to remember. His most recent book is *A Happening in Hades* (Puncher & Wattmann, 2020).

Khaing Mar Kyaw Zaw Khaing Mar Kyaw Zaw (b. 1963) was born in the Karen Liberated Area, into a family involved in Myanmar's decades long ethnic conflict. As such, she only had limited access to education and left home in order to attend school. She worked as a primary school teacher and later joined the Karen insurgency, active in the women's movement and later in indigenous media and publishing. In the borderlands, Khaing Mar began writing poetry and fiction, publishing her work in a Burmese newspapers and journals based in exile. From a precarious exile in Thailand, Khaing Mar was able to write poetry free from the Burmese censorship board and the risk of imprisonment faced by dissident poets inside the country. From Thailand, Khaing Mar was able to access a more open audience for politically tinged poetry and was able to publish her first books of poetry and short stories. Khaing Mar now lives in the USA, where she has continued to publish Burmese language poetry and prose.

Kim Haengsook is one of the best-known Korean contemporary poets. Her books include *Adolescence* (2003), *The Goodbye Ability* (2007), and *What Errands Are You Running?* (2020), which won the prestigious Daesan Literary Award. An English translation of a selected collection of her poems *Human Time* was published in 2023. She is a professor at Kangnam University.

Kim Hyesoon, born in 1955, is one of the most prominent and influential contemporary poets of South Korea. She was the first woman poet to receive the prestigious Kim Su-yong and Midang awards. In Don Mee Choi's translations, her *Autobiography of Death* (2018) was the winner of the 2019 International Griffin Poetry Prize and Phantom Pain Wings won the 2024 National Book Critics Circle Award for Poetry.

Kim Min Jeong was born in Incheon in 1976. She holds degrees in Literature and Creative Writing (Chung-Ang University), and made her literary debut in 1999 after receiving the New Literature Award. She has published a number of collections of poetry, including 날은 고슴도치 아가씨, 그녀가 처음, 느끼기 시작했다, 아름답고 쓸모없기를, 너의 거기는 작고 나의 여기는 커서 우리들은 헤어지는 중입니다, and a collection of essays, 각설하고. Her books have received the Park In-Hwan Literary Award, the Hyundai Award, and the Lee Sang-Hwa Poetry Award. Her work in English has appeared in *Poems of Kim Yideum, Kim Haengsook & Kim Min Jeong* (2016) and *Beautiful and Useless* (2020). She manages 문학동네시인선의, and works with the Korean literary publisher Nanda.

Kim Yideum has published five books of poetry – *A Stain in the Shape of a Star* (2005), *Cheer up, Femme Fatale* (2007), *The Unspeakable Lover* (2011), *Song of Berlin, Dahlem* (2013), and *Hysteria* (2014) – and the novel *Blood Sisters* (2011). Her work has been adapted into a play (*The Metamorphosis*, 2014) and a film (*After School*, 2015). She has received numerous awards for her poetry, including the Poetry & the World Literary Award (2010), the Kim Daljin Changwon Award (2011), the 22nd Century Literary Award (2015) and the Kim Chunsoo Award (2015). Having received her PhD for a thesis on Korean feminist poetics, she teaches at Gyeongsang National University. She is also a newspaper columnist and hosts a poetry-themed radio program.

John Kinsella is the author of over seventy books of poetry, fiction, criticism, plays, edited works (such as *The Penguin Book of Australian Poetry*), and collaborative works. His many awards include the Australian Prime Minister's Literary Award for Poetry, the Victorian Premier's Award for Poetry, the John Bray Award for Poetry, the Judith Wright Calanthe Award for Poetry (twice) and the Western Australian Premier's Award for Poetry (three times). Among his recent books published in Australia are *Supervivid Depastoralism* (2021),

Hollow Earth (2019), *Lucida Intervalla* (2018), *On the Outskirts* (2017), *Old Growth* (2017), *Drowning in Wheat: Selected Poems* (2016), *Crow's Breath* (2015) and *Displaced: a rural memoir* (2020). He is a Fellow of Churchill College, Cambridge University, and was Professor of Literature and Environment at Curtin University. A frequent collaborator with other poets, writers, artist, musicians, and thinkers, he lives on Ballardong Noongar land at 'Jam Tree Gully' in the Western Australian wheatbelt (north of Toodyay). In 2007 he received the Christopher Brennan Award for Lifetime Achievement in Poetry.

Elena Knox is an artist and writer based in Tokyo. She is a researcher in Intermedia Art & Science at Waseda University and performs experimental music now and then.

Koike Masayo was born in Tokyo in 1959 and graduated from the International Relations Department of Tsuda Juku College in Tokyo. Her poetry collections include *Mizu no Machi kara Arukidashite* (*I Began to Walk from the Water Town*) (1988), *Seikasai* (*Fruit and Vegetable Festival*) (1991), *Eien ni Konai Basu* (*The Bus that Never Comes*) (1997), winner of Gendaishi Hanatsubaki Prize, *Mottomo Kannohtekina Heya* (*The Most Sensuous Room*) (2000), winner of the Takami Jun Literary Prize, *Yoakemae Juppun* (*Ten Minutes before Dawn*) and *Ame Otoko, Yama Otoko, Mame o Hiku Otoko* (*Rain Men, Mountain Men and Men Who Mill Coffee Beans*) both published in 2001.

Jose Flores Lacaba, born in 1945, worked as a journalist in the seventies, wrote the screenplays of classic films by Lino Brocka and Mike de Leon, and later edited the entertainment magazine *Yes*. The moral conscience in his ironic verse is exemplary for many of his Filipino readers. He was detained for two years during the Marcos dictatorship for his political and labor activism. His first book of poems, *Ang Mga Kagilagilalas na Pakikipagsapalaran ni Juan de la Cruz* (*The Amazing Adventures of Juan de la Cruz*), came out in 1979.

Lâm Thục Nghi, Saigonese, is an admirer of the fashion industry, and she co-authors literature translation work on the side.

Mijall Lamas is a poet, translator and creative writing teacher. He has published seven collections of poetry and received the Clemencia Isaura Poetry Prize in 2012. Lamas' most recent publications include *Un recuento parcial de los incendios – selección de poemas 2007-2017* (2022), and *Memoria del Desierto* (2023), which was awarded the National Prize for Literature Gilberto Owen in the poetry category. He is also one of the editors of the online magazine *Círculo de Poesí*.

Lê Văn Tài came to Australia as a refugee in 1984. As a visual artist, he has held numerous exhibitions, individual and collective, in Vietnam, Hong Kong and Australia. As a poet, he has published three collections of poetry, two in English, Empty Arms Surrounded by *Warm Breath* (1987) and *Waiting the Waterfall Falls* (1996), and one in Vietnamese, *Thơ Lê Văn Tài* (2013).

Ji yoon Lee is a poet and translator whose most recent publication is a translation of Kim Yideum's novel *Blood Sisters* (Deep Vellum, 2019). She also translated Korean feminist poet Kim Yideum's poetry with Don Mee Choi and Johannes Göransson, the collection of which was published as *Cheer Up, Femme Fatale* (Action Books, 2015), which then was shortlisted for Lucien Stryk Prize. She is also the author of *Foreigner's Folly* (Coconut Books, 2014), *Funsize/Bitesize* (Birds of Lace, 2013), and *IMMA* (Radioactive Moat, 2012). Excerpts from her manuscript *Baby Visa Denied* are published in *Fence*.

Mabel Lee PhD FAHA is Honorary Professor of Chinese Studies at The University of Sydney and Hong Kong Metropolitan University. Her research concerns Chinese intellectual history and literature of the modern era, and her publications largely concern the writers Lu Xun (1881–1936), Gao Xingjian (b. 1940) and Yang Lian (b. 1956). She is well known as the translator of Nobel Laureate Gao Xingjian's works *Soul Mountain* (1989), *One Man's Bible* (1999) and *Buying a Fishing Rod for My Grandfather* (2004). She has also translated three books of poetry by Yang Lian: *Masks & Crocodile* (1990), *The Dead in Exile* (1990) and *Yi* (2002). She translated Hong Ying's *I Too Am Salammbo* (2013).

Takako Lento (1941-2024) translated poetry and prose from Japanese to English and vice versa. Her books of translation and critical essays include *Tamura Ryu-ichi, on the Life and Work of a 20th Century Master* (co-ed. Wayne Miller); *The Art of Being Alone: Tanikawa Shuntarō, Poems 1952 – 2009*; *Collected Haiku of Yosa Buson* (with W.S. Merwin); *Pioneers of Modern Japanese Poetry*, and *Butterfly by Kashiwagi Mari*.

Jake Levine is an assistant professor of Creative Writing at Keimyung University. He has written and translated or co-translated over a dozen books, including Kim Yideum's *Hysteria* (Action Books, 2019) which won both the National Translation Award and the Lucien Stryk Prize. He is a former Fulbright Fellow (to Lithuania in 2010), a recipient of a Korean Government Scholarship, served as an assistant editor at Acta Koreana, as a poetry editor at Spork Press, as the managing editor and editor-in-chief at *Sonora Review*, and currently edits the award-winning contemporary Korean poetry series Moon Country at Black Ocean. His latest book of poetry, *The Imagined Country*, came out with Tolsun Books in 2023.

Bella Li is the author of *Argosy* (2017), *Lost Lake* (2018), and *Theory of Colours* (2021). Her work has won the Victorian Premier's Literary Award for Poetry, the NSW Premier's Literary Award for Poetry, and the Australian Book Designers' Association Award for Best Designed Independent Book; and has been shortlisted or commended in the Judith Wright Calanthe Award, the Anne Elder Award, and the Wesley Michel Wright Prize. She holds a PhD from The University of Melbourne.

Mario Licón Cabrera (Chihuahua, México, 1949) is a poet, translator, and editor. He has published four collections of poetry, including *Yuxtas (Back&Forth)* (2009).. Licón Cabrera has translated many leading Australian poets into Spanish and is a regular contributor to two Mexican magazines, *DosFilos* and *Círculo de Poesía*, as well as *Mascara Literary Review*. He won the Premio de Poesía Trilce in 2015.

Kate Lilley is a Sydney-based poet-scholar. She is the author of 3 books of poetry: *Versary* (2002), winner of the Grace Leven Prize; *Ladylike* (2012), shortlisted for the NSW Premier's Awards; and *Tilt* (2018), winner of the Victorian Premier's Award for Poetry. She was a full-time member of the English Department at the University of Sydney from 1990 to 2021 and is now an Honorary Associate Professor.

Debbie Lim received the 2022 Bruce Dawe National Poetry Prize. She was shortlisted for the 2022 Peter Porter Poetry Prize. Her chapbook is *Beastly Eye* (2012) and a full-length collection will be published by Cordite Books in 2025. She was born in Sydney, where she lives on Darramuragal land.

Rachel Loden's Rachel Loden's book *Dick of the Dead* (2009) was shortlisted for the PEN USA Literary Award for Poetry and the California Book Award. Her first collection, *Hotel Imperium* (2008), won the Contemporary Poetry Series and was selected as one of the ten best poetry books of the year by the San Francisco Chronicle, which called it 'quirky and beguiling.' She is the recipient of a Pushcart Prize and her work appears in *Respect: The Poetry of Detroit Music* (Michigan State University), *The Paris Review* and elsewhere.

Astrid Lorange is a Senior Lecturer in the School of Art & Design. She is also a writer, researcher, editor, and artist. She studied writing and cultural studies at the University of Technology Sydney, where she completed her doctoral thesis on Gertrude Stein and contemporary poetics. *How Reading is Written: A Brief Index to Gertrude Stein*, a scholarly monograph based on the thesis, was published by Wesleyan University Press in 2014.

Ramon Loyola (1967-2018) was a Philippines-born writer of poetry, fiction, non-fiction, and legal scholarly articles. He held degrees in industrial pharmacy, law and creative writing. His writing has appeared in various online and print publications in Australia and overseas.

Lưu Diệu Vân, born December 1979, is a poet, literary translator, and co-editor of the bilingual literary magazine damau.org. She received her Master's Degree from the University of Massachusetts in 2009. Her bilingual works and translations have been published in numerous print literary journals and online magazines. Her publications include *47 Minutes After 7* (2010), *The Transparent Greenness of Grass* (2012), *Poems of Lưu Diệu Vân, Lưu Mêlan & Nhã Thuyên* (2013), *M of December* (2016), *Thế Kỷ Của Những Vật Tế* (2021), *She, Self-Winding* (2022).

Jennifer Maiden was born in Penrith, New South Wales, and has had 31 books published 24 poetry collections, 6 novels and a nonfiction work. Among her awards are 3 Kenneth Slessor Prizes for Poetry, 2 C.J. Dennis Prizes for Poetry, the overall Victorian Prize for Literature, Harri Jones Memorial Prize, FAW Christopher Brennan Award for lifetime achievement in poetry, 2 The Melbourne Age Poetry Book of the Year awards, the overall Melbourne Age Book of the Year and the ALS Gold Medal. Her book *Liquid Nitrogen* was shortlisted for the Griffin International Poetry Prize. Her latest poetry collections are published by Quemar Press: *brookings: the noun* (2019) and *Appalachian Fall* (2018), and her *Selected Poems 1967-2018*.

David Malouf was born in Brisbane in 1934. Since 'Interiors' in Four Poets, 1962, he has published poetry, novels and short stories, essays, opera librettos and a play, and has been widely translated. He is the internationally acclaimed author of novels including *Ransom*, *The Great World* (winner of the Commonwealth Writers' prize and the Prix Femina Etranger), *Remembering Babylon* (winner of the IMPAC Dublin Literary Award), *An Imaginary Life*, *Conversations at Curlow Creek*, *Dream Stuff*, *Every Move You Make* and his autobiographical classic *12 Edmondstone Street*. His *Collected Stories* won the 2008 Australia-Asia Literary Award. In 2000 he was the sixteenth Neustadt Laureate. His poetry collections include *Bicycle and Other Poems* (1970), *Neighbours in a Thicket: Poems* (1974), *Selected Poems 1959–1989* (1992), *Typewriter Music* (2007), *Revolving Days: Selected Poems* (2008), *Earth Hour* (2014), and *An Open Book* (2018).

Greg McLaren is a poet and teacher who lives on Darug and Gandagarra country in the NSW Blue Mountains. He is the author of *The Kurri Kurri Book of the Dead*, *Australian ravens* and *Windfall*. His most recent book is the dystopian verse novel *camping underground* (2022).

Philip Mead was born in Brisbane in 1953 and educated in Queensland, the U.K. and in the United States. From 2009 to 2018 he was inaugural Chair of Australian Literature at the University of Western Australia. From 1987 to 1994 he was Poetry Editor of *Meanjin Quarterly* magazine. He has edited *The Penguin Book of Modern Australian Poetry* (1991), with John Tranter, and edited selections of poetry by Frank Wilmot, *Selected Poetry and Prose* (1997) and David Campbell, *Hardening of the Light* (2007). In 2009 he published a critical study, *Networked Language: History & Culture in Australian Poetry* and in 2018 a collection of poetry from Vagabond Press, *Zanzibar Light*.

Minashita Kiryū was born in Kanagawa Prefecture in 1970 and was educated at Waseda University. Her first book of poetry *Onsoku Heiwa* (*Sonic Peace*) was published in 2005 and the following year was awarded the Nakahara Chūya Poetry Prize. Her second book of poetry *Zekkyō* (*Border Z*) was published in 2008 and was awarded the Bansui Poetry Prize.

Peter Minter is a poet, editor of poetry and writer on poetry and poetics. He teaches Creative Writing, Australian Literature and Indigenous Studies at the University of Sydney.

Mark Mordue is a writer, poet and journalist, born in 1960 and raised in Newcastle, New South Wales. He is the winner of a 1992 Human Rights Media Award and the 2010 Pascall Prize: Australian Critic of the Year. His latest book is *Boy on Fire: The Young Nick Cave* (2021).

Leith Morton (Professor Emeritus, Tokyo Institute of Technology) has written many books on modern Japanese literature and culture, including: *The Alien Within: Representations of the Exotic in Twentieth-Century Japanese Literature* (2009), *Modernism in Practice: An Introduction to Postwar Japanese Poetry* (2004), *Poems of Masayo Koike, Ishigaki Rin & Tanikawa Shuntaro* (2014). He is also a poet and translator, with over 12 volumes of poetry and poetry translations published, including *Tokyo: A Poem in Four Chapters* (2006).

Nam Đỗ is a Saigon-based Hanoian. In addition to his employment as a financial analyst, Nam is also an art aficionado and poet. Nam has demonstrated his admiration for poetry through his journey with writer Nguyen Thuy Hang, with long-term translation projects such as the Three Authors collection, published in Vagabond Press's Asia Pacific Poetry Series 2018. He has extended this support into projects with Bar De Force Press.

Robert Nery was born in the Philippines, and has made two feature-length documentaries, *Black Nazarene* and *In 1966 The Beatles Came to Manila*. His book *The Hero Takes a Walk* (2023) is an essay on a sixties childhood and education in the Philippines.

Nguyễn Thúy Hằng was a graduate from the University of Fine Arts of Ho Chi Minh City. Her first book, a triology *Current Times, Good Sensations and Reasonable Insanity*, written during her two-year stint in the US, was published by Youth Publisher, Hanoi in 2006. On return to Vietnam in 2005, Nguyễn Thúy Hằng moved to Hanoi where she published *We Haven't Been Able to Sleep for Some Time* (2008) and *They - The Powder of the Illusory* (2013). Nguyễn Thúy Hằng's works often combine various art forms: art installation, contemporary dance, cinema, painting, music. She is currently living in Ho Chi Minh City.

Nguyễn Tôn Hiệt arrived in Australia as a political refugee from Vietnam in 1983. He has been actively working as a musician, writer, poet, playwright, essayist, translator and editor. He has published several books on literary and art criticism. His creative writings have appeared in many overseas and Australian journals and anthologies, including *Tienve* and *Kunapipi*.

Nhã Thuyên is a writer born and living in Vietnam.

Kay Orchison had an art career spanning 30 years and 52 exhibitions, retiring in 2020 due to ill health. His work was primarily photographic, with occasional installations. He collaborated with Vagabond Press on the Rare Objects chapbooks and made other cover art for the press for 18 years. He now writes fiction and infrequently records music.

Ōsaki Sayaka has produced diverse collaborations with dancers, musicians, contemporary artists, and other poets and often represents Japan at international literary festivals. In 2016 her first book for children *Hey leaf, where is your home?* was published. Her second collection, *Pointing Impossible* (2014), won the Nakahara Chūya Prize in 2014, and was followed by *New Habitat* (2018) and *Freedom of Dance* (2021). Ōsaki has been invited to international festivals in Lithuania (2015), Ecuador (2017), Cuba (2018), and the Netherlands (2019). Some of her poems have been translated into English, Spanish and Lithuanian.

Ouyang Yu's eighth novel, *All the Rivers Run South*, was published in November 2023 and his first collection of short stories, *The White Cockatoo Flowers*, was out in early 2024.

Jorge Palma was born in Montevideo, Uruguay in 1961. He has worked in journalism and radio in the field of literary and cultural criticism. His first collection of poems *Entre el viento y la sombra* was published in 1989 and has been followed by four later collections. His poetry has been included in several anthologies and presented at numerous poetry festivals in Europe and Latin America. A collection of his short stories, *Paraísos artificiales*, was published in 1990.

Jasmine Nikki C Paredes was born and raised in Cebu City, Philippines. She is the author of the chapbook collections *Reclamations* (2017) and *We Will See the Scatter* (2014), from which several poems won first prize in the 2015 Maningning Miclat Poetry Competition. Her work has appeared in numerous journals and publications, including *As/Us, The Boiler, Drunken Boat* and *The Missing Slate*. She received a BFA in creative writing from Ateneo de Manila University and an MFA in poetry from Sarah Lawrence College. She works at the Academy of American Poets and lives in Queens, New York.

Allan Justo Pastrana is a writer, musician, and teacher. Many of his poems have appeared in various anthologies and journals like *Softblow Poetry Journal, Cordite Poetry Review*, and Vagabond Press' Asia Pacific Writing Series. His works have received prizes from the Maningning Miclat Art Foundation and the Don Carlos Palanca Memorial Awards for Literature. He has published two poetry books, *Body Haul* (winner of the 2013 Madrigal-Gonzalez Best First Book Award) and *Field*. Pastrana teaches at the Ateneo de Manila University.

Eddie Paterson lectures in scriptwriting for theatre, contemporary performance, new media and games at the University of Melbourne. His books include *Redactor* (2017), which was shortlisted for the Victorian Premier's Awards and the John Bray Award.

Phan Quỳnh Trâm is a poet, essayist and translator. She migrated from Vietnam to Australia in 2000 and now lives in Sydney. Her translations, micro fictions, essays and poems, written In Vietnamese and English, have been published in *Kunapipi, Ajar* and *Tiền vệ* literary webzine. She is a co-author of a collection of poems published by Vagabond in 2015.

Anupama Pilbrow's poems, reviews, and essays have been published in journals and anthologies including *Cordite Poetry Review, Rabbit Poetry Journal, JEASA, Southerly*, and *The Hunter Anthology of Contemporary Australian Feminist Poetry*. *Body Poems* was published in 2018.

Felicity Plunkett is an award-winning poet and critic. She has a PhD from the University of Sydney. Her books are *Vanishing Point* (2009), *Seastrands* (2011), *A Kinder Sea* (2020) and the edited collection *Thirty Australian Poets* (2011).

Dorothy Porter (1954-2008) pioneered the modern verse novel with her award winning modern classic, *The Monkey's Mask* (1994). Her other verse novels include *Akhenaten* (1992), *Wild Surmise* (2002) and *El Dorado* (2007), all of which garnered major awards. There were several collections of poetry, including *Little Hoodlum* (1975), *The Night Parrot* (1984), *Crete* (1996), and the posthumous collections: *The Bee Hut* (2009), and *The Best 100 Poems of Dorothy Porter* (2013). A lover of music, Dorothy Porter also wrote lyrics for Tim Finn and Paul Grabovsky, and libretti for the composer Jonathan Mills.

Stephanie Powell has published two collections, *Bone* (2021) and *Gentle Creatures* (2023) and in journals including *Ambit Magazine, Cordite Poetry Review, The Moth, Bad Lilies, Wild Court, The Rialto* and *Ink Sweat and Tears*. She is the recipient of the Melbourne Poets Union Poetry Prize, 2022.

David Prater was born in Dubbo. His works include *We Will Disappear* (2007), *Morgenland* (2007) and *Leaves of Glass* (2014). Between 2001 and 2012 he edited *Cordite Poetry Review*. He lives in the Netherlands.

Peter Ramm is a poet and teacher who writes on the Gundungarra lands of the NSW Southern Highlands. He has won the South Coast Writer's Centre Poetry Award and the Harri Jones Memorial Prize, and has shortlisted for the Bridport, ACU, Blake, and Newcastle Poetry Prizes. Peter has recently published poems with *Cordite, Westerly, Plumwood Mountain, and Eureka Street Journal*.

Kaitlin Rees is a translator, editor, and public school teacher based in New York City. She mostly translates from the Vietnamese of Nhã Thuyên, with whom she co-founded AJARpress.

Nick Riemer is a senior lecturer in the English and Linguistics Departments at the University of Sydney, and a member of the Laboratoire d'histoire des théories linguistiques, Université Paris-Diderot. He specializes in semantics and in the history and philosophy of linguistics.

Ariel Riveros is a Sydney-based writer and literary translator. He was the founding editor of Australian Latino Press and organiser for The Blue Space Poetry Jam readings. His works have appeared in various publications including *Southerly, Contrappasso Magazine, Mascara Literary Review, FourW, Verity La, ETZ, 'Forgetting is so Long' Poetry Anthology* and *Journal of Postcolonial Text*. Ariel has featured at major national literary festivals and poetry events. His chapbook of short stories, *Self-Imposed House Arrest*, was published through Blank Rune Press in 2015. Ariel was also the winner of the 2016 Schizophrenia Fellowship of NSW Poetry Prize.

Izzy Roberts-Orr is a poet, writer, broadcaster and arts worker based on Dja Dja Wurrung Country. Izzy is Creative Producer for Red Room Poetry and a 2020-2022 recipient of the Australia Council Marten Bequest Scholarship for Poetry. *Raw Salt* was the recipient of a Wheeler Centre Hot Desk Fellowship, and longlisted for the Colorado Prize for Poetry, and published in 2023.

Claire Miranda Roberts was born in Melbourne and has lived in the UK, where she completed an MFA in Creative Writing at the University of St Andrews. Claire's poetry has been published in *Antipodes, Communion, Plumwood Mountain, Text: Journal of Writing and Writing Courses*, and *Westerly Magazine*, among others. Most recently, her manuscript *Kangaroo Paw* was shortlisted for the 2021 Helen Anne Bell Poetry Bequest Award and published in 2023.

Noel Rowe (1951-2007) was a poet who lived in Sydney, Australia, and was Senior Lecturer in Australian Literature at the University of Sydney where he was also awarded the University Medal (1984) and doctorate (1989). His books include *Perhaps, After All* (2000), *Next to Nothing* (2004) and *Touching the Hem* (2006). He was co-editor of the literary journal *Southerly*, and with Vivian Smith, edited *Windchimes: Asia in Australian Poetry* (2006). In 2005, he was awarded the William Baylebridge Memorial Prize for poetry and invited to read his poetry at International Festivals in Rotterdam and Jerusalem in 2006.

Tracy Ryan lives in the Western Australian wheatbelt. She has published 6 novels & 10 volumes of poetry, most recently *Rose Interior* (2023).

Jaya Savige was born in Sydney, raised on Bribie Island, and lives in London. He is the author of *Latecomers* (2005), *Surface to Air* (2011), and *Change Machine* (2020), and has won the Thomas Shapcott Poetry Prize and the NSW Premier's Kenneth Slessor Award for Poetry. He read for a PhD on James Joyce at the University of Cambridge (Christ's) as a Gates Scholar, and has held Australia Council residencies at the B.R. Whiting Studio, Rome, and the Cité Internationale des Arts, Paris.

Susan M. Schultz is author, most recently, of *I and Eucalyptus* (2024), *Meditations* (2023), and *Lilith Walks* (2022). Several of her books have been composed of 'memory cards', which riffs off of quotations from Dōgen. She's lived in Hawai`i for over 30 years.

Joel Scott was born in Sydney and now lives in Berlin, where he works primarily as a translator. His most recent chapbook is *BILDVERBOT* (2017). His translation of *Volume II of Peter Weiss's Aesthetics of Resistance* came out with Duke University Press in 2020, and *Vol III* is slated to be released.

Soeun Seo is a poet and translator based in Suwon.

Seo Dae-kyung was born in 1976. He studied English in college. He is the author of *The Idiot Feels the Atmosphere*.

Hyemi Seok is a translator and musical writer/lyricist from Korea. She earned a BA from Yonsei University and completed the Regular Course at the Translation Academy of the Literature Translation Institute of Korea. Her original works include musical *T, Sugarcraft*, and *The Ravens' Forest*.

Kazue Shinkawa (1929-2024) was born in 1929 in Ibaraki Prefecture, Japan. Since her first book of poetry, *The Sleeping Chair*, came out in 1953, more than 30 books of her poetry have been published including many selected poems and two complete works. She also published half a dozen books of poetry for children and compiled many anthologies. With her poems appearing in a variety of media ranging from weekly magazines to national newspapers, radio and TV programs, to serious literature reviews, and many of her printed poems being made into songs and performed by chorus groups all over the country, Kazue Shinkawa was one of the most popular and respected poets in Japan.

Ella Skilbeck-Porter is a poet and artist currently living on unceded Wurundjeri Country in Naarm/Melbourne. Her poetry has been widely published in literary journals including *Rabbit, Cordite Poetry Review, HEAT, Australian Poetry Journal, Going Down Swinging* and *Otoliths*. *These Are Different Waters* was published in 2023 and shortlisted for the Mary Gilmore Award and was highly commended in the Anne Elder Award.

Peter Skrzynecki was born in 1945 in Germany and came to Australia in 1949. He has published twenty books of poetry and prose and won several awards including the Captain Cook BiCentenary Award, the Grace Levin Poetry Prize and the Henry Lawson Short Story Award. *Immigrant Chronicle*, a book of poetry, was a set text for study on the New South Wales HSC syllabus for many years. A memoir, *The Sparrow Garden*, was shortlisted for the National Biography Award. *Old/New World: New & Selected Poems* (2007) became a set text on the VCE syllabus in Victoria.

Vivian Smith taught French for many years at the University of Tasmania before moving to the Department of English and Australian Literature at Sydney University. His numerous publications include *Selected Poems* (1985) and New Selected Poems (1995). His most recent volume of poetry is *Here, There and Elsewhere* (Giramondo).

Soh Sakon (1925-2006) was one of the major postwar Japanese poets. His award-winning volume *Moeru Haha* (*Mother Burning*, 1968) is considered one of the landmark poetry books of his era, if not the twentieth century as a whole. He wrote many volumes of verse, a number of which were awarded major literary prizes.

Nicolette Stasko was the author of six collections of poetry, *Abundance* (1992), *Black Night with Windows* (1994), *Dwelling in the Shape of Things* (1999), *In Certain Light* (2001), *The Weight of Irises* (2003), and *Glass Cathedrals: New and Selected Poems* (2006).

Svetlana Sterlin, born in New Zealand to Russian/Jewish parents, writes poetry, prose, and screenplays. The recipient of the 2023 Helen Anne Bell Poetry Bequest Award, *If Movement Was a Language* is her first full-length collection. In 2023, her fiction was recognised in the Richell Prize and State Library of Queensland Young Writers Award.

Emily Stewart lives and works on Wangal land. She is the author of *Knocks* (2016) and *Running Time* (2022), which received the 2021 Helen Anne Bell Award for Poetry. Emily was formerly the poetry editor at Giramondo Publishing and she is currently completing a creative doctorate at the Writing and Society Research Centre.

James Stuart's collections of poems are *Imitation Era* (2012) and *Anonymous Folk Songs* (2013). He was a 2008 Asialink literature resident in Chengdu, China.

Thom Sullivan is a writer, editor and reviewer of poetry. His book of poems, *Carte Blanche* won the 2017-18 Noel Rowe Poetry Award and the 2020 Mary Gilmore Award. His poems have appeared in *Australian Book Review, Australian Love Poems, Australian Poetry Anthology, The Best Australian Poems* and elsewhere.

Niobe Syme is a writer and photomedia artist. Her work has appeared in numerous publications, exhibitions and awards, including *HEAT, Southerly, Island, Antipodes, Cordite* and *Notes for the Translators*. Her poetry chapbook *Beheld* was published by Vagabond Press in 2012.

Taguchi Inuo (whose pen name literally means Dog Man) was born in 1967. Taguchi's collections include *20th-Century Orphan* (1995), *General Moo* (2000), which won the prestigious Takami Jyun Award, *Armadillogic* (2002) and *St. Francis' Birds* (2008).

Ayako Takahashi is a scholar and translator teaching at University of Hyogo in Japan. Her most recent publication is a book of scholarship titled, *Reading Gary Snyder* (2018). She has published translations of many American poets such as Jane Hirshfield, Anne Waldman, and Joanne Kyger, among others.

Shuntarō Tanikawa (1931-2024) was one of world literature's major poets, his work spanning the decades from the 1950s to the 2020s. His collections include *Two Billion Light Years of Solitude* (1952), *With Silence My Companion* (1968), *Coca-Cola-Lessons* (1980), *Rather than Pure White* (1995), *Watashi* (2007), *The Art of Being Alone: Poems 1952-2009* (2011), *Kokoro* (2013) and *Ordinary People* (2020), all of which have helped to bring Japanese poetry into the contemporary world and to keep it there.

Tao Naikan is the translator with Simon Patton of *Yi Sha's Starve the Poets!: Selected Poems* (2008), and with Tony Prince of *Eight Contemporary Chinese Poets* (2006).

Rolando Santos Tinio, born in 1937 in Manila, was a playwright and theatre director, and the author of a small but original body of verse, including a number of poems from the late sixties in Taglish. Highly regarded for his Tagalog adaptations of Western theatre and opera, he died in 1997 while working on a musical.

Joel M Toledo is the author of six books of poetry – *Chiaroscuro, The Long Lost Startle, Ruins and Reconstructions, Fault Setting, The Blue Ones Are Machines*, and *Planet Nine*. He was the recipient of the 2006 NCCA Literary Prize, the Don Carlos Palanca Memorial Award, the Bridport Prize for Poetry, the Rockefeller Foundation Poetry Residency in Bellagio, Italy, and was a fellow of the 2011 International Writers Program at the University of Iowa, USA. He teaches Literature and Creative Writing at the University of Santo Tomas, Manila.

John Tranter (1943-2023), born in Cooma, New South Wales, one of the most influential and versatile Australian poets of the twentieth and twenty-first centuries, published more than twenty books of poetry in his lifetime. He was widely recognized, nationally and internationally, for the brilliant explorations of poetic form and for the range of his insights into modern life. His poetry won multiple literary prizes, including the *Age* Book of the Year in 2011, for his book of poetry *Starlight*. He also contributed in influential ways to poetic culture with the editing and co-editing of anthologies (*The New Australian Poetry*, 1979; the *Penguin Book of Modern Australian Poetry*, 1991) and his founding of the internet magazine *Jacket* in 1997 (later *Jacket2* at the University of Pennsylvania, 2010) the Australian Poetry Library and the *Journal of Poetics Research*.

Jessie Tu is a book critic at *The Age* and *Sydney Morning Herald*, and a journalist for *Women's Agenda*. She published a first poetry collection *You should have told me we have nothing left* (2018) Her debut novel, *A Lonely Girl is a Dangerous Thing* (2021) won the ABIA for 2020 Literary Fiction Book of the Year, followed by her second novel *The Honeyeater* (2024).

Suzanne Verrall has been published in *Australian Poetry Journal, foam:e, Bluepepper, Friendly Street Poets, Poetry New Zealand Yearbook, Flash Frontier, The Interpreter's House, Atlas and Alice, The Hawai`i Pacific Review* and *The Southampton Review*. *One Day I Will Go There* (2022) is her first poetry collection.

Ann Vickery is Head of Writing, Literature, and Culture at Deakin University. She is also the author of three poetry collections, the most recent being *Bees Do Bother: An Antagonist's Care Pack* (2021), which Shortlisted for 2022 Judith Wright Calanthe Award for a Poetry.

Tais Rose Wae is an artist and poet whose work explores the interconnection and imprint of maps of lineage, motherhood, and her Aboriginal ancestry. Wae's work has been published in *Australian Poetry Anthology, Best of Australian Poetry, Cordite, Overland Literary Journal, Running Dog, West Space Offsite*, and *Westerly*. Her debut collection *Riverbed Sky Songs* (2023) won the NSW Premier's Literary Award for Poetry and shortlisted for the 2024 Mary Gilmore Award.

Wago Ryoichi is a poet and high school Japanese literature teacher from Fukushima city, Japan. In 2017, the French translation of his book, *Pebbles of Poetry*, won the Nunc Magazine award for best foreign-language poetry collection. Wago has published many solo author volumes of poetry. Since March 2011, his writing has focused on the ecological devastation of the areas affected by the Tohoku earthquake, tsunami and the nuclear meltdown of the Fukushima Daiichi power station. His poem 'Abandoned Fukushima' is sung by choirs across Japan as a prayer for hope and renewal.

Corey Wakeling is a writer, translator, and scholar living in Tokyo, an associate professor of English literature at Aoyama Gakuin University. He is the author of collections *Gargantuan Terrier, Buggy or Dinghy* (2012), *Goad Omen* (2013), *The Alarming Conservatory* (2018) and *Uncle of Cats* (2024).

Maggie Walsh is a Bwgcolman woman from Palm Island. As she has spent a lot of her childhood years in the Dormitory, Walsh is still finding her family connections. Walsh was born in Townsville in 1964. Her mother Anne was in the Dormitory. She was 17 years old. When she was two years old, her mother was sent to work on the mainland. Walsh remained in the Dormitory and was cared for by the young women friends of her mother, women who had been sent to Palm Island, away from their homes and families. When the Dormitory closed in 1975, at eleven years old, Walsh was placed back into the care of her mother. Walsh has read her poetry at various events and festivals over the years, NAIDOC in Townsville, WIPCE Conference at Rod Laver Arena Melbourne, the Queensland Poetry Festival, Sydney Writers' Festival, and the Palm Island Spring Festival.

Ao Wang (1976-) is an associate professor at Dartmouth College. Wang started writing poetry when he was an undergraduate student. In addition to poetry, he has published Chinese translations of English poetry and Harold Bloom's *The Art of Reading Poetry*.

Petra White was born in Adelaide in 1975 and currently lives in Berlin with her husband and daughter. Her previous full-length collections include *The Incoming Tide* (2007), *The Simplified World* (2010), *A Hunger* (2014) and *Reading for a Quiet Morning* (2017). She received the Grace Leven Prize in 2010.

Nick Whittock lives on Djiringanj lands in the Yuin nation. For his work he uses a battery powered chainsaw charged on standalone solar. Nick works only on previously fallen trees. His publishing history includes *hows its* (2014) and an '*Australia*' calendar (2016). Nick was a convenor of the annual Brogo Poetry Symposium.

Jessica L. Wilkinson is a writer, critic, scholar and editor whose research interests include: poetry and poetics; contemporary poetry; poetic biography; 'nonfiction poetry'; experimental/radical writing; literary theory. She is the founding and Managing Editor of *Rabbit: a journal for nonfiction poetry* (2011-present) and of the Rabbit Poets Series. Jessica's poems have appeared in books, newspapers, and international anthologies and journals. She is the author of three books of poetry: *marionette: a biography of miss marion davies* (2012), *Suite for Percy Grainger* (2014) and *Music Made Visible: A Biography of George Balanchine* (2019).

Caroline Williamson is a poet and editor. Her poems have appeared in *Overland, Meanjin, Heat, Rabbit, Cordite* among other journals, and in the *Contemporary Australian Feminist Poetry*. Her first collection *Time Machines* was published in 2022.

Misbah Wolf is a Melbourne based poet. She holds a Masters in Creative Writing from the University of QLD and is the author of one chapbook, *Rooftops in Karachi* (2018), and a first collection *Carapace* (2022). Wolf has published her work through *Peril Magazine, Australia Poetry Journal, Cordite, Slow Canoe, Solid Air: Australian and New Zealand Spoken Word, Mascara Literary Journal* and has featured on ABC's Radio National Poetica.

Ed Wright is a writer, publisher, editor and educator. His latest book of poetry is *Gas Deities* (2020). He is the founding director of the Creative Word Shop which teaches Creative Writing to adults and children and provides editing and manuscript assessment services. He is also Publishing Director and part-owner of the indie press Puncher and Wattmann.

Yan Jun was born in Lanzhou, China where he began writing at age 14. He now lives and works in Beijing, where an underground music critic, organizer, producer, and experimental sound artist. His work has been translated into English, German, Dutch, and French. He has published three collections and attended the Rotterdam International Poetry Festival as well as the Berlin International Poetry Festival. *You Jump to Another Dream* (2012) was his first full-length collection in English.

Yang Lian (b. 1955) was born in Bern, Switzerland, but grew up in Beijing. His cycle of poems titled *Norlang* (1983) was criticized during the Anti-Spiritual-Pollution campaign of 1983, and he was banned from publishing for a year. In 1985 *Norlang* was reprinted twice: in his *Ritualization of the Soul* as well as together with other of his poems in Lao Mu's *Anthology of New Wave Poetry*. His poetry has been published in Chinese and also in many other languages. His English titles include *Masks and Crocodile* (1990), *The Dead in Exile* (1990), *Non-Person Singular* (1994), *Where the Sea Stands Still* (1995), *Yi* (2002), *Notes of a Blissful Ghost* (2002), *Concentric Circles* (2005), *Unreal City* (2006), and *Riding Pisces* (2008). He has been awarded two important literary prizes in Italy: the Flaiano International Poetry Prize (1999) and the Nonino International Literary Prize (2012).

Soohyun Yang was born in Seoul, South Korea, and immigrated to Canada as a teen. After earning her BA from Western University and an MA from Toronto Metropolitan University, she attended the Translation Academy of the Literature Translation Institute of Korea, a governmental organization responsible for translating major Korean literary works. She has translated and published poems of Jin Eun-young, Hwang Yuwon, Ha Jaeyoun, Kim Haengsook, and more. Her translations have appeared in *Modern Poetry in Translation and Korean Literature Now*. In many ways, she has been translating one culture for another all her life. Currently she lives and works as a translator and interpreter in Seoul.

Yotsumoto Yasuhiro is a poet, translator, essayist, editor and the author of more than 15 poetry collections, including *Starboard of My Wife* (translated into English by Takako Lento) and several volumes of poetry translations and anthologies, including *Dante Meeting Li Po*. His poetry has garnered him an Ayukawa Nobuo and a Hagiwara Sakutaro award, among others.

Maged Zaher was born and raised in Cairo, Egypt. He has lived in the US since 1995, and has published several books of poetry and translations. In 2013, Zaher won the Genius Award for Literature from The Stranger in Seattle. In 2017, Chatwin published Zaher's *Opting Out: Early, New, and Collected Poems* and in 2022 published Maged's novella *On Confused Love and Other Damages*.

Zang Di, a poet, critic, translator, and editor, was born in Beijing in 1964. He was educated at Beijing University and received his Ph.D. in literature in 1997. Now an associate professor at Beijing University, he has taught in the US, Japan, and Taiwan. Zang has published many books of poetry, most recently the collected *Horseback Riders and Soymilk* (2015), and edited several major anthologies of modern and contemporary Chinese poetry.

Zhai Yongming (b. 1955) was born in Chengdu. She was sent to the countryside to work as a peasant for two years during the Cultural Revolution, but afterwards graduated in laser technology in 1981, and in the same year began publishing poetry. Her two cycles of poems *Woman* (1984) and *Jing'an Village* (1985) stamped her credentials as one of the most significant poets of the 1980s. She became a role model for aspiring women poets who provided a powerful and distinctive voice in the world of Chinese poetry that had previously been dominated by male poets. Her collections include *Above All the Roses* (1989), *Collected Poems of Zhai Yongming* (1994), as well as the English title, *The Changing Room: Selected Poetry of Zhai Yongming* (2012).

Established in 1999, Vagabond Press is an independent literary press based on Gadigal land in Sydney, Australia. We publish poetry, prose and literature in translation from Australia and Asia Pacific more broadly. Vagabond Press began and continues out of a love of making books and the desire to open up space for new writing that is innovative, diverse, challenging and accessible. For over two decades, Vagabond Press has published a range of established and emerging poets and prose writers, working with the aim to foster and facilitate individual creativity alongside transnational collaboration and connection.

To check out our full list of titles, order a book directly, or to get in touch about supporting small press publishing, please visit our website:

WWW.VAGABONDPRESS.NET

www.ingramcontent.com/pod-product-compliance
Lightning Source LLC
Chambersburg PA
CBHW011953150426
43197CB00020B/2943